"Perry helps the reader understand that the contemporary landscape of inequality is no accident, but exists by design. *Know Your Price* is an important addition to any conversation about racial inequality in this country and is an essential tool to help refute the lies we have been told for so long."

Clint Smith,
author of *Counting Descent*

"Perry lays bare the wretched tradition that devalues black bodies and black property. By writing from the inside out, he gives the facts and figures of redlining and subsequent gentrification names and faces—their joys, desires, hopes, pain, agony, and despair. The writing itself is deft and heartfelt. It reads as if James Baldwin was a social scientist."

Rev. Osagyefo Sekou,
Institute for Policy Studies

"A powerful indictment of a white culture that persistently blames the victims of racism for the consequences of oppression, *Know Your Price* is also a hopeful and moving celebration of Black resilience. It is must-reading for American policymakers and the people who put them in office."

Grant Oliphant,
president, The Heinz Endowments

"This memoir is not another self-aggrandizing voycuristic presentation of hood triumph. Rather, it is a brave, honest, and analytically insightful understanding of dignity and worth and a challenge to society's myopic devaluation of black people and communities."

Darrick Hamilton,
The Ohio State University

KNOW YOUR PRICE

KNOW YOUR PRICE

Valuing Black Lives and Property in America's Black Cities

ANDRE M. PERRY

BROOKINGS INSTITUTION PRESS

Washington, D.C.

The Brookings Institution is a private nonprofit organization devoted to research, education, and publication on important issues of domestic and foreign policy. Its principal purpose is to bring the highest quality independent research and analysis to bear on current and emerging policy problems. Interpretations or conclusions in Brookings publications should be understood to be solely those of the authors.

Library of Congress Cataloging-in-Publication Data
Names: Perry, Andre M., author.
Title: Know your price : valuing black lives and property in America's black cities / Andre M. Perry.
Other titles: Valuing black lives and property in America's black cities
Description: Washington, D.C. : Brookings Institution Press, [2020] | Includes bibliographical references and index.
Identifiers: LCCN 2019048137 (print) | LCCN 2019048138 (ebook) | ISBN 9780815737278 (cloth) | ISBN 9780815737285 (epub)
Subjects: LCSH: Urban African Americans—Economic conditions. | Urban African Americans—Social conditions. | Valuation—United States. | United States—Race relations. | United States—Social conditions—1945–
Classification: LCC E185.8 .P43 2020 (print) | LCC E185.8 (ebook) | DDC 305.896/07301732—dc23
LC record available at https://lccn.loc.gov/2019048137
LC ebook record available at https://lccn.loc.gov/2019048138

9 8 7 6 5 4 3 2

Typeset in Adobe Caslon Pro

Composition by Elliott Beard

For incarcerated parents,
their children,
and caretakers—
You are not to blame.

Contents

Acknowledgments

Knowing your price involves understanding the value of family. I appreciate my wife Joia Crear-Perry for giving me the space and time to write the book. I thank my son for allowing me to come to my office to write on the days he wanted to play with me in the park. I thank my cousins, aunties, and uncles for sharing our family history with me. Shante, Anna, Tallulah, Kergulin, Danielle, Dorian, and Kevin provided wonderful insights into what made me into the adult I've become. My relationship with my mother Karen and sister Danielle gets stronger with time. Thank you for supporting me. I also thank my extended family, including Gemal and Erika Woods, Mattie and Gerald Woods, Stan and Monique Drayton, Darren and Dabeiba Del Rosario Hudson, and Fletcher Brooks.

Jayati Vora provided brilliant editorial support for the book. She has been my editor at the *Hechinger Report* for a few years now, and I'm never surprised and only encouraged by the rigor she demands of me. Thank you. In addition, Brentin Mock, staff writer at *CityLab*, edited the first draft of the manuscript, providing critical feedback and recommendations around structure and composition that were invaluable. He's been an editor of mine since I started writing in popular media and has been instrumental in my development as a writer. Thank you.

I'm grateful for Amy Liu, vice president and director of the Metropolitan Policy Program at the Brookings Institution, for extending an invitation to write a book chapter about education in New Orleans post-Katrina that was published in 2011. Amy would eventually hire me to join the Brookings team in 2017 as a David M. Rubenstein Fellow. My colleagues at Metro have supported this work since my arrival. In particular, I thank Alan Berube for reading an early draft of the book and providing substantive comments and criticism, which strengthened the final version. My Rubenstein siblings Jenny Schuetz and Dany Bahar helped me conceptualize the housing study. Joe Parilla and Sifan Liu's research on Birmingham proved to be invaluable. Mark Muro and Bill Frey are incredibly positive and motivating colleagues. I thank them for always leaving their door open to me.

I work with a wonderful team, for whom I am deeply grateful. From my start at Brookings, research analyst David Harshbarger has provided invaluable support during my journey. David started with me as a part-time intern, but developed a deep appreciation, forged by hard work, for my Black-majority cities work. We all benefit from his dedication to facts, justice, and coding. Not long after I met David, I befriended Jonathan Rothwell, principal economist at Gallup. Jonathan's analytic chops are unmatched. Jonathan helps me operationalize the empirical models I have in my head and enhances them. His skills are only surpassed by his kindness. I discovered Jonathan to be my brother from another mother. Anthony Fiano coordinates all of my external engagements and media requests. He makes the time for me to generate research while I engage the public. His enthusiasm is contagious. Rounding out the team are several interns who have spent some time with me: Marissa Marshall, Ally

Hardebeck, Christine MacKrell, Ananya Hariharan, Rehan Hasan, and Alex Thomas are the future of public policy.

The communications team at Brookings Metro has been vital to my success. I want to send a special shout-out to David Lanham for his careful editing and project management.

The staff at the *Hechinger Report* invested in me as writer and a person. Liz Willen, Sarah Garland, Sarah Carr, Jennifer Shaw, Jayati Vora, and the rest of the team all played a significant role in my development. Many of the ideas found in this book germinated from my weekly column in this wonderful publication. In addition, I've been lucky to have some incredible editors along the way, including Kirsten West-Savali of *Essence* magazine and Adam Kushner at the *Washington Post*. And when it comes to helping me get to the spirit of a matter, I turn to Rev. Osagyefo Sekou. Thank you, brother.

I'd also like to thank the teachers of Wilkinsburg and Pittsburgh public schools for their investment in me and others. My undergraduate faculty at Allegheny College instilled the writing and analytic fundamentals I've carried with me throughout my professional career. My graduate school faculty at the University of Maryland College Park, including Kenneth Strike, Sharon Fries-Brit, and Betty Malen, all contributed mightily to my development. I also need to acknowledge Dan Hartley, who gave me editorial insights throughout the writing process. I also thank my grad school colleagues for supporting me along the way toward completion: Shaun Gittens, Mark Lopez, Jeffrey Pegram, Jeff Van Collins, Takeyah Young, Rashida Govan, and numerous others. Go Terps!

This work and the book would not have been possible without the generous support of The Heinz Endowments, especially Grant Oliphant, Rob Stephanie, and Karen Abrams. Other folks in Pittsburgh who were instrumental in developing the book include Michael Skirpan and Community Forge, the Johnston School; Hosanna House; Mayor of Wilkinsburg Marita Garrett; William Bates, president of the American Institute of Architects; Tracy Evans; and Gordon

Manker of the Wilkinsburg Community Development Corporation.

The Detroit Artist Test Lab, Orlando Bailey, Chase Cantrell, Lauren Hood, Austin Black II, Tahirih Ziegler, Anika Goss-Foster, and SpaceLab Detroit all deserve my thanks for welcoming me into their communities and providing me with the data, knowledge, and lived experiences that made this book and the work more broadly what it is today.

In Birmingham, Alabama, my thanks go out to Brian K. Rice, Barnett Wright, Isaac Cooper, Janae Pierre, Andrew Yeager (and the rest of the team at WBHM), Deon Gordon, Brian Hilson, Waymond Jackson, Dr. Perry Ward, the Birmingham Business Alliance, Bettina Byrd-Giles, Brian Hawkins, Rob Zeigler, and Mark Martin. A special note of thanks goes out the Mayor of Birmingham Randall Woodfin and his staff, who are truly making an impact in the city.

Of course, to the people of New Orleans I owe a great amount of gratitude, including Flozell Daniels, Sharon Clark, James Meza, Jamar McKneely, Doris Hicks, Renette Dejoie Hall, Jenni Lawson, Norman Robinson, Rhonda Kalifey-Aluise, Chuck Perkins, #TakeEmDownNOLA, Victory Bar, Camille Whitworth, Daniel Victory, Maeve Wallace, and anyone who has attended one of our house parties.

KNOW
YOUR
PRICE

The Assets of Home

"He's not your son," pronounced Uncle Hotsy. "I am."

It was an ultimatum to the nearly eighty-year-old Elsie Mae Boyd.

"I'm your flesh and blood." Looking through me, he continued. "He can't stay here."

Elsie Mae may not have been my mom by blood, but that's what we called her—me, a scrawny, nappy-headed boy, and a dozen other kids who had found refuge in her yellow brick single-family home. She was in her sixties when I was born, and she had raised me since birth.

Mom listened to her eldest daughter Dot and the son she gave birth to make their case that spring day. She was too old to "watch" a house full of kids, they said, especially when one of them was as boisterous, freewheeling, and insolent as me. I did get suspended from school on occasion, mainly for mouthing off to teachers and students. Mom prepared her share of ice packs because of the "scraps" I found myself in. To Hotsy and Dot, I represented trouble. To Mom, I represented her son.

I can't remember if I had gotten into a fight that day or if a teacher had sent me home from school for bad behavior or if any specific incident triggered the intervention by Mom's grown children. She positioned herself in the doorway of the room where I had slept for most of my life and in which I now stood, frozen, petrified by anger and shame. She gripped both sides of the white, paint-chipped doorframe. The creases in her brown hands were reminders of their strength. Her well-manicured bouffant wig put her just above five feet tall. Still, she made a formidable barrier, her body between me and Uncle Hotsy—protecting me, as she always did.

The year was 1986. I was nearly sixteen. It was the first time I had to reckon with the possibility of losing my home—and my mother. "He belongs in foster care," Dot said calmly.

It is said that home is where our stories begin. The story of how this book came about also begins at home, and from what I learned from Mom. She defended her home so that it included not just her biological kin but kids from the neighborhood like me, whose families couldn't look after them for various reasons. Now, I can see that Mom rightly defined our home and family based on our circumstances, and she vigorously defended her definition of family against people and systems who would not accept it—even if those people were her children. I survived Hotsy and Dot's campaign and managed to stay in that home until I left for college at the age of eighteen.

Before that day in 1986, I didn't know what it was to be devalued as a human being. Until that day, I understood rejection only in terms of the dates with girls I couldn't get. Nothing had prepared me for that moment. Our very presence on 1320 Hill Avenue, in the small city of Wilkinsburg, Pennsylvania, was a testimonial to acceptance. I lived in a Black-majority city that we bragged about; we weren't like "those other Blacks" we looked down on, the ones who lived in neighboring Pittsburgh, because folks who lived in the city were somehow lesser. Calling Wilkinsburg home made us feel special during a time when the region was anything but.

Wilkinsburg was once a part of Pittsburgh, until its powerful

White residents seceded in 1876, setting up an antagonistic relationship with the bigger municipality early on. In the late 1960s, though, when work disappeared and demographics shifted, Whites fled Wilkinsburg, too, leaving the town half empty. Black folk trickled in, and this new Black majority eventually adopted Wilkinsburg, just as Mom had adopted me.

The adage goes that when White folks catch a cold, Black folks get pneumonia. When work disappears for White people, as it did in the Pittsburgh metropolitan area in the 1980s, Black people suffered even more, and Black women adjusted their families in ways to keep children from feeling the effects of extremely high unemployment. "In January 1983, the regional economy officially—that is, numerically— bottomed out," wrote journalist Bill Toland of the *Pittsburgh Post-Gazette*.[1] "Unemployment in Allegheny County [where Pittsburgh is located] hit 13.9 percent, a rosy figure compared to the rest of the Pittsburgh metropolitan statistical area, where the adjusted unemployment rate hit an astonishing 17.1 percent (unadjusted, the number was actually higher, 18.2 percent)." Many families struggled to realize the American Dream in Pittsburgh, but Black families, including my own, found it especially hard.

When Hotsy and Dot talked with Mom about sending me to foster care, I didn't feel I could turn to my biological family. My father, Floyd Criswell, had been killed at the age of twenty-seven in Jackson State Prison, about seventy-five minutes west of Detroit, when I was eight years old. He wasn't involved in my life prior to his death. I don't remember ever meeting him. My biological mother, Karen Perry, lived in Garfield, a low-income Pittsburgh neighborhood at the time, about four miles away, where she raised my half-sister Danielle, the youngest of her four children. Karen gave birth to my older brother Kevin when she was sixteen, me at eighteen, my younger brother Dorian at twenty, and my sister Danielle at twenty-two.

Kevin and Dorian lived in Wilkinsburg with Mom and me. Growing up, I didn't have much interaction with Karen, who I call by her first name. Every summer, a few weeks before the start of the school year, Kevin, Dorian, and I got excited about the prospect of Karen taking us back-to-school shopping. Then, taking us clothes shopping seemed to be her most important role in my life. And I was just fine with that.

Karen never talked to me about why she gave me into Mom's keeping. Mom told me Karen handed me to her at Magee-Women's Hospital in Pittsburgh, where I was born. Even as a kid who knew nothing other than our home on Hill Avenue, I always knew that the senior citizen Elsie Mae couldn't be my biological mother. Though I was quick to fight anyone who challenged my calling her Mom, I came to know through my surroundings who and what a godparent was in relation to a biological mother. I grew up knowing my "cuz," "auntie," and "brotha" could be the kin of my heart or of my blood. The similar backgrounds of many of my friends reinforced this understanding of family. In Wilkinsburg, many in my peer group lived with their grandmothers, aunties, or other surrogates. The African proverb "it takes a village to raise a child" is especially true when you factor in the economic and social realities Black people face. From our village, Black folk had developed an informal foster care system long before I became the beneficiary of that support. That system was as familiar to me as the texture of Mom's hands.

I came of age seeing how various hardships made parents give their children to surrogate parents for safekeeping. I bore witness to mothers who, to make ends meet, worked endless hours on multiple jobs as domestic workers and janitors. Mom used to be a domestic worker in the homes of wealthy White families, but she stopped her cleaning jobs around the time I was born and began watching children full-time to earn money.

Mom was the first entrepreneur and business owner I ever met. She filled a vital need in the market. Mom had help with her make-shift family; her daughter, Mary, lived with us. Mothers in our neighborhood had little choice but to entrust someone like Mom and Mary

Mary and (from left) Kevin, Dorian, me, and Angie

to love their children when, often, those Black women were taking care of White people's kids in their roles as domestic workers.

Mary also had cleaned people's homes, but she suffered a stroke, and after her recovery she assisted Mom with us kids. We called Mary our aunt, which was more believable than Elsie being our mom because Mary looked like most of the women who dropped kids off at elementary school.

Mom was married to Theodore Boyd until his death in 1977. Teddy, who served in the Second World War, was the first father figure in my life. I have fond memories of Teddy sitting on the grassy knolls outside of a nearby shopping mall. I remember him leaving for work in the mornings to go to his job as a security guard before we kids went to school. After he died from "black lung," Hotsy, also a veteran, moved into our house. But his was no benign presence— Hotsy's name was on the deed of the home we lived in, and he eventually pushed to kick us kids out (or, at least, me). Compounding matters, Hotsy had "nervous breakdowns"—psychotic breaks—every few years, something I always attributed to his involvement in the war. Now I see that the post-traumatic stress from racism in Pittsburgh may have compounded the damaging effects of war.

More than a dozen children of varying ages spent significant chunks of time in our house. Some came just when they needed to be babysat, after school every day. Others would spend long stretches with us—days, even weeks—sleeping over. Six to seven of us lived in the 2,260 square foot home at any given time. Kevin and Dorian shared the master bedroom, where other children were also occasionally housed. They would share beds, if needed, or use pillows from the couches downstairs as a makeshift mattress. I slept with Mom in her bed until Kevin and Dorian moved up to the attic, whereupon I moved into their room. Hotsy and Mary had their own bedrooms.

The condition of the house reflected its numerous, active occupants. Fallen plaster and eroded drywall left the walls pockmarked, the wood frame exposed. The house went through a paneling phase when Hotsy did his best to cover the damage we did, but sections of it eventually came down, adding to the variations and blemishes. The roof bowed and the external brickwork buckled in places. The house needed significant repairs, but it was good enough for Kevin, Dorian, me, and others until we graduated from high school.

Mom and Mary made $5 a day per child, $25 per week for babysitting—if people paid. I don't recall Karen paying Mom for my brothers and me. Instead, she helped out by purchasing back-to-school clothes and Christmas gifts. Though Mom and Mary also received Social Security and Disability, the government subsidies and babysit-

Mom, me, and Mary in Wilkinsburg

ting revenue wasn't always enough. I recall families owing money to Mom and Mary for babysitting their kids, just as Mom and Mary owed the local drug and grocery stores. When their Social Security checks arrived, Mom would have us kids pay various bills across town.

Still, I never felt poor, at least not until I went to Allegheny College, a private liberal arts institution in Pennsylvania ninety minutes north of Pittsburgh, where so many of my peers owned their own cars and had bank accounts that always seemed to have money in them. In comparison, my grandfather "Twenty" gave me $50 and a "Good luck!" when he dropped me off at the steps of my dorm. And I couldn't have had a happier upbringing—at least, not until that day when Uncle Hotsy and Dot made me realize that my belonging was conditional and that, in their eyes, I *belonged* in foster care.

Insecurities about not belonging never quite go away. I couldn't ignore the bell Hotsy rang. The belief that I had to fight to be included followed me to college and all the colleges where I ever worked, from my first, humble job as a camp counselor, helping the children of migrant workers, to the boardrooms of the Brookings Institution, where my cushy office has a nice view and my name is garnished with a flashy title. Yet I haven't outgrown my roots: I work in a unit of Brookings dedicated to making sure our economic growth includes all racial and ethnic groups. And over the weekends, I write a weekly column for the education website the Hechinger Report about how race impacts education.

But my sense of (in)security in where I live and work does not completely stem from unresolved family issues. In my office, which overlooks a main drag of one of the wealthiest areas of Washington, D.C., I constantly read insulting and infantilizing research and commentary about how Black people cause their own poverty by not getting married or by having too many children. For those writers, family planning strictly means that low-income women must figure out how to not have children. I look over my shoulder as I read these articles, thinking, "Is the researcher talking about me and my upbringing?" Well—yeah.

Privileged eyes constantly remove their gaze from root causes of social and economic despair to myopically perceive positive family adaptations as dysfunction or as causing poverty. You'd think people intuitively would know that Black people don't deliberately choose their family arrangements so they will be worse off. To be clear, we shape and create family configurations to protect children and adults. I don't think Karen, who had four children before her twenty-third birthday, could have overcome the obstacles she faced early in life to become a social worker if Mom hadn't taken in her three boys. In Black communities, it's fairly common to have women plan family based on a more expansive understanding of what a family is. A lack of opportunities for Black men and women demands innovation, creativity, and more options for family—not fewer.

The fact that many of my friends grew up with one female breadwinner doesn't mean Black people don't want to be married or that Black men are unwilling to work. Instead, maternal caregivers stepped into the breach when an economy that didn't pay women fairly, denied Black men and women job opportunities, and criminalized labor in the underground economy made it harder to form nuclear family units—if they wanted to do so. But those aren't the stories you read in much of the research on Black communities that ends up recommending changes in individual behaviors rather than endorsing anti-racism policy. Theorists who posited that poverty was mainly about individual choices produced the foundational studies undergirding family planning research. First popularized in the 1960s by anthropologist Oscar Lewis, culture of poverty theories argued that low-income people share inherent characteristics and values that keep them impoverished. Thus, children who grow up in poor communities fall victim to the decisions of their parents, replicating the intergenerational cycle of poverty. Subsequently, low-income mothers were—are—rendered culpable for putting their children in poverty. Culture of poverty theories manifest themselves in a seemingly constant focus on how Black folk aren't living up to White norms instead of probing how to dismantle systems that privilege White people at Black people's expense. I now know that my existence is a manifestation of Black women's resistance against the criminalization of poverty and the devaluing of Black lives. For me, family planning research has mostly been a thinly veiled negative reinforcement campaign that attempts to punish Black people for poverty we didn't create.

Since 1965, when Assistant Secretary of Labor Daniel Patrick Moynihan published his report, *The Negro Family: The Case for National Action*, better known as the Moynihan Report, researchers and journalists have continued framing poverty mainly as a function of individual choices—that is, mothers form families that put children in harm's way. Moynihan also offered a robust structural analysis of the economic and social conditions that help shape Black family structures. However, he set a dangerous example by identifying the main problem as Black people not living up to White middle-class ideals. This is a mold that researchers of Black people and cities willfully maintain to this day. One of the major goals of this book is to show that *there is nothing wrong with Black people that ending racism can't solve.*

What Hotsy and some researchers called a no-parent home I called family. I had multiple mothers, guardians, and father figures whose love didn't fit in a neat little nuclear family structure. In that Hill Avenue home, I learned to read, write, share, love, and accept others who didn't share my genes. Mom regularly said, "I took you from the hospital, and you were born into love." It was her way of making the single Black mother debate irrelevant for me.

Still, my struggles with Hotsy, Dot, and Patrick Moynihan are with me and manifested in my work on Black-majority cities.

In the U.S. context, we, as researchers and as residents, are bombarded with studies that project how bad Black families, students, and residents are compared to an assumed White norm. Researchers rarely ask these analytic questions: What is good about Black families? Where are the assets of Black communities? According to the research nonprofit the Institute on Assets and Social Policy, "Assets provide the tangible resources that help individuals move out of and stay out of poverty."[2] Assets include the material and nonmaterial, such as physical property, federal treasury notes, cash, stocks, bonds, brand names, savings, copyrights, and more. Assets are the physical, nonphysical, and behavioral resources that can be exchanged for quality of life improvements. People are the most important asset of all. My upbringing was an asset.

Our relentless pursuit of disparities between Black and White people often omits the policies that were designed to devalue Black assets. Those omissions help foster a sense of superiority among Whites while minimizing financial and social privileges gained from not acknowledging root policy causes of disparities.

As a way of moving toward research frameworks that look for assets in Black communities, I spoke with several of my Black colleagues who grew up in Black-majority places. I asked them two basic questions: "What are the benefits to living in a Black-majority city?" and, "Why do so many of us choose to stay in them?"

One of my peers, the Brookings fellow Makada Henry-Nickie, responded, "Home feels safe." She leaned back, sprouting a smile that spoke of relief and comfort, and added, "I don't have to explain myself." However, much of the research that is motivated to bring about equity or fairness amounts to making a case of why we should belong.

Though Henry-Nickie currently lives in Washington, D.C., home for Henry-Nickie is the Black-majority island country of Trinidad and Tobago. She acknowledges that being a Black woman and an immigrant from a Black-majority country gives her a particular appreciation of Black-majority cities in the United States. Henry-Nickie is a researcher who works with data every day. She, like many Black immigrants, feels the collateral damage of negative expectations, stereotypes, and assumptions she didn't grow up with but now has to live with in her adopted country. The expectations of Blacks in America spill over onto those who haven't been reared in our context.

Adding insult to injury, we're professionally trained and rewarded to make White people the default referent group that Blacks are measured against. In doing so, we acquire a tendency to center White people in our work.

I was first introduced to the practice of White centering later in life as a graduate researcher, when I first learned how to carry out a regression analysis, a staple of quantitative research. Regression analyses examine the relationship between two or more variables—say, the impact of race on academic achievement. For a category like race, one must pick a referent group for the purposes of comparison. I was taught to make White men (not White women) the default referent in most of my models. In the aforementioned example, achievement test scores of White women, Black women and men, as well as their Hispanic non-White, Asian, and Native American counterparts are measured against White men. Regression models are mathematically most stable if the referent group is the largest within the sample you are drawing from. For that reason, in the United States, data sources that make note of racial categories are generally presented sequentially, with "White," the largest single racial group, listed first.

But if we really are interested in improving Black communities, it's much less useful to select Whites as the referent. Historical discrimination categorically leveled against Black people makes it difficult for many research projects to make a true apples-to-apples comparison with White people. For instance, to compare a Black person's income to that of a White person without accounting for wealth that was systematically denied to Black people by federal policy is to bury one's head in the sand and ignore the roles of racism and White privilege. Racism is a common denominator for Black people; it's a given. It's much more useful, in many cases, to examine the variation *within* the Black population to see what factors and conditions can be attributed to differences.

In leading up to my study on devaluation (presented in chapter 2), I examined incomes of Black families living in Black-majority cities. It was a very simple study that simply asked, "Where are Blacks with high incomes living?" Incomes are proxies for decent job opportunities, good schools, and safe living environments. Figure I-1, a national map of Black-majority cities ranked by median household incomes of Black families, shows that 124 communities outpace the national median household income for all races ($53,889), according to data from the 2015 American Community Survey.[3] Black families are especially thriving in various city/suburbs in Maryland, which hosts more than half the top 124 Black-majority cities. The DMV—that is, the D.C.-Maryland-Virginia area—is Black bougie heaven.

Using median income as a proxy for financial status is a very imperfect practice. Measuring the middle of an income distribution—

FIGURE I-1. BLACK-MAJORITY CITIES WITH MEDIAN HOUSEHOLD INCOME ABOVE THE NATIONAL AVERAGE ($57,652) IN 2017

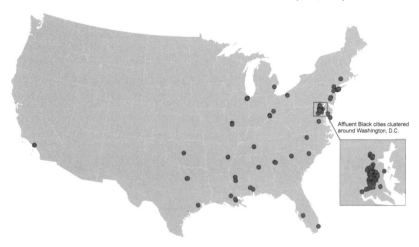

SOURCE: American Community Survey U.S. Census Bureau estimates.

median income—of a particular city often masks the earning and labor disparities of particular groups that are not employed by the dominant industries in a market. That's especially the case for Black families when popular publications put out various lists for the wealthiest places to live. Not everyone benefits from a thriving economy. That's why colleagues of mine within the Brookings Metro program encourage more robust measures of economic health that include growth, inclusion, and prosperity.[4] However, detailing strength among Black populations within Black cities offers a vantage point to opportunities that may lead to investments.

I examined home prices in these neighborhoods and found that many of the homes were of similar quality and had similar neighborhood amenities as those in similarly situated White neighborhoods. However, they were priced significantly less—the basis for my devaluation studies. One might say homeowners in Black neighborhoods received a discount. However, those same communities are hemorrhaging vital tax revenues and equity merely because of the concentration of Black people. The price difference excited me because it was clear that homes in Black neighborhoods were not the problem society portends them to be—they were devalued. Instead of centering White neighborhoods as a standard to be reached, I sought Black assets and found a path toward a solution that didn't involve fixing Black people. We can pursue solving for devaluation.

When acclaimed author Toni Morrison was asked in a 1998 interview whether she would begin to feature White characters more prominently in her work, she responded, "You can't understand how powerfully racist that question is, can you? Because you could never ask a White author, 'When are you going to write about Black people?' . . . Even the inquiry comes from a position of being in the center." Morrison continued, "There are no pluses for me. Being an African-American writer is sort of like being a Russian writer, who writes about Russia, in Russian, for Russians. And the fact that it gets translated and read by other people is a benefit. It's a plus. But he's not obliged to ever consider writing about French people or Americans or anybody."[5]

A critical disadvantage in public policy research with the use of White centering in disparity research is that it distracts our attention from finding potential solutions that can positively impact the Black community. It keeps a focus on having Black people strive for benchmarks made impossible through racism. My examinations of Black people among Black-majority cities is a deliberate attempt to look for variations, evidence that may be signs of positive resistance, adaptation, and struggle that similarly situated people can learn from and use. It's also about my learning how to tell our story.

Ultimately, the point of view of the researcher determines what group becomes the standard against which all others are measured. All researchers are filled with cultural norms and traditions that are inextricably linked to the racial setting, which ultimately influences our frameworks, methods, and findings. And it's impossible to remove our childhood experiences from our point of view. Our segregated histories influence the subtle perspectives of our work. Research can never be neutral, above the fray. All research is imbued with the norms and values of the person conducting it. Inclusion is in my family history and subsequently inseparable from my scholarship. That is to say, there is nothing dispassionate about research. This truth is especially true when it comes to privilege and racial bias. I once heard author and scholar Brittany Cooper say, "Ain't shit about White supremacy rigorous."[6] In other words, Whiteness gets in the way of quality. This is why truly rigorous research actively addresses our biases, particularly around racial prejudice.

Think tanks and universities must see diversifying the stable of researchers as a proactive solution to hedge against bias and to add value to Black communities. While there is no guarantee that Black, Latino, Asian, or Indigenous researchers will challenge the orthodoxy they were trained in, they are more likely to have insights into how the methods and findings may or may not serve the community the person lives in or is from. When the Public Health Service began studying, in 1932, the progression of syphilis—the Tuskegee Experiment—by giving hundreds of Black men the disease without their consent, it's a severe understatement to say they could have used some Black researchers (from any hood). That study went on for forty years.

Investment in researchers from underrepresented groups is an investment in rigor. It's also an ethical and moral investment. However, the methods and perspectives researchers are trained to use must also change if we are going to add value to communities that have been robbed of vital resources by racism.

All researchers need to learn how to center a community or group other than White people. The default position of Whiteness leads to horribly inaccurate and predictable interpretations of results: namely, that Blacks need to catch up. We need to focus more on real sources of disparities. The evidence that racism is directed at Black people to impede their social and economic progress keeps growing (and growing), but the focus on disparity and individual behaviors persists.

For instance, 2018 research from the Quality of Opportunity Project, a research undertaking led by noted economist Raj Chetty, shows that even wealthy Black men who live in tony neighborhoods are more likely than their White male counterparts to have sons who will grow up to be poor.[7] The researchers controlled for many factors, including the family's socioeconomic background, neighborhood, education, and wealth, among other things, and still disparities existed. The *New York Times* created a stunning data visualization based on the study that showed how Black children in wealthy families become adults in lower income brackets.[8] The graphics also represent how different racial groups that started out rich end up poor; even here, more Black children end up poor than kids of other races. Many are calling this research groundbreaking.[9]

The charts presented in the *Times'* reporting also highlighted White men's elevated position in society. Instead of focusing on the negative impact of racism on Black boys, the headline of that story could have read, "Racism enables Whites to maintain wealth." Yet the reporting on the study and most of the feedback inexplicably placed the scrutiny on Black men. So I was partly wrong. There are instances when we should center White people: when we spotlight racism and privilege.

Of all the reactions to the amazing charts in the *Times* article, you didn't hear much about White male power. Economist Arindrajit Dube summarized this in a tweet: "If you overlay the @nhendren82 (+coauthors) percentile-percentile plots, it suggests the exceptional mobility is for White men. This point should be discussed more when hypothesizing explanations for these patterns."[10] Dube is saying we need to scrutinize White privilege. What society needs is more evidence of how racism works—for the benefit of White people. Expose that. Put that in the headline.

Research that merely lays out racial disparities without acknowledging the role of racism ignores the sources of inequality. It ultimately leaves little option but to blame Black people for hurting themselves. It fuels fears that inferior populations are ruining cities. Worse, the only people empowered by these data are the people who produce them. Communities burdened by racism don't need comparison studies that, in essence, suggest they have to catch up to or become White. Disenfranchised groups need studies they can use in court to litigate against discrimination; information that can be used to build wealth; knowledge that reveals the erasing of history; and inquiries that dismantle racist systems. In addition, Black communities need research that highlights assets worth building on. By accounting for racism, researchers can better examine true value. In housing, for instance, if we can show the tax that people pay for racism, we are better able to assess the true value of homes. Then, we can begin to find ways to restore the value that Black communities deserve and identify systems that rob Black communities of the American dream.

When you get right down to it, many comparisons of Blacks to Whites are unconsciously (or consciously) asking these questions: Why can't you be more like White people? Why can't you get married and act like "normal" middle-class White families (without the leg up that federal policies have given White people over the decades)? Why can't you achieve academically like White people?

In addition, when White people are assumed to be the norm or standard, everyone else is deemed abnormal. Then, the underlying question driving the research is: Why can't Blacks be normal?

Mom never once referred to my home or my friends' homes as broken or as the source of failure. She knew the importance of narrative on the emotional well-being of children and communities. I grew up getting only tidbits about my biological parents' story from Mom and Mary, and that was deliberate. They carefully curated information about my biological family to protect them and me from incurring any shame from a world that claimed I was a deficit.

I learned about what happened to Floyd and Karen much later in life. Mom would impress upon us that Floyd died in prison while breaking up a fight. (My brothers and I did believe the "dying in jail" part, but her portrayal of him as a Good Samaritan didn't quite add up.) I mostly didn't mind the insistence on rendering my biological parents, especially my father, in a good light. I eventually learned that he was very human and had plenty of good in him. As a child, I didn't fully grasp Mom's insistence on his goodness. Now that I'm a father myself, I have a deeper appreciation of the stories we tell our children—and why we tell them.

This book picks up where Mom left off.

Mom presented the narrative of Karen and Floyd's lives so that we wouldn't be scarred by others' interpretations of their shortcomings and so we could leverage their strengths. The story we told about ourselves wasn't one of poverty and a lack of love; we were never made to feel that the way we grew up was abnormal. We had a loving home, a Mom who fought like a lioness to protect her cubs, and a city that, for the most part, shared her values.

Mom and Mary both had to leave 1320 Hill Avenue so they could receive adequate health services in their final years, leaving Hotsy alone in the home. Unable to keep up with the taxes and his own health, Hotsy also left the home, moving to an independent living facility where he resided until his death. Wilkinsburg now owns the home. Its price is nowhere near its true value in relation to the children Mom reared and the parents she undergirded, as well as its market worth—it is devalued.

I have a responsibility to restore my home and community's value. *Know Your Price* is not about viewing Black communities through rose-tinted glasses. This book, like Mom, is about seeing—not devaluing—

our true potential free from bigoted judges. It's about understanding root causes. My home, upbringing, community, and culture have significant value even though others devalue them. In addition, my children's future—and your son's, and your daughter's—is linked to our abilities to give value back to Wilkinsburg and other Black-majority cities. Those children could live in a Black-majority city. Approximately 9 million Black people do, roughly 20 percent of the country's Black population. And many other ethnicities live in these cities, as well.

Know Your Price is not an argument for creating all-Black cities. Wanting one's culture and background not to be insulted, invalidated, or erased isn't an argument for segregation. White, Hispanic, and Asian people already live and love in Black-majority places. And we love this multiculturalism (especially when we're not targeted by 911 calls) because Black folk are inherently diverse, representing different ethnicities, socioeconomic classes, and gender constructions. To disavow the presence of others is to deny parts of ourselves.

If there is a direct message to White people in the book, it's to relay that helping individuals doesn't require fixing them. Try fixing policy, instead. Likewise, we can't wait for White folks to see that Black people aren't broken. Researchers will write yet another (and another) Moynihan Report, so *Know Your Price* is also a call to researchers. We need the tools, analytics, and frameworks to properly assess the cities, neighborhoods, and people others devalue.

In addition to calling attention to assets (investment opportunities) in Black-majority cities as well as structural change, I write this book for people who find themselves in the same situation I was in that day in 1986—fighting to belong, to stay in your homes, your communities. It would be foolish to assume that investors will immediately reverse their thinking upon reading my work and start financing Black people, firms, and institutions instead of exploiting devaluation as a path to make profits. Seeing value in inner-city housing stock has helped spur gentrification—just ask the residents of Harlem, Oakland, or Washington, D.C.

Mom moved to Wilkinsburg during the massive intra-city migration in Pittsburgh in the 1960s. I should say that Mom was displaced. In 1961, city officials voted to raze approximately 1,300 structures within the heart of Black Pittsburgh, the section known as the Hill District, to make room for the construction of the Civic Arena sports complex. Over 1,500 families, approximately 8,000 people, were displaced, which spurred a migration to the East End section of town—the Homewood-Brushton neighborhood of Pittsburgh and Wilkinsburg. Mom's story of how she got to Wilkinsburg is one many Black families in Pittsburgh can tell; Pittsburgher and Pulitzer Prize-winning playwright August Wilson captured one aspect of it in his play *Two Trains Running*, which offers a framework for a solution to positive change (as well as the title for my book).[11]

The play, which is set in 1969, the year after the Civil Rights Act was passed and Martin Luther King Jr. was assassinated, illustrates the economic injustice Black people still face. It presumes that Pittsburgh's Urban Redevelopment Authority (URA), which seized land in the neighborhood of the Hill District throughout the 1960s as part of an urban renewal project, purposely undervalued Black residents' homes and businesses to purchase the land on the cheap. The protagonist, Memphis, owns a building and restaurant, both of which are slated to be seized by the city through an eminent domain clause in his deed. A Black man, Memphis is certain the city would assess his property differently if he were White. Referring to the eminent domain language in his deed, Memphis says, "They don't know I got a clause of my own . . . They can carry me out feet first . . . but my clause say . . . they got to meet my price!"

Another character in the play, Hambone, painted a fence for a grocer who promised him a ham upon completion. Hambone painted the fence, but the owner never paid Hambone the ham. "He gonna give me my ham" is a refrain throughout the play. It's unclear if Hambone suffered from a mental illness before the incident or developed one after, but waiting for the grocer to pay what he promised drove him mad. He died demanding what he was owed.

Memphis, meanwhile, went back and forth with city officials, armed with an accurate valuation of his property and a demand that the city meet his price. The last scene of the play epitomized the kind of result Black business owners, home owners, and all residents can realize if we are collectively as committed as Memphis was in not selling himself short.

"I went down there to the courthouse ready to fight for that twenty-five thousand dollars I want for my property," Memphis said. "I wasn't taking no fifteen. I wasn't taking no twenty. I want twenty-five thousand. They told me, 'Well, Mr. Lee . . . we got a clause, and the city is prepared to put into motion'—that's the part I like, 'prepared to put into motion'—'the securing of your property at 1621 Wylie Avenue'—they had the address right and everything—'for the sum of thirty-five-thousand dollars.'" Memphis, elated to receive the compensation he demanded and deserved, starts making plans for a new restaurant. In real life, Mom, like so many other Black families, was forced to move from the Hill District to Wilkinsburg.

Knowing the worth of our homes, businesses, and communities—assets—starts with knowing that our assets are constantly being devalued. The devaluation of our assets affects us physically, psychologically, and economically in negative ways, one of which is to rob us of our sense of self-worth and dignity. Demanding our proper price helps us achieve just and equitable distributions of needed resources and reinforces the notion that there is nothing wrong with Black people that ending racism can't solve.

Racist federal, state, and local policies created housing, education, and wealth disparities. Policy must work for Black people in the same way it has supported White people's efforts to lift themselves up. Bootstrapping, financial literacy, and other things we wrongly attribute to White success didn't save them from urban plight and rabid unemployment during and after the Great Depression. Federal housing, transportation, and employment policies did, and the U.S. government largely excluded Black people from those efforts.

When upliftment is too rigidly viewed as a zero-sum game, there is no incentive for an overwhelmingly White U.S. House and Senate with mostly White constituents to re-create policy history for the benefit of Black people. Therefore, change must emanate upward from the neighborhoods to the halls of Congress. To be clear, I'm not disguising a call for bootstrapping as activism. Bootstrapping won't solve many of the problems Black people face, especially those around economic mobility. Pragmatically speaking, Black people must leverage the assets we possess to excite change. As Frederick Douglass said in his 1857 "West India Emancipation" address at Canandaigua, New York, "Power concedes nothing without a demand. It never did and it never will."[12] Knowing your price is about leveraging the power we possess.

There are certainly plenty of Black people who know they have value—folks like Memphis and Hambone. However, communities need researchers to provide enough frameworks and information so leaders and families can challenge governments and markets that devalue, dehumanize, and demean us for economic gain. This book is about understanding those processes as well as how our agency and assets can dismantle those structures. We have little choice but to mobilize the resources at our disposal, but we must deploy them toward structural change if we want outcomes free of the influences of racism.

I represent Wilkinsburg. My ups and downs as a person are undoubtedly rooted in many of the struggles of my hometown. Our fates are intertwined. The childhood conflict I related earlier has shaped my entire adult life, which has been beleaguered with unpredictable outbreaks of rage, largely stemming from reminders of past feelings of vulnerability and worthlessness. Minor disagreements with lovers, friends, colleagues, and strangers often turned into blowout arguments, for reasons unknown to them. To those whom I verbally assaulted, I apologize.

In my late thirties, I "progressed." Instead of outright verbally assaulting people, I aggressively debated with those who consciously or unconsciously reminded me of Hotsy, still taking people to the brink of hurt feelings and broken friendships. Again, I apologize. While many interpreted my anger as passion, I hurt the people in my life and myself. The stain of unresolved contempt toward Hotsy and others kept me trapped in internal conflict. I deeply wanted to belong, to matter.

This book is written using different styles to convey a state of my personal development and my varied levels of connection with certain Black-majority cities. Sometimes my internal conflicts will emerge in my writings about cities. Chapters are part memoir, part essay, and part *cri de cœur*, with a splash of "dispassionate" analysis, varying in degree. I hope people will turn to the associated research reports on the Brookings website.

Some chapters are emotionally distant; others are very personal. The degree to which I insert my personal narrative into each chapter reflects the level of personal and professional investment I have with each featured Black-majority city. Nonetheless, the goal at the onset of the project was to highlight assets in Black-majority cities, which in and of themselves should be viewed as assets to our democracy. I aimed to push back against the harmful narrative, rooted in White supremacy, that Black people are deficits in need of fixing. And, finally, I set out to identify potential solutions that can be used in Black-majority cities to restore some of the value lost from racism.

I start with using my hometown as a case study of sorts, illuminating the dynamics of devaluation and how it throttles economic growth in geographic areas with high concentrations of Black people. By retracing my old high school cross-country training route, I illustrate in chapter 1, "Who Runs the City," how Pittsburgh's tech boom was spurred by common economic development practices that overlooked and ignored Black people and institutions worthy of investment, reifying structural inequality. Consequently, cities need help in identifying assets that have been devalued. To illustrate how research methods can be used to identify assets, in chapter 2, "A Father Forged in Detroit," I show how racism lowers the prices of owner-occupied homes in Detroit's Black neighborhoods, lessening past and current residents' (including my father) abilities to climb the proverbial social ladder. If we can solve for devaluation by restoring value in our homes, we should be able to lift our communities and the people in them. In chapter 3, "Buy Back the Block," I examine one man's efforts to restore value through real estate development in the historic Black neighborhood of Ensley, which is in Birmingham, Alabama.

White and middle-class flight leaves many physical structures unoccupied, including school buildings, that are tactically placed to optimize a neighborhood's access. Adding value to communities will require converting some of these vacant properties into organizations and firms that meet communities' needs. Chapter 4, "A Different Kind of School," examines one effort to convert my first school into a business incubator.

There will be mistakes in adding value to communities. In chapter 5, "The Apologies We Owe to Students and Teachers," I show how my own efforts to reform schools devalued Black teachers of New Orleans. In chapter 6, "Having Babies like White People," I return to family. The devaluation of property is really a manifestation of the debasement of Black people. Restoring value in our communities will require the expansion of options to make family, gaining reproductive justice rather than restricting it through family planning. I will show how social connections and reproductive justice literally make Black lives matter through an examination of racism, infant mortality, and surrogacy.

Restoring value in communities will require a legislative agenda delivered by the people we elect. Chapter 7, "For the Sake of America, Elect a Black Woman President," highlights the Atlanta mayoral race to show how Black women voters and elected officials provide a vantage point that can unify communities in an era of fractured politics. In closing, I show in chapter 8 that, in spite of many efforts to remove Black culture from city landscapes like Washington, D.C., chocolate cities can't be erased because our brilliant culture won't allow it.

I work toward fixing systems instead of people. I can help my hometown forge a new path in the face of new challenges caused by devaluation. But I'm also creating a new path for my own development. Like many Black men, I directed my unresolved anger at people I should have loved instead. I do my best to atone for those actions throughout the text. However, I choose to keep some of my anger—an anger we all should have when our home, our hometown, is taken from us without a fair hearing—for this project. This time, I will direct my indignations toward biased policies instead of people.

1

Who Runs the City

In 1985, when pop stars convened to perform at Live Aid concerts around the world, singing "We Are the World" to raise awareness of starving populations in Africa, I decided to join the Wilkinsburg cross-country team. One of my team's primary training routes was a straight six-mile down-and-back on Penn Avenue, the main street running through the heart of town. Single file, the team would patiently weave between shoppers and workers, who animated the physical assets shops and transportation hubs that Wilkinsburg possessed. As it did then, Wilkinsburg still has the infrastructure and location that should sustain investment in the borough. But as I was coming of age, the percentage of Black residents grew, which seems to alter the value of assets beyond what their intrinsic qualities would suggest.

Historically, Penn follows the same military throughway that was known as Forbes Road, or, during the colonial period, Great Road.[1] In the late 1700s, Forbes became a "de facto civilian highway, providing settlers and traders from eastern Pennsylvania with a land route to . . . the fledgling community of Pittsburgh that took root in its shadow."[2] It would later be named the Greensburg and Pittsburgh Turnpike before it was called Penn Ave.

The road ran east to west through the 266-acre tract purchased in April 1769 by European settler Andrew Levi Levy Sr.; he named it Africa. Wilkinsburg was later sited within that tract.[3] It's unclear when the original name of Africa was dropped (or why Levi Levy called it that in the first place). In 1788, Levi Levy sold the tract to General William Thompson, who died a year later. Thompson's heirs transferred the deed for the land to Colonel Dunning McNair, an officer in the Pennsylvania state militia who became a prominent Pittsburgh area legislator, businessman, and land speculator.[4] McNair named some of that land McNairstown and laid out its street plan. McNair would later rename the tract Wilkinsburgh in honor of his friend General John Wilkins Jr. (the "h" was dropped in 1878). The name Wilkinsburg stuck, and the fledgling borough grew rapidly.

Because of Penn Avenue, Wilkinsburg has been favorable to commerce since its christening. The 1841 *General Business Directory* listed twenty-two businesses and people, but the village of "Wilkingsburgh" had fewer than 100 people.[5] When the railroad began stopping in Wilkinsburg in 1852, more people and businesses came to the municipality. "In 1880, there were 3,000 residents; by 1910, there were 19,000," according to the Wilkinsburg Historical Society.[6] Although the city has realized many ups and downs since the turn of the last century, I grew up seeing the productivity of generations' past.

Wilkinsburg High School sat only two blocks off Penn Avenue. In 1985, Wilkinsburg's downtown offered something for everyone. Heavy street traffic kept our cross-country training runs confined to Penn's busy sidewalks. George Westinghouse's extremely profitable company, Westinghouse Electric and Manufacturing, was on the cutting edge of technology and was based in the adjacent borough of East Pittsburgh, and a good many of its 20,000 workers used Penn to get there. Westinghouse was good for Wilkinsburg business, bolstering the borough's retail corridor on Penn Avenue.

Mom's daughter, my auntie Mary, routinely took the family to the same establishments I passed on my training route. G. C. Murphy, the local five-and-dime, anchored the corridor. Mary would go there to collect the money that Cheryl, a manager at Murphy's, owed for watching her sons David and Jamar. From there, Mary would take us to the Red, White, and Blue Store, a second-hand clothing store also located on Penn Avenue. Mary often stopped in Don's Appliances as well as Steel City Vacuum on her way to Mellon Bank down the street to make a deposit.

Eateries like Smith's Bakery and Angelo's Pizza were always busy after school. My classmates bought candies from the Pittsburgh Asian Market, which was a full-scale supermarket catering to the Asian diaspora. I bought my first pair of name-brand tennis shoes from David's Shoes, which was conveniently nuzzled up next to Sol's clothing store, whose owners smoked cigars while they showed you their goods. They'd size you up on the spot and hem your smoke infused pants within minutes. Next to Sol's sat the Montgomery Ward department store, the classic catalog store from back in the day. Touch of India sold Indian clothing and curios, but it also catered to the edge of Black culture, with its ten-karat hollow gold chains, New York fashions, baggies, and pipes for drugs. New comics came out on Tuesdays, and the family would head to Zern's magazine shop; Marvel's Kung-Fu was my favorite.

Once the team crossed the above-ground bus expressway, East Busway All Stops, better known as the EBA, we got a little more elbowroom. The two-lane bus-only highway in Wilkinsburg connecting Pittsburgh with the Black neighborhoods in the eastern part of the city. We passed Columbia Nursing Home and Forbes Hospital, which sat cattycorner from each other on Penn Avenue. Back then, I didn't realize how much economic power our tiny borough wielded. Wilkinsburg was so busy I would sometimes not even realize when we crossed over into Pittsburgh proper, sitting cheek by jowl as the cities do, with only the lonely street of Point Breeze as border. Writer and Wilkinsburg native Damon Young wrote in a column about Wilkinsburg, "I've lived in Pittsburgh for practically my entire life, and I'm still not quite sure where Pittsburgh ends and Wilkinsburg begins. I suspect it occurs when Braddock Avenue is crossed, but again I'm not certain."[7] The buildings looked the same to me, too, as well as the people. Wilkinsburg was Pittsburgh without the "h."

At the point when we started building up a healthy sweat, the smells of the Nabisco cookie factory, located in the Black-majority neighborhood of East Liberty, hit us in the face. The changing color of the street signs from green (Wilkinsburg) to blue (Pittsburgh) was supposed to let people know they were leaving one municipality and entering the other. A more substantive indication for me was the smell of cookies. Pittsburgh was so close you could smell it.

Sometimes we ran past my biological mother's house. Karen lived about four miles away, in the Garfield neighborhood, another Black area along my Penn Avenue running route, closer to downtown Pittsburgh. To break up the monotony of a down-and-back run on Penn, we often headed west on Fifth Avenue into the Oakland neighborhood, home of the University of Pittsburgh, Carnegie Mellon University, and Carlow College. If the timing was right, we'd see runners from one of the local college teams. Occasionally, we stopped to watch them doing intervals in the nearby parks of Schenely or Frick.

I didn't realize during my cross-country days that Wilkinsburg was in transition, becoming majority Black. When I was born in 1970, Wilkinsburg was approximately 20 percent Black. By 1990, the Black population rose to 52 percent. From 1990 to 2010, its population fell to 15,930 from 21,080, and the population changed to more than two-thirds Black. Those who remained were more likely to be poor. The poverty rate among Wilkinsburg families rose to 20.9 percent in 2016 from 14.3 percent in 1990.

Those of us who lived in Wilkinsburg in the seventies and eighties were flush with pride from all the assets that were in front of us, and understandably so. We taunted kids from Pittsburgh by saying we lived in Wilkinsburg. The economic anchor of Westinghouse Electric and Manufacturing Company sat on the outskirts of Wilkinsburg, as did the ABC television affiliate WTAE Channel 4. We saw the bustling activity generated by those companies on the commercial corridor of Penn. I saw my friends' parents come from Westinghouse to shop in Murphy's and donate clothes to the Red, White, and Blue store. My peers got their first jobs in those businesses. As a skinny ninth-grade runner from Wilkinsburg, I had prestigious postsecondary institutions, retail outlets, banks, libraries, parks, and Black people in my sights. I saw the flow of commerce and the resulting prosperity pass into Black communities and Black families. The world was at my feet.

When I returned to Wilkinsburg for an all-class reunion in 2017, I retraced my old Penn Avenue running route. Whereas the foot traffic of Wilkinsburg's sidewalks had constricted my runs in the past, the distractions of what used to be slowed my steps this time. My alma mater, Wilkinsburg High School, no longer exists. In 2016, the Wilkinsburg School District dissolved its middle and high schools, conceding its educational responsibility to Westinghouse High School of Pittsburgh Public Schools.[8] The high school building designed for big kids now houses elementary school students. Twenty-five students comprised Wilkinsburg High's last graduating class. Wilkinsburg graduated about the same number of male graduates that year as ran on the cross-country team in 1985.

The primary school I attended, Johnston Elementary, is now Community Forge, a nonprofit business incubator dedicated to speeding up the growth of Wilkinsburg start-ups. The building had sat vacant since 2012 when Community Forge purchased Johnston from the school district for $225,000, and opened in 2018.[9]

Traditional business incubators strive to do just as their name suggests—they incubate or help develop businesses so they can eventually leave the nest to fly on their own. Incubators provide a physical office space and offer business services such as printing and internet, conference rooms, and even management training to those who apply and/or pay rent.[10] Accelerators (not to be confused with incubators) are businesses that provide intensive technical assistance (most often not offered in college) and access to practitioner-mentors in the field to selected entrepreneurs. It's comparable to the TV show *Shark Tank*, with similar pitch competitions to attract potential investors. Some incubators and accelerators help germinate an idea or business with investments of private capital in exchange for an ownership share or profit percentage. Incubators and accelerators are central elements of the start-up tech culture that has proliferated in the last decade. Community Forge, which is featured in chapter 4, hopes to make incubators a community development tool.

The Borough of Wilkinsburg integrated its fire department into Pittsburgh's in 2011, after the department became financially insolvent.[11] Pittsburgh also manages the borough's waste removal. Wilkinsburg's downtown today is but a shell of its previous self. The loss of so many businesses and stores only throws into relief the typical poverty shops; cell phone dealers, discount stores, and check cashing places offer a monotonous set of options for passersby.

As I moved closer to the city of Pittsburgh on my 2017 run, the once-invisible border between the cities became remarkably apparent. The intangible aroma of buttery Ritz crackers had vanished, the fragrant boundary between the two cities replaced by a physical one— the colorfully decorated offices Google had set up in East Liberty where Nabisco used to be. Apart from the new windows, multicolored lighting, and pressure-washed brick, the outside looked familiar. But inside, the heavy machinery of the past had been replaced by an open-space cubicle farm for software developers, featuring playrooms with musical instruments, videogames, and hammocks, and with snack stations throughout.

The tech giant anchors a ballyhooed innovation hub in East Liberty, not too far from Peabody, the high school I transferred to in my junior year. In 2009, that high school became the Barack Obama Academy of International Studies. A year later and a mile away, Google established a second Pittsburgh office, also on Penn Avenue, complete with famously fanciful workspaces, on the grounds of the old Nabisco factory renamed Bakery Square. The mixed-use development includes apartments, fancy retail, a commercial gym, and many work-play-live conveniences that highly paid employees expect. Google employees can walk across a footbridge to the latest addition to the campus, Bakery Square 2.0, which opened in 2017. Bike trails wind from the square to adjacent Mellon Park with its walking paths, basketball and tennis courts, and grassy knolls for those who just need some quiet and sun.

The conversion from East Liberty to Bakery Square illustrates how urban planners institute a process for community development that "capitalizes on a local community's assets, inspiration, and potential, and . . . results in the creation of quality public spaces that contribute to people's health, happiness, and wellbeing," according the Project for Public Spaces, a nonprofit that helps people create and sustain public spaces.[12] This process is described by the jargon "placemaking"—a verbal waffle that is quite deceiving.

"Places already exist," said New Orleans based architect Bryan Lee, who heads his own planning firm. Placemaking minimizes architects and planners' sordid history of transforming a place into what they feel is best for Black communities, which in actuality is rooted in what the architect would do for him/herself. In 2017, only 2 percent of all architects were Black. When Whites are the default placemakers, the projects taken on will undoubtedly carry implicit biases. When it comes to community development in Black-majority neighborhoods, the person, firm, or group orchestrating the actual development can't be ambiguous. Black communities need reimagined spaces just like everyone else. But architects and planners must be deliberate about not imagining Black-majority spaces as places that are suitable for White, middle-class residents.

If community development is the goal, architects and planners should invest in how people of a particular place already use an area. "Rather than trying to reinvent space, planners should try to accentuate how they are already being used," said Lee. For instance, the areas in which elders use milk crates as stools and card tables can be resourced and developed to emphasize its current functions. Lee explained that people will adapt a place based on the amount of resources in it but needs and desires for the space can still present themselves. But overall community development wasn't the goal in the development of Bakery Square. Developing Pittsburgh's then-budding tech sector was.

Bakery Square helped spur growth along Penn Avenue in one reimagined neighborhood after another, cascading to downtown Pittsburgh, well beyond my old running route through Karen's old community. Chic restaurants and bars have opened where time-worn buildings and blight used to be. Driverless cars zip through the streets, made conspicuous by a spinning contraption, a lidar,[13] sitting atop their roofs. Two new hotels—the notoriously hip Ace and the cool Indigo—have sprung up in East Liberty to accommodate those flying in for job interviews with Google or any number of other tech companies and ancillary businesses.

Something else is noticeable. East Liberty is visibly much less Black than it used to be. It looks more like a home for the pale male tech industry that is struggling with its lack of diversity. The online magazine *Business Insider* reported in 2016 that Black people made up less than 5 percent of the field nationwide.[14]

Uber, Amazon, Argo AI, and dozens of other tech companies have all found the Steel City accommodating in the last decade. The *Pittsburgh Tribune* reported that investments in the city's tech scene exceeded $687 million in 2017, and will grow to more than $3.5 billion in ten years.[15] East Liberty represents the kind of neighborhood transformation old industrial cities lust after. The town that once spun a narrative of brawn, smoke, and iron now peddles brainpower, innovation, and technology, as well as neighborhood revitalization. Bakery Square, the capital of Pittsburgh's intellectual revolution, sits two miles from the University of Pittsburgh, University of Pittsburgh Medical Center, Carnegie Mellon University, and Chatham University, as well as my hometown of Wilkinsburg.

The tech boom and the development of East Liberty didn't happen by chance. Millions of dollars were invested in grouping the powerful intellectual institutions of the city, and that clustering was used as the basis for placemaking strategies for areas such as East Liberty. The city sought to develop an "innovation district," which, according to one of its proponents, Bruce Katz, an urban scholar with Drexel University, is "a small geographic area within cities where research universities, medical institutions, and companies cluster and connect with start-ups, accelerators, and incubators."[16] Those efforts proved successful.

Clustering is another term loosely used in economic development circles. My colleagues at the Brookings Institution define industry clusters as "groups of firms that gain a competitive advantage through local proximity and interdependence . . . [Clustering] offers a compelling framework for local and state leaders to analyze and support their economies."[17] Black economists and business owners recognize that clustering is mostly a euphemism for some form of exclusion when it comes to economic development. Who's included in a business cluster almost always reflects the racial dynamics of a place. Pittsburgh leaders' clustering and placemaking efforts largely excluded Black talent, firms, and associations. The competitive advantages that are gained come at the expense of the quality of life among those who are not included. If deconstructing racism isn't a primary goal of a cluster, then you're more than likely going to increase inequality.

In many ways, I recognize East Liberty as everything Wilkinsburg used to be. Everything to accommodate the residents is within walking distance, built and anchored by industry. You'd think Wilkinsburg and other Black communities would be benefiting from Pittsburgh's resurgence as a tech force, maybe even serving as home base for these businesses. Proximity to economic growth and technological expansion should increase opportunities for Black and Hispanic people.

My hometown has the history of Westinghouse Electric and Manufacturing Company, which was as close to Wilkinsburg's downtown as Google is to Pittsburgh's. Wilkinsburg has its own exit off Interstate 376, which transitions to Penn Avenue. The same two-lane bus-only highway that has a stop in East Liberty starts in Wilkinsburg. Closeness to Black and Hispanic communities should be an opportunity for disproportionately White industries looking to develop people of color. The tech industry is important because it makes up the "traded sector" of the economy, which comprises everything traded outside of the region (from raw materials and algorithms to cars and software) as opposed to skills in the non-traded sector that are related to industries that serve local residents (such as schools, construction, and healthcare). Economist Enrico Moretti found that for every high-tech job produced in this era another five is created in non-tradeable, locally serving jobs.[18] However close in proximity many neighborhoods are to these booming industries, the evidence shows there are limited career pathways for low-skilled residents—at least for Black people in places like Pittsburgh. Worse, pay for low-skilled laborers may decrease from the presence of the tech industry.

In a 2019 study, researchers Neil Lee and Stephen Clarke found that high-tech industries do, indeed, have a multiplying effect.[19] Using data on UK labor markets from 2009 to 2015, they found with each ten new high-tech jobs another seven local, non-tradeable service jobs were produced, six of which go to low-skilled workers. "Yet while low-skilled workers gain from higher employment rates, the jobs are often poorly paid service work, so average wages fall, particularly when increased housing costs are considered."

Pittsburgh's tech boom offers a cautionary tale; the median wage of Blacks in the Pittsburgh metro area from 2005 to 2015 dropped by nearly 20 percent while Whites realized an increase of almost 10 percent, according to a 2017 Brookings Institution analysis.[20] Being proximate to economic growth isn't enough.

Wilkinsburg still has potential. The assets it possessed in the past are still there: affordable real estate and ample space. Its library remains, along with parks and other amenities that all residents enjoy. But it hasn't gotten anywhere near the level of investment Pittsburgh has, outside of organizations that seek to leverage or save aging and vacant real estate. The Pittsburgh History and Landmarks Foundation has invested roughly $13 million in Wilkinsburg in recent years.[21] There is a small nonprofit business incubator and a project by the Wilkinsburg Community Development Corporation (WCDC), a nonprofit that promotes revitalization in Wilkinsburg through business and residential development, with the aim of raising $6 million toward its Train Station Restoration Project, the largest restoration project in the municipality.[22] Restoring the train station as a retail hub is an attempt to connect the local bus hub (East Busway All Stops) and Penn Avenue, "which together host over 50,000 people every day," according to the WCDC video.[23]

People in Pittsburgh will say that folks won't invest in Wilkinsburg because of the history of violence in the borough. The Larimer Avenue-Wilkinsburg gang, also known as LAW, became one of the most lethal in the entire country around the time I went to college, between 1989 and 1993. Because my home situation was so insecure during those years—a crowded house, an aging matriarch, and a fraying relationship with Mom's son Hotsy—I found ways to do summer research projects, camps, and short-term jobs in other cities, living with college classmates.

But the streets talked. I'd get messages from my younger brother Dorian about some of my family and peers. David and Jamar Dorsey, whom Mom and Mary used to watch, were swept up by gang life and eventually found guilty of multiple crimes. Between 1993 and 1999, dozens of my former classmates and friends were sent to jail on racketeering, murder, and kidnapping charges. At least sixty of my friends (yes, sixty; I counted) got caught up in the drug game, and dozens of those were killed. Many are just now being released from prison. What seems like a lifetime ago was my hometown's twenty-five-year rush of violence compounded by economic and social depression.

Just as Wilkinsburg showed a sustained period of relatively low levels of violence between 2010 and 2014 (figure 1-1), as did in the entire city of Pittsburgh, my hometown made national headlines in 2016 for an incident dubbed the "Wilkinsburg massacre."[24] That spring, Cheron Shelton and Robert Thomas opened fire on fifteen people during a backyard party and killed five people and a pregnant woman's fetus. In response, a local broadcaster and Emmy Award–winning anchor Wendy Bell, of the television station WTAE (located about a quarter of a mile away), offered this commentary on her Facebook page, before any arrest was made: "You needn't be a criminal profiler to draw a mental sketch of the killers who broke so many hearts two weeks ago Wednesday," Bell posted.[25] "They are young Black men, likely in their teens or in their early 20s. They have multiple siblings from multiple fathers and their mothers work multiple jobs. These boys have been in the system before. They've grown up there. They know the police. They've been arrested."

WTAE's parent company Hearst Television fired Bell, saying in a statement that her comments were "inconsistent with the company's ethics and journalistic standards." Bell and Hearst reached a financial settlement, but the deficit thinking inherent in her commentary is shared by others throughout the region, particularly among those involved in economic development. This downward, nihilistic gaze is what educators call "the deficit perspective"—the conscious or unconscious belief that members of a disenfranchised cultural group don't have the skills to achieve because of their cultural background, or, in plain terms, that they're not White or middle-class enough.

The deficit thinking inherent in Bell's mental sketch of the killers

FIGURE 1-1. DECLINING CRIME IN ALLEGHENY COUNTY, PA.
VIOLENT AND PROPERTY CRIME RATE PER 100,000, 2010-2014.

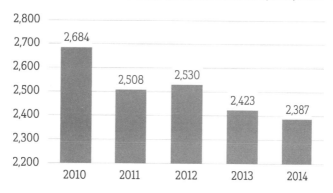

SOURCE: UCR crime data estimates.

is a significant reason why resources that are requisite for economic growth never get to the people who need the boost. The mental sketch of the killer isn't dissimilar to a description of Black young people who had nothing to do with the murder. In general, investments are made in assets as well as problems in which there is a potential for a positive return; however, they are not made in people who are perceived to be problematic or who aren't expected to add value—my friends and family in Wilkinsburg.

Today's East Liberty would be indistinguishable from Wilkinsburg if no one had thought to invest in the *people* of Carnegie Mellon, University of Pittsburgh, Google, and the assets in that section of town. Economic development has always been chiefly about people— except when it comes to Black people in Black neighborhoods. When it comes to Black people, economic development becomes about investing in inanimate objects, like buildings in which Whites are the assumed beneficiaries. Phrases such as *urban development* and *urban planning* are misnomers, because in practice they are mostly real estate deals that aren't substantively connected to the Black and Hispanic business and homeowners (or potential owners) closest in proximity.

As a result, many affordable housing and tax incentive programs in inner cities facilitate White people's growth and end up displacing Black residents in the long run.

Many of the academic institutions and businesses that regularly receive investments in the Pittsburgh area have no deep ties to Black communities. Consequently, those dollars don't go beyond those social networks. The placemaking efforts leading to the development of Bakery Square exemplify what can happen when Black people aren't seen or valued. Inclusive growth can't happen without investments in existing talent and social networks within the neighborhoods where they reside.

The invisibility of Black institutions, firms, and social clubs in various economic strategies is so stark that many cast doubts on whether many Black-majority cities like Wilkinsburg should even exist. "Merger with the central city is an option more physically contiguous inner-ring suburbs should consider," writes Aaron Renn, a researcher at the Manhattan Institute for Policy Research.[26] Journalist Eduardo Porter, commenting on small cities' struggles to adapt to economic downturns, writes, "As technology continues to make inroads into the economy . . . it bodes ill for the future of such areas."[27] If Black-majority cities are a problem, making them less Black through annexation becomes the solution.

We know too well that merging with a larger city isn't a foolproof path to prosperity. Indeed, there are Black neighborhoods within Pittsburgh that are struggling just like Wilkinsburg; Homewood and Beltzhoover are almost indistinguishable from my hometown. Not only is Wilkinsburg small, it hosts many undereducated single moms and fathers who've been to jail or prison: people whom many believe are incapable of adapting.

Restoring value is, indeed, possible. It was returned to East Liberty. The rationale of Pittsburgh's transformation from a rust belt to a brain belt city can be applied to thinking about how to revive struggling, Black-majority communities. White Pittsburgh's revitalization didn't happen from talent alone. Economic growth and advancements in technology are a direct result of strategic investments in people who are trusted. Those who aren't trusted are left behind.

When I run the Wilkinsburg streets now, my heart pounds, not from fear but from encountering some of my former classmates on Penn Avenue. One classmate who I'll call Frank told me that, after a long bid in prison in the nineties, he has been doing odd jobs, trying to survive. He looked depleted, like he'd run a distance he couldn't handle. Back in the day, I was scared of him. Now, I'm fearful for him, and for the residents of Wilkinsburg. It's the same palpable fear I feel when in Detroit, Ferguson, Baltimore, and other Black-majority cities. The town is realizing the impact of divestment and devaluation and there is no hope in sight, because no one invests in perceived deficits or problems. Still, the people and property have value. The assets in Wilkinsburg are made invisible by the negative perceptions of Black people. However, instead of running away, I'm learning to run toward distress, learning how to fight back.

2

A Father Forged
in Detroit

The deliberate deployment of racist policy toward Black neighborhoods has been documented, measured, and accounted for when looking at outcomes of people like my father Floyd, yet we would rather blame Black parents and parenting for the economic and social trajectory of people in Black-majority locales. We often hear "It all starts at home" when searching for reasons why someone ends up poor, incarcerated, or murdered. Some would rather find cause in poverty instead of policy. In this vein, "It all starts at home" covers for the belief that people's deficits are to blame for negative outcomes. "Individuals are left without the norms that middle-class people take for granted," *New York Times* columnist David Brooks wrote in a column about urban poverty.[1] His commentary shows how subtle blaming people while ignoring policy can be. Brooks adds, "It is phenomenally hard for young people in such circumstances to guide themselves."

Behaviors don't exist in a vacuum. Life and death are shaped by forces larger than oneself. Factors like generational wealth, property taxes, and bias baked into home valuations all limit or expand the choices a person can make. According to my research highlighted in this chapter, the value of homes in Black-majority neighborhoods across the country is $156 billion lower than their equivalents in similar White neighborhoods. In addition to eliminating wealth, the devaluation of housing throttles educational, vocational, and recreational opportunities for residents.[2] Whether you are in Wilkinsburg or Detroit, the neighborhoods where many of us reside are devalued, and our educational and career choices reflect the impacts of that extraction of resources caused by racism. As Notorious B.I.G. rapped in the song "Things Done Changed":[3]

> *If I wasn't in the rap game*
> *I'd probably have a key knee-deep in the crack game*
> *Because the streets is a short stop*
> *Either you're slinging crack rock or you got a wicked jump shot*

When societal biases lessen the value on homes in Black neighborhoods, residents and communities lose the wealth and revenue to develop themselves as well as the institutions that expand the number of options residents have. Home values drive property taxes, which generates the revenue that helps determine school quality, infrastructure improvements, public safety, and recreation.

Absent is the culpability that policy should share with behaviors. While de facto and de jure segregation and housing discrimination unquestionably influenced housing markets, the residents most burdened by U.S. policy continue to shoulder the blame of its effects. The retort "it all starts at home" should be about policies that devalue homes, people, and places rather than family behavior.

"Your father just got caught up," explained Kergulin Cunikin, who ran the streets with my father in the 1970s. "It was a good time in Detroit. People worked; they had money. Drugs were flowing . . . People had a good time . . . Your father just got caught up."

Getting caught up with heroin led my father, Floyd Allen Criswell Jr., to a life of crime that didn't last very long. Floyd died in prison a day before his twenty-seventh birthday—stabbed in the heart by another inmate.

But Floyd didn't just get caught up in his own personal issues—drug use and criminal activity—as many of my family members and his former friends believe. He lived in neighborhoods that were devalued, limiting his choices. My father made bad decisions, and he paid the ultimate price. Racism was also culpable for his development, but society has not paid its debt.

All my life, I never took the time to learn much about Floyd. I don't think I had the chance to call him Dad. I can't recall ever talking to him, even though my mother Karen charitably says I did. Floyd bounced between Detroit and Pittsburgh throughout his life, so if I did talk to him, it was fleeting. The only address of his I knew was the one on his criminal record: Whitcomb Street on Detroit's west side. His father, Floyd Sr., and my Grandma Doris were both born in Detroit. Grandma Doris reared her four children—Sherdina, Raymond, Floyd, and Boo—in an apartment on Pingree and 12th Streets, also on Detroit's west side. Floyd bounced between various apartments, the Herman Gardens Housing Projects, and single-family homes amid prison bids and trips to Pittsburgh.

Three of Grandma's four children died before she did—two killed in the Detroit area. Floyd's older brother Raymond was a pimp who was stabbed to death in 1963 by a woman who, I presume, he tried to traffic. Although Grandma Doris and Floyd Jr. moved to Pittsburgh when he was about eight years old, they stayed connected with Floyd Sr.'s brother, Uncle Rufus, in Detroit.

I don't remember seeing Floyd or talking with him, but I frequently saw my immediate biological family throughout my time in Pittsburgh. I learned most of the details I know about Floyd's life only recently, from my cousin Shante. Gregarious and sharp-witted,

Shante interpreted for me the police records and other legal documents I had about Floyd. But she was a witness to his story too. At about twelve years younger than he, she was old enough to remember the major events in his life. Shante wasn't sure when Floyd started using, but by the time he was nineteen, he was a father of three and a full-blown addict. Floyd and Karen conceived my older brother Kevin and me. In 1971, five months after I was born, Floyd had another child—Diona—by a woman named Bernice.

When I visited Grandma Doris on holidays, she repeatedly grabbed my face to tell me how much I looked like Floyd. It was like she couldn't say hello without commenting on the physical resemblance. When she talked about Floyd the person, the exchange seemed to drift into a conversation about Detroit. Given the trauma Grandma Doris experienced in Detroit, you'd think she would avoid conversations about the Motor City. To Grandma Doris, despite it being the backdrop for much suffering, Detroit also represented a sacred land full of opportunity that attracted Black folks with its promise of freedom. Detroit may have been a painful place for Grandma, but it was a place she could claim for her own.

Grandma Doris represented a people's unrequited love for Black-majority cities. Many of us are unquestionably committed to Black-majority cities, but that love is not reciprocated by public policy. Considering the devaluation of our lives and property, my family's losses reflect an abject failure of policy to protect us against discrimination. History shows that policy proactively degraded us. The extent of White residents, politicians, and employers' efforts to make conditions as difficult as possible for Black people to thrive in Detroit reveals how today's $156 billion in losses is rooted in antagonistic policies and people bent on debasing our lives and property—*in the past and present.*

"There's never been a place designed for Black people to live in large numbers," said comedian D. L. Hughley in an interview on VLAD

TV, an online video and news website run by DJ Vlad. "The only place they build for niggas to live was jail, was prison."[4] The history of White antagonism toward Black people in Detroit, including my family members, makes Hughley's point.

Blacks relocated to Detroit largely from the South in two waves of the Great Migration: first after World War I and later with the coming of World War II, seeking jobs in the auto capital of the world. The rapid migration of Blacks who already had limited options where they could live created a severe housing shortage. In anticipation of grants from the federal government, the Detroit Housing Commission in 1941 approved two housing developments—one for Blacks and one for Whites—to provide some relief for a growing Black population. However, the federal government rejected Detroit's plan to build homes for Black folk while allowing a development for Whites. Intense protests ensued from housing advocates, resulting in a single development for Black occupants that was to be named Sojourner Truth Homes in honor of the nineteenth-century abolitionist and women's rights activist.

Soon before the U.S. Housing Authority (USHA) planned to open the housing units, on February 27, 1942, a mob of dozens of White residents participated in a cross burning at the site. The next morning, approximately 150 White dissidents blockaded the lot to prevent Black residents from moving in.[5] Chronicled in the book *Black Detroit* by City College of New York historian Herb Boyd, Blacks retaliated by driving two cars through the gang. What ensued is now known as the Sojourner Truth riot, which ended with police placing the Black residents under protective order. To allow for time to calm a tinderbox situation, the National Housing Agency took two months to ready themselves for another effort to move Black tenants, who were given temporary housing, into their permanent homes in Sojourner Truth. The mayor deployed 1,000 police officers and had 1,600 National Guard troops to assist and eventually clear the way. The many physical disputes and police envoys highlight the degree to which Whites fought to show that Black people didn't belong in Detroit.

While racist Whites tried to make housing insecure for Black people, they also applied aggressive tactics in the workplace. In 1941, during World War II, car manufacturers had to convert assembly lines that made cars into lines that produced tanks. The war demanded more workers—regardless of race—to produce enough war machines. Before and immediately after World War II, Blacks were relegated to service work like janitorial services or given dangerous jobs in the foundries, pouring melted metals into castings.

A worker described working in the foundry in the early twentieth century in an oral history project cited in a 1979 *Journal of Negro History* article:

> As I looked around, all the men were dirty and greasy and smoked up. They were beyond recognition. There were only three or four Whites. These were Polish. Negroes told me later they were the only ones able to stand the work. Their faces looked exactly like Negro faces. They were so matted and covered with oil and dirt that no skin showed. My friend and I went home discussing how it was that they could say everyone was free with equal rights up North. There was no one in the foundry but Negroes. We didn't believe those men wanted to be in the foundry.[6]

Blacks were most often excluded from the assembly lines because White laborers refused to work with them, limiting the amount of quality jobs available for Blacks. Frank Hadas, a Ford engineer during the period, described in an oral history project cited in a 1979 *Journal of Negro History* article on how employers justified putting Blacks in inferior roles and dangerous positions in the early twentieth century. "You could have them on some dirty, rough job where there wouldn't be many Whites to complain against them," said Hadas. "But if you tried to mix them in the assembly lines or any place else where Whites predominated and hung their coats touching those of the Whites you know, 'that nigger is poison;' you couldn't do that."[7] Again, the federal government intervened. Apparently, when it comes to winning wars, patriotism had little patience for racism.

In 1941, Navy Secretary Frank Knox attempted to squelch racial harassment that may have slowed production. Knox issued warnings to White employees who refused to work with African Americans, according to Boyd. Refusals were to be seen as being disloyal to the government and the war efforts. Knox proclaimed that those who refused to work with Black laborers would be subject to dismissal and banishment from other wartime production jobs.[8]

Civil rights organizations such as the NAACP and unions like the United Auto Workers fought alongside the federal government to eradicate employment discrimination in the factories. People knew then, as they do now, that many problems in Black communities stem from a lack of job opportunities. In 1943, the preeminent scholar W.E.B. Dubois recommended in his column in the *Amsterdam News* these crime reduction strategies: employment at a livable wage, the eradication of African American illiteracy by 1980, healthcare for all people, and a social security system that included eliminating unemployment.[9] Today we know that those who are out of the labor force for reasons that generally are not socially acceptable (such as retirement and disability) and who also are not looking for work are much more likely to commit burglary and robbery, according to a 2016 study published in the *Journal of Quantitative Criminology* by researchers Gary Kleck and Dylan Jackson.[10]

A national Black labor movement led by A. Phillip Randolph pressured the auto industry for greater inclusion in the 1940s. Organizers put enough pressure on President Franklin D. Roosevelt in 1943 that he issued an executive order to get more Blacks hired in the factories, resulting in the hiring of more than 75 thousand Black Detroiters, highlighting the role the federal government could play today in improving employment outcomes.[11]

While labor organizers helped Black Detroiters acquire housing and jobs, victories for equity didn't assuage hardline prejudicial attitudes of White residents, and back then they were the majority in the city: 91 percent in 1940; 84 percent in 1950; and 71 percent in 1960. The attitudes that fueled racial tensions in the 1940s and 1950s helped motivate White people to move out of Detroit. And the federal government's housing and transportation policies facilitated those desires. White Detroiters abandoned Detroit at the expense of Black residents' assets rather than make it a place everyone could call home.

The establishment of the interstate highway system in 1956 literally paved the way for White flight to the suburbs. Freeway construction, most notably the Edsel Ford Expressway, which was completed in the 1950s, also known as I-94, tore through predominately Black neighborhoods. Black businesses and homes were seized through eminent domain polices. More than 2,800 properties were removed for that project alone, debilitating Black wealth and economic growth. Detroit's population dropped from 2 million to approximately 1.5 million during the 1960s when Whites moved to the suburbs, taking their tax dollars and discretionary incomes with them.

"Whites were able to use the government guaranteed housing loans that were a pillar of the [GI] bill to buy homes in the fast growing suburbs . . . But Black veterans weren't able to make use of the housing provisions of the GI Bill for the most part," wrote David Callahan of the left-leaning think tank Demos about the discrimination against Black veterans that occurred across the United States, including Detroit. "Banks generally wouldn't make loans for mortgages in Black neighborhoods, and African-Americans were excluded from the suburbs by a combination of deed covenants and informal racism."[12] The Home Owners' Loan Corporation established in 1934 the practice of drawing red lines around precise geographic areas the government-sponsored corporation classified as "hazardous," disqualifying potential homebuyers from using federally-backed, low-interest loans to purchase homes in these neighborhoods. Racially restrictive housing covenants that prohibited Blacks from buying in certain areas throughout the twentieth century, isolating Blacks in areas that realized lower levels of investment than their White counterparts. "As the wealthier White population left Detroit, the overall population shrank and the city's tax base shrank, too, leaving Detroit less able to support public schools, public safety, and its huge, geographically spread-out infrastructure," wrote research fellow Ross Eisenbrey of the Economic Policy Institute in a 2014 blog post.[13] People like my father Floyd were negatively impacted by a school finance structure based on local property. Born in 1951, Floyd attended severely underfunded schools in the city White people abandoned.

In the late 1950s, Floyd moved out of the Black neighborhoods of Detroit and into the Black sections of Pittsburgh. Unlike his White peers, he could not escape harsh conditions. Urban development across the country had decimated Black neighborhoods in cities everywhere, hurting the economic and social fabric that supports people. Less than a decade after developers in Detroit displaced Blacks by building highways through Black areas, city planners in Pittsburgh displaced Blacks in the 1950s by building the Civic Arena sports stadium in the economic and social center of the Black community.

The devaluing and abandonment of Black people by White Detroiters, facilitated by the federal government, left those who remained behind without a government-backed means to uplift their own social status like their White peers had done. For instance, the Black soldiers who could not use the GI Bill because of redlining and racial covenants had no choice but to pull themselves up by their bootstraps.

The Civil Rights Movement did produce gains during the period: President Lyndon B. Johnson signed the Civil Rights Act of 1964. But that legislation was followed with the assassination of Malcolm

X in 1965. The next month, police sicced dogs on 600 civil rights marchers in Selma, Alabama. When President Johnson signed the Voting Rights Act of 1965, racial tensions were at a breaking point. White people's resistance to integration around the country led up to the turbulent "long hot summer" of 1967 in which 159 race riots erupted nationwide.

In Detroit, racial tensions exploded after police raided an unlicensed bar known as the Blind Pig. What police officers thought would be a standard police raid turned into "five days of violence, leaving 43 people dead, thousands of others injured and much of the city looking like a smoldering war zone," according to *Detroit Free Press* reporting.[14] Black Detroiters set the city ablaze, proclaiming that their lives matter. "The insurrection was the culmination of decades of institutional racism and entrenched segregation," according to an account offered by the Detroit Historical Society.[15] The conditions in which my grandmother reared Floyd were the same as those the protesters were willing to burn down.

After the riots, Blacks continued to press for economic justice in the face of flagrant discrimination. The intense labor demands of the high-growth automotive industry pressured companies to meet those needs with Black workers. Approximately one in five Detroit autoworkers was Black when I was born in 1970, up from 16 percent in 1960.[16] The proliferation of unionized jobs in the auto industry empowered Black people in Detroit like few other places in the country. In terms of labor participation, Detroit had become a Mecca for Black people, just like Grandma Doris talked about.

University of Pennsylvania historian Thomas Sugrue found that, in the late 1960s and early 1970s, unionized companies hired more Black people for higher pay than their non-unionized peers; the positions came with benefits, including health insurance and pensions. Union rules privileging seniority helped protect Black workers from discrimination by their supervisors, encouraging longevity in their jobs and, subsequently, creating much-needed opportunities for wealth building. Unions also created fair employment practice departments for autoworkers to seek redress for grievances.

"Because auto industry jobs were unionized and relatively well-paying, Black autoworkers formed a Black labor 'aristocracy,'" wrote Sugrue in a series of articles on Blacks in the auto industry.[17] General economic growth in the region in the 1960s and 1970s spurred business activity among Black-owned companies.

Floyd's Uncle Rufus, who also lived in Detroit the late 1960s, saw an opportunity in the growth of the auto industry to start a trucking company. Rufus Criswell's Trucking Company hauled lumber from the ports to the factories in Detroit. His business supported about a dozen employees and his immediate family who also lived in Detroit. When Rufus' trucking business was growing, Floyd lived in Pittsburgh, and he soon got a call to return home and help with the business. It was an opportunity for a fresh start that he desperately needed, and it would help him take care of his two young sons and his daughter. In addition to giving him a job, Rufus also invited Floyd to stay with him in his house on Whitcomb Street.

Moving back to Detroit made sense. In 1970 in Detroit, the overall unemployment rate was 7.2 percent; Black unemployment was 10.3 percent. In many U.S. cities, the unemployment rate for Blacks was double that of Whites. Floyd took Rufus up on the offer. He married Bernice, the mother of his daughter, packed their bags, and moved to Detroit. My brother Kevin and I stayed at home with Mom and Mary in Wilkinsburg about 300 miles away.

Floyd landed a solid job, had a family who supported him, and was living rent-free in a single-family home in a solidly middle-class neighborhood where the lawns were maintained and light decorations in the front gave the neighborhood an upright identity. But it didn't take him long to return to his old life of drugs and crime. Floyd was an addict. And the criminalization of the underground economy of drugs, prostitution, and other activities made Floyd vulnerable to incarceration.

In 1971, two years after he moved to Detroit, Floyd was sentenced to two and a half to five years for attempted larceny in Jackson State Penitentiary (now Michigan State Penitentiary), located about seventy-five miles outside of Detroit. He was released in 1974, but police records show he received another sentence of one to two and a half years for carrying a concealed weapon the year he was released. Floyd entered Jackson on a third charge of unarmed robbery in 1977 for a ten-year bid. Between his stints in prison, Floyd fathered another child in Detroit with his wife Bernice, as well as two children with another woman. When Floyd was killed in prison in 1978, he left behind six children born of three women. The kids ranged in age from ten to one.

He died the day before his twenty-seventh birthday. Records say he was stabbed in the heart at 7:50 a.m., dying of a single, fatal wound. My family says someone killed Floyd while he tried to break up a fight. The records are painfully inadequate. I believe Floyd died because he entered a prison instead of a drug treatment center. Many will point to his drug use and his criminal activity as causes. Floyd's personal story is about so much more than his individual choices. Floyd's story is about the devaluation of Black people as well as the places and homes in which he lived. That story of devaluation is being played out in the lives of countless others today.

RACISM COMES OUT IN THE WASH OF RESEARCH

Racism can be defined as the systemic devaluation of *people* because of their race, ethnicity, and/or immigration status. However, people and places are inextricably linked. When it comes to housing discrimination, it's hard to see where bigotry against people begins and where place-based injustice ends. Discriminating against place leads to people of color being subjugated to racism en masse. That kind of discrimination involves the devaluation of the cities and towns as well as the physical structures within them. Policymakers, captains of industry, and private citizens all have used place-based strategies to throttle Black people's development, restrict our movement, as well as imprison us based on racialized criminal justice policy. For proof, you need go no further than past and present redlining; predatory lending practices; environmental racism that subjects our communities to disproportionate exposure to pollution and hazardous waste; harmful zoning practices that make us susceptible to flooding and post-disaster displacement; as well as discriminatory drug sentencing and stop-and-frisk laws that reflect policymakers' extreme disregard for Black people.[18] All these injustices take years off our lives and value from our homes.

In a study I coauthored with my colleagues Jonathan Rothwell of the survey company Gallup and David Harshbarger, also at Brookings, we examined how prices in Black-majority neighborhoods convey value; we compared home prices between Black-majority neighborhoods and White neighborhoods. We examined homes of similar quality in neighborhoods that were comparable—except for the racial demographics—to make an apples-to-apples comparison between places where the share of the Black population is 50 percent or higher and those where there are few to no Black residents. After controlling for factors such as housing and neighborhood quality, education, and crime, we found that comparable homes in neighborhoods with similar amenities are worth 23 percent less in Black-majority neighborhoods, compared to those with very few or no Black residents. The percent difference is the devaluation. In real dollars, owner-occupied homes in Black neighborhoods are undervalued by $48,000 per home on average, amounting to a whopping $156 billion in cumulative losses nationwide.

Take the metropolitan statistical area (the urban core and surrounding areas) of Rochester, New York, for example. With a Black population of 11.5 percent, this metro area sees a 65 percent difference between the actual price of a home in a Black neighborhood and the adjusted rate for equivalent housing in one of the area's White neighborhoods, amounting to a $53,000 loss in price per home. In the Durham-Chapel Hill metro area of North Carolina, which has a Black population of 26.8 percent, there is a 12.5 percent difference, resulting in $26,000 loss in price per home. In the Pittsburgh metro area, which has a Black population of 8.2 percent, there is an 11.6 percent difference, resulting in $12,000 loss in price per home. And in the homes in the Detroit metropolitan area—Detroit being the largest Black-majority major city in the nation—there is a 37 percent difference, resulting in $28,000 in average loss per home to a sum of $4.36 billion.

Let's break all this down. Most people intuitively know that homes in Black neighborhoods are priced lower than those in White areas. This is certainly true. In the average U.S. metropolitan area, homes in neighborhoods where the share of the population is 50 percent Black are priced at roughly half the amount of homes in neighborhoods with no Black residents. There is a strong and powerful statistical relationship between the share of the population that is Black and the market value of owner-occupied homes (figure 2-1). Location in a Black neighborhood predicts a large financial penalty for 117 out of the 119 metropolitan areas with Black-majority neighborhoods, though the valuation gap varies widely between them.

Federal and local governments as well as private citizens, as explicated in the Detroit example, certainly had a role in degrading property. The practice of redlining didn't formally end until 1977 with the passage of anti-housing discrimination policy, the Community Reinvestment Act. That loss of revenue kept individuals and municipalities from investing in neighborhoods, which negatively impacted the housing stock.

Most people will attribute the price difference to perceived flaws in people and communities. Many will say lower school quality, crime, poor housing stock, and other problems with either the home or the neighborhood are the reasons for the lower prices. We con-

FIGURE 2-1. NEIGHBORHOOD MEDIAN HOME VALUE BY BLACK POPULATION SHARE, U.S. METROPOLITAN AREAS, 2012–2016.

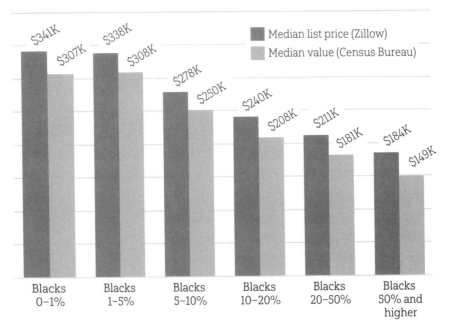

SOURCE: Zillow and 2016 American Community Survey five-year estimates.

trolled statistically for many of those variables. Taking the common beliefs about what lowers home prices off the table, we found that differences in home and neighborhood quality do not fully explain the lower prices of homes in Black neighborhoods. Black-majority neighborhoods do exhibit features associated with lower property values, including higher crime rates, longer commute times, and less access to high-scoring schools and well-rated restaurants. And these factors do have a negative impact on price. Yet, these factors explain only roughly half of the undervaluation of homes in Black neighborhoods.

Given that homes in Black-majority neighborhoods are devalued by 23 percent as compared to White ones, with a cumulative loss of $156 billion nationally, we need to reframe the "it all starts at home" refrain. It does start at home, but what that means is bigotry and implicit bias impose a "Black tax" on residents of Black-majority neighborhoods that White neighborhoods simply don't have to pay. To put it plainly, racial bias is taking away money from Black families that could be put toward college tuition or a small business. Notwithstanding the elimination of discrimination in employment, policing, education, and other areas, if homes in Black neighborhoods bought and sold at market rates, our neighborhoods would have significantly more resources. Home sellers don't get their proper value, and certain buyers don't necessarily get the return on investment they deserve. Devaluation also means municipalities with a significant percentage of African Americans lose tax revenue that could be put toward government services and infrastructure. This is a vicious cycle: Devaluation leads to divestment, which leads to people moving out of the community; social services decline and crime and unemployment rise. Given the large amount of money that is stripped from communities because of racism, it's illogical to think Black folk should be faulted for community decay.

Put that $156 billion in cumulative, national losses into perspective. That $156 billion could have started 4.4 million Black-owned businesses, based on the average amount of $35,205 Blacks use to start a company.[19] It could have paid for 8.1 million four-year degrees based on the average tuition of $19,189 at public universities in 2016.[20] These are real wealth-building opportunities that could have catapulted the Black population to greater heights.

More perspective: The cost of replacing all the water pipes in Flint, Michigan, was estimated to be about $55 million, and the cost of the damage related to hurricane Katrina was $161 billion. That means the $156 billion could have replaced pipes in Flint nearly 3,000 times over and paid for the nearly all (97 percent) the damage caused by Hurricane Katrina.[21] The nation's yearly economic burden due to opioid abuse, dependence, and overdose is an estimated $70 billion (excluding criminal justice costs, which account for 10 percent of the total). The $156 billion is a sum large enough to more than double our efforts to combat the opioid crisis, according to a 2013 analysis of Centers for Disease Control data published in the academic journal *Medical Care*.[22] All this is to say that 23 percent and $156 billion are big numbers.

Our study also looked at devaluation in the same neighborhoods studied by lead author Harvard economist Raj Chetty, which linked records from the Internal Revenue Service to the Census Bureau to understand intergenerational income mobility for people age thirty-one to thirty-seven who were born between 1978 and 1983.[23] We found that Black children born into low-income families could achieve higher incomes as adults if they grew up in metro areas where homes were less devalued. If properties in Black neighborhoods were priced equally to those in White neighborhoods, Black children coming of age in the 1990s and 2000s would have had much more wealth to draw upon to pay for tutoring, travel, and educational experiences, as well as higher education and greater access to other neighborhoods. Greater property wealth also may have facilitated higher rates of entrepreneurship among Black parents, which may have positively affected children.

Contemporary work from social scientists has tried to sort out whether these lower valuations are caused by differences in socio-economic status, neighborhood qualities, or plain discrimination.[24] The findings are in agreement that discrimination is at play.[25] In one study published in the academic journal *Social Forces*, Valerie Lewis, Michael Emerson, and Stephen Klineberg collected detailed survey data on neighborhood racial preferences in Houston, Texas.[26] Researchers asked 1,000 participants from each racial group from a variety of neighborhood types to imagine that they were looking for a new house and to find one within their price range and close to their job. Respondents were then told about the neighborhood context using randomly generated combinations of characteristics about the public schools in the area, property values, the crime rate, and racial percentages. Consistent with previous research, they found that certain neighborhood features strongly predicted whether someone said they would buy the house. Racial composition strongly predicted the preferences of White buyers in neighborhoods that were otherwise identical, meaning White buyers refused to buy houses in Black neighborhoods but bought identical-seeming houses in White or mixed neighborhoods.

Researchers Jacob Fabera and Ingrid Gould Ellen, in the academic journal *Housing Policy Debate,* examined rising housing prices through the housing bubble from 2000 to 2007 and through the bust of 2008.[27] They reported that Blacks and Hispanics gained less equity than Whites during that period and were more likely to owe more than their home was worth in 2008. In addition, their findings show that "Black-White gaps were driven in part by racial disparities in income and education and differences in types of homes purchased." The researchers hypothesized that racial segregation and the resulting economic and education stratification between neighborhoods exacerbated equity disparities within neighborhoods that already had high concentrations of poverty. Consequently, the recession hit impoverished neighborhoods disproportionately harder, creating intense volatility in those markets. Declining incomes reduced people's ability to purchase homes, thus further deflating prices in those neighborhoods. The findings around education and income may result from the disparities in wealth as it is "a powerful predictor of individual educational and economic outcomes, and despite their significantly lower homeownership . . . the long-run consequences of these gaps are substantively important and difficult to overcome."[28]

But how does the concentration of Black residents in a given neighborhood affect demand among all buyers? In other words, what is the cost of racial bias? Real estate agents have been shown to direct Black and White home buyers differently based on racial stereotypes, reinforcing patterns of racial segregation. Researchers Sun Jung Oh and John Yinger reviewed four different national studies on the topic in a 2015 academic article published in *Cityscape* and found a common thread: There is "evidence of statistically significant discrimination against home seekers who belong to a historically disadvantaged racial or ethnic group."[29] Some of this research is not about devaluation per se but about steering and price discrimination. It indicates that Blacks actually pay more than Whites for equivalent housing.

It's clear that much more is at play regarding Black people's outcomes than our individual behaviors. Our findings show researchers must put the onus on those who use a tool of racism—devaluation—rather than on the people effected by racism, which ultimately leads to blaming the victim. Black homes are worth much more than they are priced, and isn't that just the perfect metaphor for living while Black in America?

But how can we bring value back to these communities? There are some practical steps. The areas our research demarcated as being devalued by race provide a geographic unit by which we can restore value through different kinds of investments. But we must tread lightly. If we waved a magic wand and priced devalued homes at market rates, we would price out many of the long-term residents, particularly renters, who ostensibly live in these neighborhoods in part because of the lower rents. We must restore value iteratively in ways that empower and support those who have been committed to the neighborhoods without pricing them out.

That starts with incentivizing homeownership among current renters. After reaching a high of approximately 69 percent in 2004 and 2005, the U.S. Black homeownership rate has declined significantly (figure 2-2). Today, the rate is about the same as it was when the 1968 Fair Housing Act was turned into law, but it has been relatively stagnant since the Great Recession.

Homeownership in devalued communities may not offer the greatest wealth building assets because of the low market values, but ownership would make people less vulnerable to displacement or gentrification. However, devalued areas could offer tremendous

FIGURE 2-2. HOMEOWNERSHIP BY RACE,
UNITED STATES, 2009–2017.

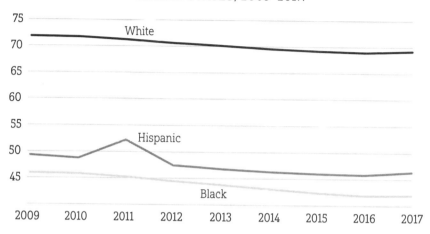

SOURCE: American Community Survey U.S. Census Bureau estimates.

returns as the price of entry is significantly lower. Incentives for renters to become homeowners can come in the form of first-time buyer down payment assistance to people who have lived in devalued areas since before the Great Recession—a time of incredible volatility and movement.

There is a plethora of affordable homes that long-term renters would purchase if they had access to low-dollar, low interest mortgage loans. Alanna McCargo, researcher at the D.C. think tank the Urban Institute, reported in her 2019 congressional testimony that "In 2015, there were over 630,000 home sales recorded under $70,000. Only one in four of those sales was mortgaged."[30] I agree with McCargo's analysis. We must create a robust small-dollar mortgage market designed for low- to moderate-income residents in areas with significant devaluation. Income and residency criteria must be in place to prevent the hording of property discounted for those who benefited from a biased housing market.

If not for racism, White families would have long sought to move into Black neighborhoods en masse. White homebuyers are moving into Black neighborhoods that are near downtown, according to an analysis by *New York Times* reporter Emily Badger.[31] Our study on housing devaluation found significant assets in Black communities that everyone deems desirable. For instance, Black-majority neighborhoods are more walkable, have higher public transportation usage, and have comparable commute times to work as their White counterparts (table 2-1). Consequently, eligibility for first-time homeownership programs should employ wealth scores (the total value of all financial and property assets owned minus financial debts like credit cards and student loans) as opposed to using income criteria.

We also must restore value to neighborhoods with investments in current homeowners. The devaluation metric can help determine the amount of tax credits that can go to owners who occupy property and have lost significant wealth because of racism. Devalued communities could also benefit from the distribution of micro-loans for deferred maintenance to current homeowners who have less discretionary spending because of the lost equity in their homes.

Universal place-based strategies will be insufficient in restoring the value lost by racism. Many have assumed, including some of the 2020 Democratic candidates for president of the United States, that reuse of the old redline maps—employed by the Home Owners' Loan Corporation (HOLC) from 1933 to 1977—can be a place-based strategy to address some of the residuals of historical discrimination against Black and Latino people. Prohibited from using race-based remedies by the Constitution, politicos assume they can repair some of the damaging financial effects redlining had on Black residents with this strategy. However, the assumption that maps made more than sixty years ago can redress Black people effected by discrimination or that the same racial proportions remain in these places isn't a strong one.

The University of Richmond's *Mapping Inequality* project has digitized scans of the HOLC redlining maps held in the National Ar-

TABLE 2-1. SAMPLE OF NEIGHBORHOOD CHARACTERISTICS BY BLACK POPULATION SHARE IN U.S. METROPOLITAN AREAS, 2012–2016

Black population share, percent	School test scores (Standardized)	EPA Walkability Index	Number of restaurants	Number of gas stations	Percent who use public transportation	Average commute time (minutes)
0–1	0.29	−0.31	53.2	6.9	3.6	26.7
1–5	0.28	−0.03	69.3	8.1	5.1	26.5
5–10	0.17	−0.01	69.7	9.2	4.7	26.6
10–20	−0.01	−0.01	67.5	10.0	5.4	26.5
20–50	−0.27	0.01	61.9	10.6	7.7	27.1
50 or higher	−0.85	0.23	50.0	10.8	15.0	29.2

SOURCE: Analysis of data from 2016 American Community Survey five-year estimates, Department of Education, Environmental Protection Agency, and County Business Patterns

chives.[32] David Harshbarger's and my examination of the maps, numbering over 200, reveals that about 11 million Americans (10,852,727) live in once-redlined areas, according to the latest population data from the Census Bureau's American Community Survey for 2017.[33] This population is majority minority but not majority Black, and, contrary to conventional perceptions, Black residents also do not form a plurality in these areas overall. The Black population share is approximately 28 percent, ranking third among the racial groups who live in formerly redlined areas, behind Latino or Hispanic (31 percent) and White residents (31 percent). In addition, the total percentage of Blacks living in formerly redlined areas is only 8 percent (figure 2-3).

Redlining was one form of housing discrimination that contributed to the wealth gap. Racial housing covenants, discriminatory lending, biased appraisals, as well as steering behaviors on the part of real estate agents also robbed Black people from benefiting from the housing market. Most Black people did not live in redlined areas, so any proposal that uses just this place-based strategy will be insufficient—not unuseful, but insufficient. Consequently, there should be multiple approaches to restoring value to homes, communities, and institutions and wealth to individuals.

The federal government should make reparations for people who were robbed of opportunities and wealth due to slavery, segregation, and housing discrimination. "Broach the topic of reparations today and a barrage of questions inevitably follows," wrote Ta-Nehisi Coates in his masterpiece "The Case for Reparations" published in the *Atlantic*.[34] "Who will be paid? How much will they be paid? Who will pay? But if the practicalities, not the justice, of reparations are the true sticking point, there has for some time been the beginnings of a solution." Addressing specific remedies for reparations was not a goal of this book. But I must say, the usual response that reparations are too hard to figure out simply doesn't fly. "You can use sound historical research to connect individual institutions to descendants of enslavement for purpose of reparations," wrote Marcia Chatelain,

FIGURE 2-3. MOST RESIDENTS OF REDLINED
AREAS ARE NOT BLACK

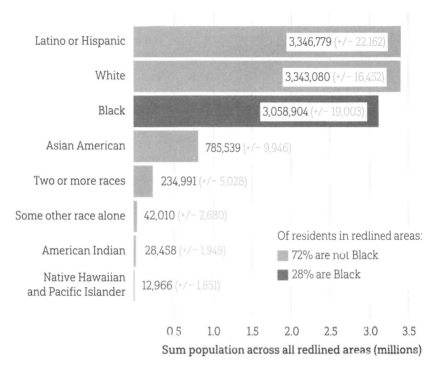

SOURCE: University of Richmond *Mapping Inequality* project and Brookings analysis of 2017 ACS block group estimates.

NOTE: Margins of error calculated at a 90% confidence interval.

associate professor at Georgetown University, in an email to me for a column I wrote about the university's reparations plan.[35] Chatelain is one of the advisers for the student group that formed the idea of a reparations fund. "The archive is deep and rich and we need to use it. So, the excuse that the history is too in the past to facilitate financial repair is not always the case."

In addition to reparations, the federal government simply has a responsibility to uplift struggling communities stunted by discrimination. Just like the federal government assisted White families with federal housing and transportation policy after World War II, it must be involved with the restoration of Black families who were burdened by said policies. Those strategies proved effective in building wealth for many White Americans. Why not for others? Well, we know why, but that's not an excuse.

Because an immediate correction to housing prices would prohibit homebuying for low-income Black residents, we must also iteratively restore wealth to the people targeted by racist federal policy. Darrick Hamilton, who serves as the director of The Ohio State University's Kirwan Institute for the Study of Race and Ethnicity, and Duke professor William Darity proposed savings securities called "baby bonds" as an attempt to reduce wealth inequality among Americans, but the plan offers the kind of restorative program that could also help with devaluation. Under Hamilton's and Darity's baby bond plan, every child born in the United States would receive $1,000 in a bonded savings account run by the Treasury Department.[36] Each year, the government would make contributions based on each family's size and income. The lower a family's income, the greater the contribution would be. Children would receive an average of $25,000 upon turning eighteen. Those from the poorest backgrounds could expect as much as $60,000, according to Bloomberg reporting.[37] The money would then be restricted to wealth-building activities such as attending school, starting a business, or purchasing a home. The program would cost less than 3 percent of the federal budget. This kind of program would benefit all Americans, but those who've been negatively impacted by racial discrimination would certainly welcome a renewed commitment to social security.

The federal government must also renew its commitment to holding people responsible for discrimination that's illegal and legal. The devaluation we found based on 2017 data provides evidence that discrimination is baked into current policy. On June 20, 2019, I testified before the U.S. House of Representatives Committee on Financial Services Subcommittee on Housing, Community Development, and

Insurance for a hearing titled "What's Your Home Worth? A Review of the Appraisal Industry."[38] Representative Al Green of Texas asked a few pointed questions to a panel of witnesses composed of members of the appraisal lobby as well as me.

"Do you believe that invidious, invidious is harmful . . . , invidious discrimination plays a role in the devaluation of property in neighborhoods that are predominated with minorities, but more specifically Black people. If you do believe this, raise your hand."

I was the only one on the panel who raised a hand.

Nonplussed, Green asked another question for fear the panel didn't understand. "If you feel Black people are not being discriminated against when their property is being appraised . . . kindly raise your hand." No one on the panel raised their hand, but many guests (seemingly all White) of the panel seated directly behind the witnesses raised their hand in unison. Green responded, "Now we're getting some consternation."

After the hearing, many of the guests who raised their hand approached me to tell me they never did anything illegal or racist. The appraisers explained how they follow strict procedures and guidelines to prevent illegal activity. I reminded them that for decades housing professionals legally discriminated against Black people and the neighborhoods they lived in. Nevertheless, 87 percent of appraisers identify as White, 4 percent Latino, and 3 percent Black and 75 percent identify as male, according to a 2017 study by the Appraisal Institute;[39] professionals don't have to break any laws to discriminate when structures that govern their rules and practices are tilted against Black people.

Congress should restore value to families the federal government extracted wealth from in the past. And we must root out discrimination that still occurs today. We can look no further than the president of the United States, Donald Trump, as an example of someone who debases Black-majority neighborhoods with racist rhetoric, setting the tone for professionals within the housing market.

Approximately ninety minutes from Detroit in August 2016, hot on the campaign trail, presidential nominee Donald Trump said, "Look how much African American communities have suffered under Democratic control."

He was speaking at a rally in Dimondale, Michigan, where the crowd seemed to reflect the town's population: 98 percent White, by 2017 Census counts. Trump then made his pitch for the Black vote: "You're living in poverty, your schools are no good, you have no jobs, 58 percent of your youth is unemployed—what the hell do you have to lose?"

The message resonated with his mostly White audience, which roared in response.

There are $609 billion in owner-occupied homes, 10,000 public schools, and over 3 million businesses in Black-majority places nationwide to lose, according to my analysis. Trump's fatalistic appeal to the Black community mirrors a widely held view in Black communities that there is nothing of value there. It's a perspective that Trump has taken upon himself to reinforce in other Black-majority places.

In a tweet attack on July 27, 2019, directed at the late U.S. Representative Elijah Cummings (D-MD), who was Black, Trump disparaged the congressman's district of Baltimore as a "disgusting, rat and rodent infested mess."[40] Trump isn't the first leader to debase a Black-majority district with words, and he likely won't be the last. Trump's words are taken from the same poisoned well that bigots regularly spoon from. In March 2019, the *Washington Post* reported that a state delegate from Harford County, Maryland, referred to a neighboring county, Prince George's, which is 62 percent Black, as an "[n-word] district."[41] In July 2018, the news outlet the *Daily Beast* reported that Rick Shaftan, an aide for 2018 Senate candidate Corey Stewart in Virginia, tweeted that Memphis, New Orleans, and Baltimore—all Black-majority cities—were "shitholes," mimicking the term President Trump reportedly used in an Oval Office discussion to describe Haiti, El Salvador, and certain African countries.[42]

Shaftan attempted to use a proven campaign strategy—demonize Black cities and people.

Racism is not a mere distraction.[43] Inserting racist language has been the reliable prelude to codifying bigotry into law. Racial attitudes baked into Baltimore's housing policy in 1910 became a model for racial housing covenants across the country. Baltimore's then mayor J. Barry Mahool's negative view of Black people was laid bare in his explanation of the policy: "Blacks should be quarantined in isolated slums in order to reduce the incidence of civil disturbance, to prevent the spread of communicable disease into the nearby White neighborhoods, and to protect property values among the White majority."[44]

The neighborhood-based discrimination we accept as a given has helped normalize stereotypes of Black people and devalue the places in which we live.[45] Racist words not only diminish home values, they undercut Black leadership as well. Blaming Black-majority city councils, school boards, and housing authorities for corruption is a sport passed on from one generation to the next. Notwithstanding the high-flying scandal that is former Detroit Mayor Kwame Kilpatrick, who was found guilty in 2013 for multiple counts of racketeering and extortion, Black leadership in Detroit, chiefly the Black city council, bore outsized culpability for the city's financial woes in the same year, when it became clear the city didn't have a path toward paying its debts. Those totaled approximately $18 billion if you included outstanding bonds and unfunded liabilities for its employee pensions and retiree healthcare plans.[46] A White governor and a majority-White legislature took over the city and forced it into bankruptcy—the largest municipal filing in U.S. history—handing political and economic control over the budget to a state-appointed emergency manager.

Without question, prior city administrations bore some responsibility for Detroit's bankruptcy, as they cosigned the corporate welfare given to auto manufacturers. But to cast blame squarely on city officials for Detroit's decline is irresponsible and dishonest. "Corrupt mayors or antagonistic mayors are a sideshow compared to the gigantic outmigration of White people that began in the 1950s and turned Detroit from a wealthy White city into a desperately poor Black city," wrote Economic Policy Institute's Ross Eisenbrey in his 2014 blog post.[47]

The auto industry, like many other influential business sectors (see Amazon's HQ2 Competition), punked the city officials into dishing out tax breaks and other incentives to keep companies from leaving Detroit proper. By relenting to pressure from the auto industry, city officials dug themselves into a hole by not appropriately addressing spending needs and revenue shortages. At some point, governments must represent the entire public, not just private interests. (See New York City residents' backlash to Amazon's plan to build its new headquarters in Long Island City.)[48]

However, the impact of city officials' decisions on Detroit's economic and social situation pale in comparison to the divestment of "the big three"—GM, Chrysler, and Ford—from Detroit by leaving the city for the suburbs starting in the late 1940s, essentially to dodge taxes.

"From the very start, auto manufacturers preferred to locate in the suburbs—often as a tax dodge," Kevin Boyle, Detroit native and Northwestern University historian told the *Washington Post* in 2013.[49] Companies even moved major factories to countries like Brazil and Mexico to save costs. In addition, a significant source of the auto crisis was the inability of executives to properly account for their spending.

"Some observers cite labor contracts that prevent layoffs and guarantee high-cost health care coverage that can continue for decades after workers leave the company," wrote Chris Isidore for CNNMoney.com in 2008.[50] "Others say the companies are the victims of executives who overproduced gas-guzzling SUVs and pickups and ignored the fuel-saving technologies of their Japanese rivals. Either way, it's easy to see why so many people are troubled at the prospect of rewarding the automakers' management and workers with billions of taxpayer dollars."

The big three received an $80 billion federally backed bailout between 2008 and 2014.

A more balanced analysis of the city's bankruptcy would tell "the stories of the downfall of GM and Chrysler on the one hand and Detroit on the other as being intertwined and deriving from the same causes," as *Washington Post* columnist Todd Zywicki's examination indicated.[51] If Detroit was forced into bankruptcy on grounds of mismanagement, then the auto industry didn't deserve a bailout. I tend to believe that both the auto industry and the city of Detroit needed a bailout because both were "too big to fail," but clearly Black-led entities weren't given the same benefit of the doubt that they could rebound from a bankruptcy.

Instead, the old narrative that Black leaders should not be trusted ruled the day as state leaders stripped, in 2013, budgetary control from Detroit's elected Black city council members, who were against the state takeover.[52] Forcing the city into bankruptcy reinforced the thinking that preceded White flight: It's better to leave Black people to their own devices than to overcome racism or live alongside them. Black elected leaders were scapegoated for failing to harness an unsustainable fiscal situation that White flight and corporate subsidies created. The state of Michigan punished a Black-majority city via a Black city council by wresting away control of the city, abdicating responsibility for addressing the city collapse's root causes: White flight and corporate divestment.

The city came out of bankruptcy a year after it filed and after the emergency manager had shed $7 billion in debt.[53] As a consequence, retirees who were too young for Medicare lost their healthcare insurance, forcing most of them to purchase plans under the federal Affordable Care Act, also known as Obamacare. In addition, workers on the city's pension plan took a 4.5 percent base cut, including the elimination of an annual cost-of-living increase.[54] The cut in employee pensions affected 20,000 people.

The lens through which all Black-led institutions (city councils, school boards, housing authorities) are viewed is the same one used to see people like Floyd. Like many of its current and past residents, the city government of Detroit needed support. In the United States, there is a belief that you have to punish Black people for them to grow or learn. Whether it's a drug-addicted parent, a student who violates a dress code policy, or a city struggling with its finances, punishment is offered in lieu of the support that would be proffered to White people and White-led organizations.

In February 2019, I traveled back to Floyd's last two known addresses—first Whitcomb Street in Detroit, then Jackson Prison—to see for myself where my father lived, to learn more about my family, and to record how I felt about the experience. In the process of writing this book, Floyd became more than a subject for my analysis about Detroit. I developed a connection I didn't expect. I stood outside both of his last addresses, just to be in the same areas he used to be. My academic approach to learning about Detroit through my father didn't prepare me for what I felt. His last home, with Uncle Rufus, felt like the kind of place where Mom and Mary raised me. The neighborhood looks like your neighbors will snarl at you if your grass isn't cut. It felt familiar.

As I rode through Jackson, the town where the prison was located, I saw Black men in orange jumpsuits through the fences, walking around the yard. I could visualize many of my childhood friends, including David and Jamar from Wilkinsburg, behind those gates. I learned I had a psychological disconnect—a defense mechanism, of sorts—that was confirmed by the closure I got by reading his death certificate outside the county clerk's office in Jackson. "Stab wound to chest—lac[eration]—right ventricle." As I read, I felt a connection to a father I never knew and to a city I had never lived in. When I began writing this chapter, I felt strange typing *Floyd* and *father* in the same sentence because I had never uttered those words together growing up. Mom and Mary will always be my parents. However, after taking this journey, I realize I did have a father, and I have ownership of his story. I choose not to devalue him.

Close friends and colleagues often ask me, "What was the difference between you and your father?" After visiting where my father lived and died, I know for sure there wasn't much difference. The same underground economy that supplied drugs to an addict gave rise to mothers like Mom and Mary. None of us were exceptional and none were defective. However, we were all devalued. Some of us "make it" in spite of circumstances. Many of us don't. The trials and tribulations my father faced are the same I confront. Sure, there were choices I made that shifted my trajectory: I have a Ph.D., for instance. My father had an eighth-grade education—but so did Mom. Education didn't save me so much as the people in the 'hood and in boardrooms who gave me back the opportunities that had been taken from me.

Detroit *can* be that place of opportunity that Grandma Doris talked about. But at some point, corporate leaders and those who left must reckon with the devaluation of people and property that's holding Detroit back. White and middle-class flight significantly influenced the concentrations of families who make less than $50,000 in the suburbs (30 percent) and in Detroit (75 percent), according to findings in Detroit Future City's *139 Square Miles* report.[55] We owe a debt to people who stayed in Detroit through the good times and the bad. They are the assets that are worthy of investment.

There's a simple, universal concept concerning economic, social, and educational growth that must be front of mind when planning the expansion of the Black middle class: Authentic development and growth requires deliberate investment. If we want to see more Black people enter the middle class, we must invest in endeavors and interventions that lead to better paying jobs, affordable housing, efficient transportation, and effective schools. Though these amenities will attract middle-class people back to Detroit, the focus on development must be directed at uplifting a greater percentage of current residents so they have the necessary tools to enter the middle class. This means that growing the Black middle class in Detroit should not result from pushing low-income people out of the city.

Not just a matter of policy, devaluation is also a mindset that will have some thinking that a strategy to attract people back to the city should take priority. Bringing suburbanites back into Detroit would alter these racial and economic percentages, and we most certainly want conditions that are attractive to all middle-class families. However, we also don't want to return to the days when the devaluing of low-income and Black people hastened the flight to the suburbs. The concentration of Black people who stayed in the city is an asset worthy of investment. Increasing the percentage of the Black middle class is vitally important. But building from within is more so. Adding value to communities requires community development in the truest sense of the term. We must build up the people in neighborhoods, block by block.

3

Buy Back the Block

When people talk about real estate and community development in Black communities, they think mostly about building inanimate physical things, revitalizing property and infrastructure, and alleviating the outward signs of poverty.[1] Instead of people, traditional developers pay most of their attention to the built environment, making physical structures in a community suitable for residents to use. Consequently, conversations about urban development have focused largely on vacant lots, affordable housing, propping up storefronts, and creating bike lanes.

Black communities need to go beyond traditional community and real estate development. Rehabbing a bunch of buildings in hope of prosperous tenants falls short of the kind of investments Black communities need, particularly in a business district. We need real estate developers and urban planners to build endeavors that meet residents' basic needs while exciting economic growth in areas that goes beyond suppling affordable housing, creating jobs that generate a living wage, and assuring safety. In other words, developers should build community.

There is a clear tie and distinction between community and place.

Community represents people who share a culture, history, and traditions, all of which are held in neighborhoods, towns, and cities. Adding value to communities means constructing spaces that nurture human potential. It means incubating businesses in high-growth sectors of the economy as well as schools in which students and teachers reach their fullest potential. In a financing environment that is seemingly unreachable to Black people who didn't reap the wealth created by the New Deal, we also need real estate developers and urban planners to think holistically about financing, self-determinism, and claiming space. All this must be done at a scale that is both practical and inspirational.

Over most of this decade, rapper, entrepreneur, and community activist Ermias Joseph Asghedom, aka Nipsey Hussle, began investing in technology and community development projects such as Destination Crenshaw (an outdoor museum celebrating Black arts and culture) and Vector 90 (a co-working space that connects youth interested in STEM to Silicon Valley investors). He co-owned the brick-and-mortar "smartstore" Marathon Clothing, a retail outlet in South Los Angeles with an accompanying smartphone app. Nipsey realized that Black-majority cities and neighborhoods need developers who can cocreate with residents as well as other Black professionals who are from or are highly engaged with the devalued communities.

"I wanted to redefine the lifestyle and what we view as important," he said. "When you hear 'buy back the block' as the narrative, that's powerful. That's a step toward redefining the expectation." On March 31, 2019, Nipsey Hussle was fatally shot. The shooting took place in front of a clothing store that Hussle co-owned.

In the spirit of Nipsey, we can buy back the block.

In 2018, I met real estate developer Brian Rice, who, by buying an entire neighborhood block, is attempting to do that in Birmingham, Alabama. While highly motivated, Rice is clear-eyed about the difficult road he and others must take. Right before Rice and I entered a building he is rehabbing on a half-blighted commercial corridor he plans to refurbish, he repeated the same question many people had asked him: "Why, Brian? What are you thinking?"

Blighted, vacant buildings interspersed with crumbling, if occupied, storefronts surrounded us. Rice had purchased nine buildings on the block in 2018 and planned to bring them and the commercial corridor they were once part of back to life. Rice is developing the commercial properties on 19th Street in downtown Ensley, the largest of the ninety-nine neighborhoods within Birmingham. At the turn of the twentieth century, Ensley was its own municipality, with two business thoroughfares—one Black, the other White—where merchants sold their wares to people who worked in the nearby steel factory of Tennessee Coal, Iron, and Railroad Company (TCI).

Today, only a small number of businesses operate in the former White thoroughfare of Ensley. Trés' Fine Dressing at Cotton's and Gilmer Drug Store are community staples. African American Attorney Antonio Spurling developed several properties in the area, including his own office, which sticks out because of the building's new appearance. Mostly vacant, dilapidated structures sit idly between occupied ones. Half-demolished lots overshadow the occupied businesses in buildings that could very well pass as condemned. Very few people and cars passed us as we walked and talked. On this walking tour of Ensley, we stopped at one of Rice's buildings that was partitioned into multiple units; it was constructed of brick and wood seemingly held together by decay.

Large sheets of rice paper covered the inside of the windows, which prevented me from seeing the interior. Rice opened the padlocked wooden door to a unit that had definitely seen better days. He had to kick the door several times to unstick it. When we stepped inside, what I saw inspired me to join the chorus: "Why, Brian? Why?" Why develop this crumbling edifice?" Most of the roof had fallen to the floor. Sunlight illuminated the jumbled piles of wood, plaster, brick, and metal that covered the ground. Pieces of tin ceil-

ing tiles dangled perilously over our heads. The padlock was clearly
more to keep people out of harm's way than to protect the contents
of the condemned building.

Rice exuded a sense of confidence and purpose that made me feel
safe in this hazardous structure. The stocky Black man introduced
the wrecked building like a new friend. A large industrial printer
sat quietly in the back, the only trace of what this space might have
been. He didn't know its history.

And the state of the building held a mirror to the unemployment,
divestment, and devaluation in the entire neighborhood. The residents
of Ensley have been waiting for someone like Rice to develop the strip
with the neighborhood amenities they deserve. To outsiders, Rice
would no doubt seem to have made a bad investment by purchasing,
with the help of family and friend investors, nearly an entire crumbling, commercial city block in a low-income Black neighborhood.

Between 1970 and 2010, the East Ensley neighborhood lost 81
percent of its residents, the most of any Census tract in the city.[2]
When bank lenders and outside observers ask Rice, "Why?" they
are seeing the low-incomes, high unemployment, and high crime
in Ensley. But Rice is not looking at those realities; instead, he is
focused on its potential.

As we walked down 19th Street, Rice began sharing pieces of
his vision. Facing an open area, he said, "I want to turn that into an
outdoor pavilion patio-type space. A place for food trucks to set up."
We walked a few dozen feet, and he pointed out the three accounting firms on the block. He wants to convert one of the buildings to
a place for nonprofits and mentoring programs. He plans to use a
walkway between two buildings to host pop-up businesses. "As you
look down the street a little bit more, you will see there's three more
buildings . . . I want to turn that into a conference space for us and
the community." He was also clear about what he didn't want: "I
don't want . . . ABC stores or easy money stores."

Rice believes that crime in the area reflects a lack of purchasing power. "Of the 79 homicides that happened in Birmingham, Alabama, by October 2018, 52 of those were of either ex-felons or convicts," Rice exhorted. "But of the 52, seven of them were employed. Seven of 52." Rice is saying that if he can put people to work, he will automatically reduce murder in the area. AL.com, the web portal for Alabama newspapers including the *Birmingham Times*, reported in October 2018 that among the eighty-four victims of homicide that year only seven were employed; thirty-seven had graduated from high school. It's unclear why the *Birmingham Times* reported employment and educational status of the victims and not the perpetrators—probably because the perpetrators in many cases were unknown. Of the eighty-four victims, fifty-six were acquaintances with the killers, and investigators cited retaliation as the motive for many of the murders. We are left to assume victims and perpetrators represent the same population in need of an intervention. Nonetheless, Birmingham ended 2018 with 107 homicides—the second highest number in the last twenty years, with the lion's share in the city's west side around the Ensley neighborhood.[3]

Each building represented the multiple lives Rice intended to save through his development. He explained that the unit we were standing in was the easiest one to clean out. "It's already half on the ground." Pointing to openings in the crumbling plaster, he said, "We'll start showing that red brick again." Rice's desire to showcase the original brick reveals the motivation driving many Black developers: restoring past assets that have been forsaken by racism and neglect.

BLACKS' HISTORIC CONNECTION TO ENSLEY

What lies behind the façade of Ensley's disintegrating structures is a complicated history of Black uplift and White suppression. From Ensley's beginnings in the late nineteenth century, Black people have sought refuge in this historic neighborhood to weather economic and social storms. Birmingham was rich in coal and iron, which drew TCI to the region. The company acquired upstart local coal and iron firms, becoming a force in those and related industries.[4] The town's namesake, Enoch Ensley, was born of a wealthy White family in Nashville, Tennessee. Enoch Ensley received a large inheritance, which enabled him to purchase companies and land in both Tennessee and Alabama. After several failed attempts to purchase TCI, Ensley eventually became its president in 1886, and soon after, he sought to form a town. Ensley officially became its own city in the same year its namesake took the helm of TCI. The company built four blast furnaces in the new municipality, paving the way for a conjoining steel mill and stimulating population growth among Black people. Before the city of Birmingham existed, only 10 percent of residents were Black. By 1910, Black workers held 75 percent of iron and steel jobs in their area. TCI went on to build houses for the Black employees who worked in the furnaces.[5]

When U.S. Steel Corporation purchased TCI in 1907, executives decided to build a new plant north of Ensley in the area now known as Fairfield, signaling that company leaders did not see value in the part of town with a significant number of Black families. The move checked Ensley's economic and population growth. Nonetheless, the area remained an important commercial and cultural hub. Three years later, in 1910, Birmingham annexed Ensley, making it one of the most important neighborhoods of the city.

The establishment of a Black middle class through the formation of labor unions characterized the turn of the twentieth century in Birmingham. Black and White miners in the United Mine Workers (UMW) organized together for union recognition and better wages, which they gained. The Alabama Federation of Labor (AFL), another labor union, originally dominated by mine workers, adopted the same approach of integrating its membership. The success of the UMW and the fear that non-unionized Blacks would replace striking workers motivated the group to build a union that represented, in terms of membership, a racially united front.

As a result, Blacks earned positions of leadership and spots in every committee of the AFL, and the first five vice presidents all were Black.[6] Alonzo Gaines, a Black worker for the Sloss Iron and Steel Company between 1925 and 1940, described in an interview with the University of Alabama Oral History Program how the factory owners treated him like "a man instead of an animal."[7] Gaines worked on the "floating gang," which worked on tasks as needed in the machine shop, boilermaker, and other parts of the factory. According to the interview transcript, Gains said, "Black workers hauled all the pig iron, Whites didn't do that. Blacks handled all the iron. There were more Blacks at Sloss than Whites because there were more harder work to do."[8] This work environment posed acute and long-term health risks, but miners didn't need specialized skills to enter the middle class.

Ensley's Black middle class derived from more than industrial employment. Black-owned businesses provided goods, services, and entertainment along 17th and 19th Streets as well as Avenue E, which became the Black business district, approximately ten blocks south of Rice's development project.[9] Though many of the actual buildings were owned by White people, Blacks laid claim to it as an area of their own. With Blacks unable to work at or frequent many White-owned businesses in Birmingham, Ensley's Black business district provided access to shopping and entertainment, from hardware stores to movie theaters.

To unwind, Blacks patronized a part of the Black business district known as Tuxedo Junction—so named because performers purchased and rented tuxedos and other formal wear at a tuxedo shop in the neighborhood—located at the intersection of Ensley Avenue and 19th Street, where the Pratt City and Wylam streetcars once stopped to turn around.[10]

The Black commercial corridor in Ensley included a park, local businesses, and dance halls where jazz greats made a stop to perform en route to larger cities. "This was the place where . . . the big band leaders in the jazz era . . . would come and sit in," artist and poet Brian "Voice" Hawkins, who also leads the nonprofit Ensley Alive, told me. The Glen Miller Orchestra memorialized Tuxedo Junction in the 1940s by recording a popular song of the same name, written by jazz musician Erskine Ramsay Hawkins.

The two-story commercial Belcher-Nixon Building, also known as the Tuxedo Ballroom, anchored Tuxedo Junction as a commercial, social, and political hub. Since its construction in 1922, mostly Black-owned ventures occupied the building that was central to the economic and social prosperity of Blacks in Ensley.[11] Belcher-Nixon originally housed the offices of Dr. Andrew F. Belcher, an African-American dentist, on the second floor, and three commercial businesses on the first. "Once upon a time, it was a warehouse, then it became a doctor's office and attorney's space; it's been a lot of things over the years," said Hawkins.

Throughout the years, Belcher-Nixon became more than just an office building with tenants; it resembled what we now would call a business incubator.[12] The Belcher-Nixon building was a similar resource for the businesses it housed over time.

Ensley has a rich history to build on. Dozens of companies started and died in that building, harnessing the resources and strength of the other firms housed there. Civic leadership was a by-product of that cohabitation. Belcher's business partner, fellow dentist Dr. John Nixon, became a key figure in the civil rights struggle, serving as president of the local chapter of the NAACP in the pivotal years of the 1960s. Belcher's moderate style of leadership is cited in David Schneider's historiography of Ensley as instrumental in implementing some of the civil rights policies later adopted in the city.[13]

"Dr. Nixon was among a group of Black business leaders who called for moderation rather than confrontation," wrote historian David Schneider in a historiography of Ensley for the city of Birmingham.[14] "While the work of [Martin Luther] King and [Fred] Shuttlesworth was the precursor to The March on Washington in August 1963, and ultimately the passage of more effective civil rights legislation, the established relationships moderate Black professionals like Dr. Nixon had with their White counterparts paved the way for the successful implementation of many of the local reforms that the protests had initiated." Belcher and Nixon's economic and political presence in the business district provided leadership in a racially hostile environment and paved the way for endeavors like Rice's block purchase many decades later.

Although Blacks in Ensley flourished during the early twentieth century, racism limited their advancement thereafter. In the mid-1920s, many White residents of Birmingham joined or affiliated with the Ku Klux Klan, influencing the political and social decisions of the time.[15] Color-coded maps of the city's boundaries in 1926 show clear race-based divisions, restricting the neighborhoods in which Blacks could live.[16] Civic leaders relied on Jim Crow laws to limit the degree to which Black residents could advance socially. In the 1930s, U.S. Steel began restricting job promotions to Blacks, limiting access to senior positions previously enjoyed under TCI.[17] During the cycle of layoffs and rehiring of industrial workers during and after the Great Depression, one in four Black workers were laid off while the number of White workers increased by the end of the 1930s.[18] The loss of Black workers was White workers' gain. In 1930, the city was home to 259,678 people. By 1940, the population had barely changed, with 267,583 people living in the city, according to the Census Bureau.[19] Over the next decade, the proportion of Black residents in the city increased while that of White residents decreased.[20]

In 1941, President Franklin D. Roosevelt appointed the Fair Employment Practices Committee, which sought to end employment discrimination in defense industries, exacerbating White Southerners' fears that the federal government supported Black workers' rights.

Integrated unions appreciated Blacks' loyalty, but when U.S. Steel purchased TCI, they abandoned efforts to advocate on Blacks' behalf when presented with the risk of Whites' losing power. "TCI [Owned by U.S. Steel] and the Steelworkers locals agreed to a system of segregated lines of promotion that preserved White supremacy and expanded the seniority rights of White workers. Whites could 'bid' up and 'bump' down the line of promotion within an all-White seniority unit. Black laborers were put on occupational ladders that led nowhere," wrote historian Robert J. Norrell in the *Journal of American History*.[21]

With a coinciding decline in mining during the 1950s, seven of ten Blacks in the industry lost their jobs in Birmingham.[22] As national attention to civil rights grew, the intensity of segregationists' efforts to maintain Black subordination increased.

In 1961, Klansmen attacked the Freedom Riders, the racially integrated groups typically composed of college-age students who took bus trips throughout the south to test court ordered desegregation. A second bus was burned in Anniston, Alabama, en route to Birmingham.[23] The ill-famed segregationist Bull Connor served as Commissioner of Public Safety for the City of Birmingham and used that position to order the use of police dogs and firehoses on civil rights activists throughout the Southern Christian Leadership Conference's Birmingham campaign of 1963 to end segregation.[24] In that same year, the infamous 16th Street Baptist Church bombing occurred right outside the Black business district of Ensley, killing four young Black girls—Addie Mae Collins (fourteen), Carol Denise McNair (eleven), Carole Robertson (fourteen), and Cynthia Wesley (fourteen)—which helped galvanize the Civil Rights Movement.[25]

Even policies aimed at increasing the rights and liberties of Black Americans had damaging effects. On paper, the Civil Rights Act of 1964 gave Blacks greater protections and freedoms against outright discrimination—a significant start on the long road to economic and social liberty.[26] However, as Black people started shopping at

White-owned businesses, Black-owned businesses began to lose revenue, forcing many of them to close. With business waning, White landlords neglected building maintenance, allowing for both a void of economic activity and neighborhood deterioration to occur in the once-bustling district in Ensley.[27] In the same decade that saw the country pass historic civil rights legislation, Whites in Birmingham fled to the suburbs, declining in population from 60 percent in 1960 to approximately 44 percent in 1980. The neighborhoods that Whites abandoned, then, are the spaces we must claim and reimagine now.

TOWARD A VISION OF BLACK URBAN PLANNING

In Angel David Nieves book *We Shall Independent Be: African American Place-Making and the Struggle to Claim Space in the United States*, he explains how the struggle over landownership and property rights began with our arrival as slaves to the Americas. When Blacks were enslaved, we sought places that outlawed slavery. During Reconstruction and Jim Crow, Blacks had to claim land, businesses, and schools without the start-up capital that Whites were able to gain through public policy. Black economic, social, and political uplift has been about stringing together our assets to lay a claim. Development in this vein requires investment in Black people who can see the good in a Black community. It also requires investment in their projects, which includes the building of homes, businesses, schools, and community centers, not taking for granted how current and past segregation and discrimination rob Black folk of the space to think.

We need the freedom to see ourselves beyond White norms and bigotry to define our own needs. That kind of activity is currently being done by Afrofuturists. Writer Jordi Oliveres defines Afrofuturism as "a sweeping, cultural aesthetic that examines issues around Black representation, the Black future and Black agency using music, novels, visual media, history and myth to create something else entirely."[28] Afrofuturism is most accessible through the works of science fiction writers who create fantastical worlds in which blackness challenges our everyday conceptions of it. Think Wakanda in the blockbuster motion picture *Black Panther*, a fictional place in Africa with the most advanced technology and a culture that is still familiar to Africans and their descendants in America.

Writer Octavia Butler, winner of the Nebula and Hugo awards for sci-fi literature, is largely considered the mother of Afrofuturism.[29] Butler regularly critiques racial hierarchies with her reimagined worlds and characters. Afrofuturism can also be seen in protest art. Artist Alisha Wormsley created a billboard installation atop a prominent building in the gentrifying neighborhood of East Liberty in Pittsburgh in 2018.[30] Against a black background, the billboard read in white block lettering, "There Are Black People in the Future." Afrofuturism can be seen and heard in the works of musician Janelle Monae, who in the music video *Many Moons* sells off her cyborg clones in a fictional android sale posed as a futuristic fashion show, conjuring the imagery of a slave auction.[31] Monae's entire album was an Afrofuturistic concept.

There is a growing number of urban planners, architects, and writers about cities, including me, who deem ourselves Black urbanists, the Afrofuturists of urban planners. Black urbanists include architect and urban planner Toni L. Griffin, planner and writer Kristen Jeff, and engineer and transportation expert Richard Ezike. Also included are Eric Walker, who works on energy management in Buffalo, New York, and Jeana Dunlap, who works on converting vacant properties to improve the quality of life for residents. There are practitioners like Brian Rice who may not see themselves as Black urbanists but are actively reimagining spaces where racism has left Black neighborhoods desolate in its wake. Our growth depends on us creating new formulas that determine the value of a prospective project. Black people need fresh, imagined spaces that can be constructed to provide affordable housing and areas for commerce. Residents need more stores to shop for fresh vegetables and meats, to pick up hardware, and shop for clothes. We also need spaces to exemplify quality policing and energy use. These neighborhoods and business districts can't be separated from our need for spaces to ideate and theorize—to not see ourselves against the foil of racism or White people, but as something much more distinct.

"Just imagine that [building] being a Black arts gallery," said Rice on our walking tour. "Imagine this being two or three restaurants. You know, just imagine you've got a place for spoken word, you've got a place for poetry. Imagine you've got a place for a coffeehouse."

In her book *Sister Outsider*, poet and political activist Audre Lorde wrote an essay titled "Poetry Is Not a Luxury."[32] Lorde made clear that women need safe spaces to express, feel, and simply be. For purposes of community and economic development, I include Black men as needing this type of space. Poetry clubs may not seem essential to economic and social growth, but these are the very kind of enterprises Black people need to grow at scale.

In her essay, Lorde wrote, "But as we become more in touch with our own ancient, Black, non-European view of living as a situation to be experienced and interacted with, we learn more and more to cherish our feelings, and to respect those hidden sources of our power from where true knowledge and therefore lasting action comes." Lorde continued, "The White fathers told us, I think therefore I am; and the Black mothers in each of us—the poet—whispers in our dreams, I feel therefore I can be free." Lorde challenges us to break out of the frameworks ascribed by traditional economic developers (the White fathers of development) of the world who would deem Black poetry and mom-and-pop coffee shops as ancillary to more profitable financial and tech businesses.

Our business is to find space—the mental and physical as well as the commercial and anti-commercial. We need places to foster creativity so tech entrepreneurs can develop the next multibillion-dollar app or open the first Black owned grocery store in an area.

Notwithstanding research and development departments in some corporations and banks, these entities typically don't fund people to simply think and plan, especially Black people. However, philanthropic organizations can and do. Philanthropy can play a definite role in funding Black urbanists—architects and planners—to imagine, research, design, and strategize. Real estate developers such as Brian Rice need the support of planners to properly execute a culturally relevant vision.

Business corridors in the cities that White people abandoned and where Black people stayed often make great places for Black firms to cluster and grow. Again, clustering doesn't capture the nature of how White industries excluded Black business leaders from economic development plans.[33] Blacks need clustering in a spirit of the Kwanzaa principle of Ujamaa, or cooperative economics, which means to "build our own businesses, control the economics of our own community and share in all its work and wealth."[34] Kwanzaa is the pan-African, seven-day holiday in which a different principle is celebrated each day. We need to cluster to gain control and ownership of our businesses and communities, which have been throttled by biased housing, tax, and business practices. These clusters deserve the same kind of investments that built up the innovation district of East Liberty in Pittsburgh.

Black-owned businesses can complement and support each other while providing a comprehensive suite of products and services for neighboring communities. Taking over a city block is the kind of entrepreneurialism that is required to cluster a group of businesses that can meet communities' basic needs while creating a support system for the people managing them. Buying the block to create a new kind of corridor will take blackness out of the museum and put it in the open air. Customers of all shades need to see Black people's cultural selves as an affirming trait in the marketplace.

A NEW VISION

In 2009, when Brian Rice lived and worked in Charlotte, North Carolina, he recorded himself on video talking about moving back to Birmingham. "I think I was still speaking with my lisp," he remembers. Rice, whose reclamation project started with himself, sought help from a speech therapist to learn to speak without the lisp. Looking back at the video, Rice believes he spoke his current actions into existence. In 2013, Rice moved back to Birmingham to execute his vision.

"I knew I wanted to come to a Black community that was struggling, that was distressed," plus, it already had commercial infrastructure, Rice said of his decision to buy most of the buildings. "You have the same issues of a lot of Black neighborhoods in this country—you got crime; you got school issues . . . So I'm like, this could be the place to create that model that can eventually be used around the country."

On January 1, 2018, Rice posted a Facebook status update that included an illustration of downtown Ensley and adjacent residential areas. He recalls writing in that post, "We need to stop saying we need to buy the block and actually start buying the block."

He then requested his Facebook followers to message him if they were interested in restoring downtown Ensley. About thirty people responded, and Rice set up a time to talk with them. On February 2, approximately forty-five people showed for the meeting. However, the group spent most of its time discussing the need to restore the nearby homes of the residents who most likely would utilize the downtown. He left that day with pledges of financial support from twenty-five attendees. Rice said that some attendees said they could buy thirty homes and renovate. Others said they could purchase one or two homes or partner in an acquisition. A week after that meeting, Rice, for the first time, presented his larger vision for the downtown area to a group of neighborhood associations and city officials. And Rice took his first major step toward making his vision a reality.

FINANCING

Community development for places that have been ravaged by racism calls for multiple investments in people and places at a scale that can truly make an impact. Similar kinds of policies that created wealth for Whites after the Great Depression could be applied again but for Supreme Court decisions barring racial preferences. For the devalued price on property, there are Black developers who can buy a city block with family and friend investors, but those individuals need financing structures to redress the systemic and historic exclusion to wealth creation in this country.

"It should be easy," Rice said, when describing getting financing to develop the properties he'd already paid for. Rice's initial investors provided him with the cash to pay for all the buildings. He still struggled to receive a loan from a traditional bank to develop the properties. Six months after the purchase, Rice had been able to secure only $50,000, from a local bank. After an extensive process of sending numerous forms to several banks, the only returns he received were requests for more documents. Rice says he realized then that "they're trying to burn me out, but they don't want to say no."

Banks account for the majority of real estate development funding. Loans from large banks are the most sought-after source of funding by businesses, regardless of the racial background of owners.[35] However, White individuals receive more loans and lower interest rates than people of color.[36] Additionally, since the 2008 financial crisis, traditional banks have had more restrained lending practices. The Federal Reserve found that 70 percent of banks have tightened their standards for lending to small businesses, and many have increased the cost of a line of credit for businesses according to size.[37]

In 2011, 50 percent of the money received in mortgages came from the three largest traditional banks in the country (JPMorgan Chase, Bank of America, and Wells Fargo). By September 2016, these banks offered only 21 percent of all bank loans.[38] Despite the restricted availability of loans, some banks have developed grant programs to support select organizations with inclusive development aims. These programs include JPMorgan Chase's Entrepreneurs of Color Fund,[39] Wells Fargo's initiative to increase loans and grants to diverse small businesses,[40] and U.S. Banks Community Possible Grant Program,[41] among others.

Rice points to the history of redlining in Ensley. Comparing Ensley to other parts of town, Rice says, "We're in an area where banks have chosen not to invest." With banks across the area delaying, denying, and not even responding to his requests for loans, Rice is currently recruiting Community Development Financial Institutions (CDFIs) and banks to open branches in Ensley, which currently has only one bank (Regions) and one credit union (America's First Credit Union).

CDFIs serve lower- and moderate-income individuals or communities by providing accessible financial resources.[42] In 2018, there were more than 1,100 government-certified CDFIs located across the country managing $150 billion in total assets collectively, according to the Community Development Financial Institutions Fund, which is a government agency established by the Riegle Community Development and Regulatory Improvement Act of 1994, as a bipartisan initiative.[43] According to the Opportunity Finance Network, the national association of CDFIs, of those served by CDFIs in 2017, 55 percent were people of color and 82 percent had low-income or low-wealth, or were from historically disinvested communities. Additionally, 27 percent of those served were from rural communities and 45 percent were women.[44]

Birmingham, with only two certified CDFIs (NRS Community Development Federal Credit Union and Sabre Finance-Venture South

Loan Fund), receives significantly less CDFI funding compared to its peers of similar size (figure 3-1).

Brian Rice's development is exactly the kind of endeavor the Opportunity Zone provision of the 2017 Tax Cuts and Jobs Act is supposed to support. Opportunity zones are a community development tool that give tax relief on unrealized capital gains—profit from the sale of property and other investments—if those revenues are reinvested in a dedicated opportunity fund, which deploys resources in designated distressed areas (opportunity zones). Governors identified the low-income urban and rural communities that fit certain criteria designated as an opportunity zone, and there are fund managers across the country who are ready to take in funds to invest in commercial real estate, housing, infrastructure, and even existing and start-up businesses.[45] However, there are significantly fewer Black-owned real estate developments of the size and scale of

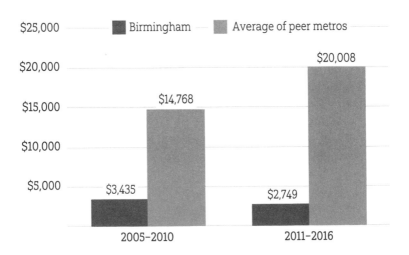

FIGURE 3-1. BIRMINGHAM CDFIs RECEIVE LESS INVESTMENT. AVERAGE ANNUAL LOAN VOLUME PER 1,000 WORKERS.

SOURCE: Brookings analysis by S. Liu and J. Parilla of Community Development Financial Institutions Fund data.

those owned by other racial groups. In addition, there are a limited number of Black and Latino managers of funds from which the investment dollars would be directed. Consequently, the reinvestment of an estimated $6 trillion in unrealized capital gains would not build wealth for the people who need it.[46] The inability to create wealth within the Black community is the reason so many Black-majority places are distressed. Nonetheless, Rice's projects fell outside of the opportunity zone that covers parts of Ensley, precluding him from those investment dollars.

Still, real estate developers like Rice need support from government agencies. Needing to meet construction and zoning requirements outlined in city charters, developers can't build anything without municipal leaders' approval. But city officials represent more than checkboxes for building permits and quality control audits. Council members and mayors sit on a perch where they can see the overall economic landscape beyond the city limits. Local elected officials control federal, state, and local resources—financial, human, and administrative—that can be deployed to help move a developer's concept toward completion. So local government leaders should be considered partners in any major project.

Developers have a much better chance of getting a project approved and financed if a mayor recognizes a project's value relative to the mayor's broader agenda. Mayors' political futures hinge mightily on the accomplishments of developers like Rice. New commercial corridors and housing projects can be the physical signs of progress that voters and funders love. More importantly, great commercial and residential projects improve the quality of life for residents and consumers. Nevertheless, city hall can't stand in as a bank, but it can provide much-needed resources that increase the likelihood that financial markets embrace a development project. Rice and the City of Birmingham share a fate—if only they could see that.

In lieu of an equitable financing structure, Rice is relying on bringing in private financiers. "It's unfortunate that I have to find somebody that's not even local, but it's a reality for me and a lot of other people," he said.

SMART BLOCK INVESTMENTS

We need to encourage Black developers who can transform several blocks located in disenfranchised and distressed parts of town into havens of social and economic growth. But it's clear that buying the block for the purposes of Black community development calls for more than just property acquisition. Smart block investments require purposeful, intentional investments in Black and Hispanic real estate developers and planners who want to create comprehensive commercial corridors designed to meet communities' needs, incubate and finance businesses, validate the community's identity, and add value to devalued property.

Individuals should buy blocks in areas of severe property devaluation, where it's actually cheaper for disenfranchised groups to buy parcels. Planners must work with or develop a merchant association that can help recruit a CDFI or other banking entity to the block project. The developer must tactfully select firms that address local/immediate needs—grocery stores, gas stations, barbershops, restaurants—as well as first-order services such as schools and urgent care clinics. In addition, there should be a business incubator that includes high-growth start-up companies that have the potential to expand well beyond a block. All the businesses collectively should help promote the rich cultural heritage of the community. The incubator should also provide support to all businesses on the block. These components make up what I call smart block investments.

WE'VE BEEN HERE BEFORE

History shows that Rice should not shoulder all the blame for his struggles. His situation is far from unique. White resistance to and disregard of Black success has been a primary impediment to the growth of Black businesses and neighborhoods. Since the Civil War, Blacks have consistently demonstrated their ability to build great neighborhoods with thriving business districts. Developers can draw upon the past as inspiration for the present and future. However, Black communities' economic and community development goals have always been tied to our civil rights, for good reason. Historically, where we see Blacks' economic success, we have found the not-so-invisible White hand of economic suppression.

Jackson Ward in Richmond, Virginia, became one of the first notable Black neighborhoods of this sort. The migration stemming from the Civil War and Blacks' emancipation from slavery led to their influx to Richmond in the mid-1800s.[47] By 1886, community members chartered and opened the True Reformer's Bank in Jackson Ward, the first Black-owned bank in the country.[48] By the turn of the century, rowhouses and townhouses with porches and columns began to fill Jackson Ward streets. Residents opened a myriad of businesses to cater to the community: restaurants, banks, barbershops, medical practices, and insurance companies.[49] As the economy flourished, influential figures such as John Mitchell Jr., editor for the newspaper the *Richmond Planet*, and Maggie L. Walker, the first female president to charter a bank in America, moved to the neighborhood. Both Mitchell and Walker brought their businesses with them.

The forty blocks making up Jackson Ward developed into a notable cityscape of Richmond. Its buildings displayed decorative wrought iron detailing. Second Street hosted a number of theaters, evincing the ward's national reputation as a premiere entertainment district. At the Hippodrome Theater, residents saw jazz greats Ella Fitzgerald, Cab Calloway, and Duke Ellington perform. In the 1950s, the ward became known as the Harlem of the South, attesting to its economic success, artistic brilliance, and social cachet.

But also in the 1950s, the federal government proposed construction of an interstate highway, I-95, through the community. Jackson Ward, like many other Black neighborhoods, was viewed as an obstruction to White business and community development. White planners and business leaders deemed Black communities as unimportant places that could be razed. The plan for Richmond, which focused on improving the business district in downtown, contributed to the decline of the Black community in the Jackson Ward. The introduction of department stores downtown pushed out small businesses that couldn't compete, and Jackson Ward's vibrancy wilted.

Tulsa, Oklahoma, is the location of the most emblematic story of Black business success and White resistance to it. In 1906, O. W. Gurley, a wealthy Black man from Arkansas, moved to Tulsa, where he purchased over forty acres of land that was available only to African-Americans.[50] Gurley's acquisition became the foundation for Tulsa's Greenwood District, which included a business strip that became known as Black Wall Street. Jim Crow laws made it illegal for Blacks to shop at White-owned establishments, so, as a result, Greenwood residents spent their dollars within the community, with bills changing hands between thirty-six to 100 times before being spent elsewhere.[51]

"What we're talking about really are sole-proprietorship mom-and-pop businesses," Tulsa historian Hannibal Johnson told the online news magazine *The Ringer*.[52] "Things like pharmacies, dry cleaners, haberdasheries, barber shops, beauty shops, movie theaters, pool halls. Professional services like doctors, lawyers, dentists. Just the kinds of small businesses that make a place vibrant and engaging for folks."

Black businesses prospered, and residents experienced a high quality of life. The average wage of Black families in the area exceeded the adjusted minimum wage today. While the entire state of Oklahoma only had two airports, six families who had businesses on Black Wall Street owned their own planes.

Blacks flocked to the prosperity of Greenwood, the buzz of Black wealth spreading throughout Tulsa. And Whites looked on in contempt.[53] When the *Tulsa Tribune* reported that a Black man had been accused of trying to rape a White woman in 1921, the city's White residents found a reason to destroy a thriving community.[54] Mobs set fire to entire blocks. The police force abetted the mob, arming White protestors. Thirty-five blocks of the city were scorched, leading to the deaths of 300 Black residents and injury to 800 others. The Tulsa Race Massacre, as the butchery is named, led to the destruction of 1,256 residences, the loss of 600 businesses, and left 10,000 people homeless.[55]

Nonetheless, the headline of the *Tulsa World* front page story read, "Two Whites Dead in Race Riot."[56] "There are no known negro fatalities," the staff reporters wrote. "Negroes finally driven into little Africa." Reporters cited White retaliation against Black aggressors.[57] A later edition of the paper headlined "Many More Whites are Shot," maintaining the narrative of a violent and dangerous Black community.[58]

Olivia Hooker, a six-year-old witness of the massacre, had a different experience. In a 2018 interview, Hooker told the *Washington Post* of her experience hiding with her mother beneath their kitchen table as torch-carrying White people ransacked their home. "They took everything they thought was valuable. They smashed everything they couldn't take," Hooker recalled.

These reports provided Whites with a narrative to rationalize policies to put Blacks "back in their place."[59] Following the massacre, government and private industry used the city's reconstruction period to solidify White dominance and devalue property in the Greenwood district. Colorado State professor Chris Messer wrote that, ultimately, Greenwood residents posed a "geographical problem because their community was situated in an ideal location for business expansion."[60]

Following the 1921 massacre, Whites were able to gain a grip on the neighborhood and exploit it for their political interests. Homes and businesses were rebuilt in Greenwood, but Black Wall Street never regained its old status.

Blacks in Ensley know too well how racism stifles economic growth in Birmingham. On Birmingham's Fourth Avenue, approximately five miles from Ensley, Black residents had another thriving business district, with shops ranging from barbers and tailors to lawyers and physicians.[61] With little choice but to invest their money in their Black district due to segregation, Black businesses thrived. "It was a jewel. And a jail," wrote Stan Diel of the *Birmingham Times*, noting the limits to Black economic success. Fourth Avenue North was so packed with shoppers and businesspeople that it was coined Little Harlem. Whites, however, owned virtually the entire district, with landlords living out of the area or in the neighboring all-White communities.

History tells us you can't have sustainable economic growth with racist social policies. After Bull Connor ordered the use of police dogs and firehoses on civil rights activists on Fourth Avenue, the business district became a shell of itself. Soon after, White owners of the buildings neglected to maintain their properties, and the district further deteriorated. Today, vendors and investors are trying in earnest to restore Fourth Avenue to the stature it once knew.[62]

Since the civil rights movement, some progress has been made to redevelop the Ensley community. In 1979, the first Black mayor of Birmingham, Richard Arrington, created a land bank that assisted with brokering property sales between absent White owners of property in Ensley and its present Black residents.[63] In 2013, the Urban Studio at Auburn University, an outreach program of the College of Architecture, Design, and Construction, worked to create a master plan for business development in the neighborhood.[64] Much of the current energy around the revitalization of Ensley's business corridor has focused on the vacant Ramsay-McCormack building. In 1930, the newly constructed ten-story Ramsay-McCormack building opened less than a mile from the Black business district on Avenue E, becoming Ensley's first skyscraper.[65] Though built to house businesses and corporate offices, the imposing building's location in the center of Ensley increased general interest in the Black- and White-owned business in the neighborhood. The size and location certainly make it a symbol of Ensley. Having been vacant since 1986, Ramsay-McCormack is more of a symbol of Ensley's decline.

Antonio Spurling, a Black lawyer and prominent business owner with several enterprises in downtown Ensley, sued the city of Birmingham in 2009 and 2012, asking to demolish or renovate the Ramsay-McCormack because he felt the massive vacant structure negatively affected the value of his properties on the same street. Spurling and the city under former Mayor William Bell, who is also Black, reached a settlement agreement in 2012 that entailed remodeling the building so it would house a municipal court. In 2016, Bell also proposed investing $40 million toward the creation of a public safety complex that involved moving the police and fire departments from downtown Birmingham to Ensley, around the Ramsay-McCormack.

The current mayor, Bell's successor Randall Woodfin, who is also Black, scotched those plans. AL.com reported that Woodfin did not believe Bell's proposal made much sense, given there was no other model across the country to replicate; fire and police departments are usually located in the central city. Woodfin prioritized Ensley in his election campaign. In 2018, the city began working with the Brookings Institution to create a strategy that would revive unused facilities in Ensley, including the former U.S. Steel industrial park. Woodfin also seeks to help landowners develop a retail corridor, extending transit lines to the area and relocating city departmental services in the section of town.

In 2018, the city of Birmingham accepted proposals from organizations to redevelop the Ramsay-McCormack building.[66] The city chose REV Birmingham, a local nonprofit focused on place-based revitalization, awarding it $338,000 to develop the ten-story structure.[67] "Under the nearly $400,000 contract REV Birmingham will work with the city to manage the process of finding a developer for Ramsay McCormack building," WBRC reported.[68] In April 2017, Architecture Works, LLC, gave a quote to the city that a makeover of Ramsay-McCormack would cost $12 to $14 million to actually develop the building.[69] After receiving notification of the award in November 2018, David Fleming, the president and CEO of REV Birmingham, told television station WVTM 13 that he believed "that building is a game changer for the part of the city. It is the physical symbol of Ensley."[70]

In October 2019, the City of Birmingham entered into a development agreement with Ensley District Developers, an Alabama limited liability company, to develop the Ramsay-McCormack Building and adjoining land on Avenue E. The Black-led firm has a history of doing historic preservation tax credit projects with an emphasis on African American properties. In addition, the City of Birmingham purchased the vacant Ensley High School from the school district. Officials plan to issue a request for proposals to develop the property as a mixed-use site.

Having campaigned on improving the Ensley neighborhood, the Woodfin administration announced in the fall of 2019 plans to deploy resources in the corridor that Rice is developing, including the distribution of $450,000 of community development block grant funds toward the beautification of neighborhood and commercial areas in Ensley and the Fourth Avenue business district.

Rice is largely ambivalent about the political and legal maneuverings over the years. "If they're not moving forward and they're holding a property like this stagnant then it's stagnating the rest of the community," says Rice.

Rice is right. The built environment, parlance for human-made surroundings, includes roads, homes, parks, businesses, and monuments. Our buildings and statues symbolize the values of the community. The built environment also represents human values and culture. The Ramsay-McCormack building has become a monument to White flight that is keeping Ensley from realizing an identity that is more inspiring and authentic to the current residents. It's a constant reminder that U.S. Steel left town and that many White and Black middle-class families did also, because they didn't see opportunity in a community of their poorer Black neighbors. People like Rice want it developed in a manner befitting the community or to have it demolished. If the building can be revitalized and repurposed, then it should be done in a way that gives committed residents of Ensley a useful physical asset and a symbolic victory in their existential battle for control and representation.

The people who left took their racist and classist attitudes with them. While I want people to repopulate Ensley, current residents should not want the Birminghamians of old to return. As Rice rebuilds his block, he should work with current community members to serve their basic needs, but the built environment should honor them too. There should be a process that allows current residents to rename the building if it's too much of a reminder of a segregated past or, if the project manager determines that demolition is more feasible, then residents should be solicited for their input in deciding what goes in its place. Removing monuments is about making history, not just erasing it.

But there is a much deeper issue that planners who are interested in buying the block must tackle. Successful Black corridors of the past were predicated on Black dollars circulating within them because business owners and patrons had little other choice. Jim Crow forbade them from spending or saving their money elsewhere. These conditions are different today, and Black people can—and regularly choose to—spend their money nationally and globally. The question is: What does it mean for Black people to circulate Black dollars within Black communities in the age of Amazon when people can spend money nationally and globally thanks to the internet?

The reality is that while Blacks can spend anywhere, sadly, support for start-up and existing businesses, financing structures, economic development organizations, and merchant associations is still very much running along separate and unequal tracks. For instance, the economic development organizations in Birmingham are highly racialized in terms of staffing and mission. Urban Impact Incorporated is a place-based economic development agency—staffed mostly by Black people—that has focused on Black neighborhoods and business districts.[71] REV Birmingham, which won the contract to manage the Ramsay-McCormack building in Ensley is perceived to be a White organization, as reflected in its staffing.[72] As part of their plan to invest in Ensley, the City of Birmingham proposed funding Urban Impact to reestablish the Ensley Merchants Association and manage a façade improvement program.

Black developers need every opportunity afforded them in Black neighborhoods because they are at a disadvantage in cities like Birmingham that have over time built an infrastructure that gives White-led companies more opportunities. The history of Birmingham should make this apparent. Black firms and communities are further disadvantaged every time they miss opportunities to circulate dollars.

Adding value to Black communities demands a disruption in cities' current business development and financing infrastructure, which have over time created advantages for White-led organizations. By creating new organizations that are focused on extending opportunities for Black organizations on projects informally designated for White firms, the city or region can begin to develop a more equitable infrastructure. In addition, Black neighborhoods and business corridors need advocates and conveners who can help identify opportunities for Black firms and commercial corridors. There isn't a merchant association in Ensley at present.

Black communities have built leadership muscle and civic infrastructure around combatting racist attacks aimed at destroying the development of Black communities. However, that substructure largely focused on civil rights broadly. Notably, Black pastors in Birmingham founded the Alabama Christian Movement for Human Rights (ACMHR) to further the work of the NAACP.[73] One of those pastors was Reverend Fred Shuttlesworth, a prominent figure of the civil rights movement during the late 1950s and early 1960s who mobilized the network when hate groups attacked the Freedom Riders, and he used that network to extend voting rights to Blacks and register them, modeling organizational strategies for generations.[74] However, there is no corollary movement today around economic development issues.

"Why, Brian?" Rice asked himself on another stop of our tour of downtown Ensley. Finally, he answered the question: "Living in Charlotte, living in Knoxville, living in Milwaukee, living in Richmond, Virginia, and living in Houston, you see renovation happening everywhere. You even see it in other parts of Birmingham. I've seen it so many times, I'm like, how do I get on the front end of the next opportunity? I believe Ensley and other neighborhoods in Birmingham could easily be those neighborhoods."

Alas, while buying a block is relatively easier in devalued neighborhoods, developing it is another challenge. In June 2019, Brian Rice called me, seething. I could barely understand him. "They basically said my property is worthless," he bellowed. Brian Rice shared the appraiser's report with me. His bank took more than eight months to complete the appraisal process, although the buildings had been paid off completely. The appraisers valued 43,125 square feet of land at $1.04 per square foot. All eight of his properties were compared to buildings such as an abandoned car wash and a rural farm, parcels of land more than ten miles outside of the city. The report lists the total value of his block at $45,000, which accounts for $170,000 indicated land and property value minus $125,000 in demolition costs. The low appraisal will make it difficult to get the kind of loan needed to develop an entire block.

Rice alleges that his appraisers intentionally devalued the eight Ensley properties. According to Rice, the appraisers willfully selected the worst property comparison scenarios, comparing his properties to dissimilar rural parcels more than ten miles away. The appraisal recommends demolition as the best use, although none of the properties have been placed on a condemnation list by the city of Birmingham. The Jefferson County property tax division has also placed a much higher value on the properties than the appraisers. Rice argues that this devaluation is evidence of racism. Rice also argues that his bank is complicit in this bias, as they avoided ordering an appraisal for seven months. Rice harbors concerns about communication between the bank and the appraisers in efforts to give his properties the lowest value possible. He calls for an independent appraisal that allows him to help select the appraisal company.

"I have no choice but to go public," he told me. "I truly believe the bank is trying to force me out of business and into bankruptcy, so they can get my properties for very low." Based on local and national history, Rice's claims must be taken seriously.

4

A Different Kind
of School

On the subject of taking on challenges, the late great tennis master
Arthur Ashe said, "Start where you are; use what you have; do what
you can."[1] In places like Wilkinsburg, these principles must apply
to economic and community development. If corporate and university leaders, economic development professionals, and other external
actors don't see or value resources in Black-majority cities, residents
of municipalities like Wilkinsburg have little choice but to leverage
the assets at their disposal to stimulate growth. My mom used to tell
me that sometimes you have to rub two sticks together to make fire.
It was her version of the Ashe quote. To Ashe's and Mom's point,
vacant schools may not seem like much but they have a lot more
potential than two sticks.

Recognizing the potential of school buildings in a neighborhood,
Bill Bates, Pittsburgh native and president of the American Institute
of Architects, told me: "Schools were built to last . . . I think it's easier
and more sustainable to rehabilitate a building than to close or destroy

it. They are already in place. You don't have to import materials and do a lot of work to build them; to renovate them."[2]

Bates has an intimate understanding of the dilemma Wilkinsburg faces. His father and grandfather worked in the steel mills thirty minutes outside Pittsburgh in the early 1970s. Bates himself inhaled the heat and smoke of the mills as he toiled alongside his father to earn enough money to pay for and get through college. Bates is also the board chair of the Landmarks Development Corporation, a subset of Pittsburgh's History and Landmarks Corporation Foundation. In that capacity, Bates uses historic tax credits to revitalize old buildings for residential purposes. His organization builds one home at a time in an attempt to avoid displacing residents, something larger-scale projects have the potential of doing.

"There's some DNA to community that's important. And that's some of the history and the nature of the families who've grown up there," Bates said. "Having that connection is important."

Bates also believes the architectural assets that schools provide help sustain communities. "Architecture is the skeleton, the bones of the community that you build the next generation upon." He added, "People understand what that history is and they pass that history on so that they want to stay here and keep the living organism, if you will, the community alive."

So if communities are to apply the Arthur Ashe principle and start where they are; use what they have; and do what they can, re-purposing their schools makes perfect sense. But who you give the keys to and for what purpose is also critically important.

"Community-based services are really important," explains Bates. He believes community-focused endeavors give locals more opportunities for jobs, training, and development than do businesses that don't have ties to community.

Mom's husband possessed a car, a luxury for families on my block. My brothers, friends, and I bobbed joyously on the sidewalk next to his tan sedan, ecstatic about the first day of school at Johnston Elementary in Wilkinsburg in 1975. That tan car and that first day are some of my earliest memories growing up in Wilkinsburg. Usually, Teddy left for work before the break of dawn. But that day, he must have wanted to extend to us that luxury and celebrate our first day of school. After a three-month summer break, the day after Labor Day represented an un-calendared holiday in the 'hood. In Black America, an education represents freedom in a literal and metaphorical way—a real opportunity to escape the hardships of life.

Abolitionist, statesman, and civil rights leader Frederick Douglass once said that denying a person an education means adding another link in the chain of their servitude. Quoting his owner in his book *Life of an American Slave*, Douglass wrote, "If you teach that nigger (speaking of myself) how to read, there would be no keeping him. It would forever unfit him to be a slave."[3] Mom would always tell us to get as much education as we could. She didn't necessarily show us how in deed; she only had an eighth-grade education. But she always encouraged the kids toward academic achievement.

It was the month before I turned five. Knowing me, I probably clung to my brother Kevin's side. I remember the sense of security he provided. And Kevin already had two years of school under his belt, so he was accustomed to school; that day meant something different for him. My lifelong friend Dave Brown, who was also starting kindergarten with me, joined us beside the car, along with a few other children on the block. I remember piling inside Teddy's car, sans seatbelt, with our parents in the front.

I have a vivid memory of passing the school as we found a place to park. We all moved to the driver's side window. Jaws dropped as we slowly passed the sturdy, three-storied, concrete facility, which sat along one of the busiest intersections in town just off the highway. I remember thinking the school was enormous. In reality, it *was* fairly large. The entire facility takes up 45,000 square feet and housed twenty 900-square-foot classrooms, a playground, and ample parking space.

Whereas the trip to the school was rowdy, we held silence on our walk up the steps, in awe of the school. I recall my anxiety and how I looked for Kevin; when he was nowhere to be found, I clutched Mom's hand for support. The concrete steps leading up to the entrance seemed so big at the time, and they probably were for a five-year-old. But Mom was there for me. Looking back, schools represented some of the most loving and violent places in my life. In high school, the regular fights in Wilkinsburg reflected a divestment of the civic and social infrastructure of Wilkinsburg. However, I deeply treasure the memories of parents rallying for their children throughout my time in Wilkinsburg schools.

Schools are linchpins of a community's overall physical landscape and what researcher Eric Klinenberg defines as social infrastructure: the physical places and organizations that shape the way people interact.[4] Schools in cities are located mostly for convenience. People can walk or drive to them fairly easily. It's why we use them as polling stations and for neighborhood association meetings. Many students have fun on the playgrounds when the school is closed. In addition, a school's vitality helps support the economy; they employ numerous workers, many of whom are middle-class professionals. And they help hold the history and culture of a place through yearbooks, trophy cases, and photo archives. School traditions often connect one generation to the next, providing a sense of community stability and cohesion.

They can provide social and emotional support for educational and noneducational purposes. And they help shape residents' identity. It's not uncommon for people to try to figure out other people by asking what school they attended. Schools go well beyond helping develop youth for citizenship and the workforce. Schools bring people together. They help us organize our communities. However, many schools are falling apart or closing, sending our social infrastructure into a tailspin.

"When social infrastructure is robust, it fosters contact, mutual support, and collaboration among friends and neighbors," writes Klinenberg in his book *Palaces for the People*. "When degraded, it inhibits social activity, leaving families and individuals to fend for themselves."[5]

In 2013, the federal government estimated that schools nationwide needed a $550 billion investment to bring them up to standard just from deferred maintenance issues—damage from postponing repairs.[6] In addition, many districts are closing schools due to low enrollments. Of the 22,101 public schools that have closed since 2004, 3,927 (17 percent) of them were in Black-majority census tracts—and 3,395 of those schools (86 percent) were in urban areas. If a district has to close a school, something else needs to fill the educational, economic, and social voids. These needs don't go away because there are fewer children in an area. So what do you do with the community asset when a school does close? What do you replace it with? How do you leverage the building, the playground, and the meeting space?

I walked up the Johnston School steps again more than forty years later for the writing of this book. Traffic streamed by in the morning, making it difficult to park. The school still felt vast as I as walked up the staircase and entered the spacious foyer that doubled as an auditorium. Ornate ivory columns buttressed the balcony I had leaned over as a third and fourth grader. The openness invited me to run the halls, but my old teachers' instructions were still exerting sway. I walked dutifully, instead, to my old kindergarten classroom, in room 5.

I felt again the warmth of Ms. Hogan, my teacher, a young African American woman and the anxious knot in my stomach dissolving when I first saw the books, play spaces, and other kids in class. Now, butterflies fluttered in my belly from seeing the white ceramic sink and fountain I sipped from as a child. I recalled how proud I was of my very own cubby where my favorite yellow raincoat hung. Nothing could diffuse the self-importance of this forty-eight-year-old so swiftly as recalling my five-year-old self.

But this time around, there weren't any children in the class-room. No one read books in the library or played basketball in the gymnasium during my visit. Kids weren't playing with the blocks or puppets. The classroom held materials for children, but they were more or less being stored, just in case. The only buzz came from a filtration system of a fish tank nestled in a corner. The loneliness of being one of a few adults in the room eventually replaced the nostalgia that had washed over me.

In June 2012, the Wilkinsburg School District decided to close Johnston after enrollment declined to 180 students, less than half the student population when I attended. Students were assigned to the two other elementary schools in the district at the time. In addi-tion to moving the students, forty-three employees were furloughed. "School directors had to close a $3.1 million budget shortfall created by factors including statewide budget cuts, increases in school district employees' health costs and declining enrollment," Bruce Dakan, director of business affairs told the *Tribune-Review*.[7] In March 2013, the Wilkinsburg School District was placed on the state's financial watch list, an early-warning system created by the state legislature to identify districts besieged with budgetary difficulties and revenue shortages.[8]

The Wilkinsburg School District had been struggling fiscally and academically for more than a decade when it decided to close Johnston. Fewer children lived in the district than had in the past, which meant fewer dollars coming into the district. The district had no choice but to cover costs with local revenues by increasing taxes, which makes the city less attractive for prospective home buyers and residents.

The closing of Johnston didn't stop the bleeding. In 2015, the *Pittsburgh Business Times* ranked the Wilkinsburg School District at number 492 of 493 school districts in the state, largely based on academic performance.[9] As a fiscal and academic stopgap measure, the district agreed in 2015 to contract with the Pittsburgh Public

School District (a separate, much larger school district) to educate all the Wilkinsburg's seventh- through twelfth-grade students at the Westinghouse High School located in nearby Homewood, a neighborhood in the city of Pittsburgh, in the 2016–2017 school year. This was a way for the district to save money, giving Wilkinsburg taxpayers some relief. The move made the border between Wilkinsburg and Pittsburgh blurrier than it already was. The Wilkinsburg School District continued to educate the students in the primary grades.

Although families always used addresses of other family members to cross into either Wilkinsburg or Pittsburgh schools, moving the students was controversial, as beefs between the two neighborhoods were historic and often violent. (I have not-so-fond memories of getting chased on foot to get home to Wilkinsburg after attending parties in Homewood.)

While the threat of neighborhood rivalries resulting from the merger was real, neighborhood fights never really came to pass. School and community leaders took many steps to prevent major conflicts.[10] The cohorts of students that transferred, seemingly unified under the Westinghouse banner, suggests you can break a legacy of community rivalry with the careful social integration of schools through mergers. But not having fights in the hallways is not the way we should measure success.

"It's a shame that they were willing to settle for sending their kids to Westinghouse, because if there was one school in Western Pennsylvania, if not the state, that is academically as poor as Wilkinsburg, it's Westinghouse," Jake Haulk, president of the conservative think tank Allegheny Institute for Public Policy, told the *Pittsburgh City Paper*.[11] "I'm not sure their kids are going to be uplifted by being around kids who are failing as bad as they are, if not worse."

Haulk has a point. The *Washington Post* reported that, at 9 percent, Wilkinsburg actually had a higher percentage of high school students who were proficient in math in 2014, as compared to Westinghouse at 3 percent.[12] Both schools posted comparable SAT scores, below the national mean, and both fell in the bottom 3 percentile in the state. The Wilkinsburg-Westinghouse merger exemplifies research that shows most students who are displaced from closures due to academic reasons don't end up in better schools.[13] However, school districts don't have the time or resources to keep open a school that doesn't have the enrollment to support it. A school enrolled at half its capacity drains districts' budgets, throttling programs in other schools, which also puts a drag on a community's potential growth. The reality is that there are times that schools must close for fiscal and academic reasons. But when it comes to Black schools, shuttering them seldom comes with alternatives that give families better educational options. In the case of my old school, Johnston Elementary is now Community Forge, a nonprofit business incubator dedicated to speeding up the growth of Wilkinsburg start-ups.[14]

A 2012 study from the National Business Incubator Association found 1,400 incubators scattered across the United States, an increase of 300 since 2006.[15] Ian Hathaway, a nonresident fellow at the Brookings Institution, found that American accelerators increased by an average of 50 percent each year between 2008 and 2014.[16] Hathaway's analysis included video footage of an interview he conducted with Brad Feld, cofounder of TechStars, one of the most successful accelerator programs in the world, with over forty sites, mainly in the United States but with locations in Africa, Australia, and Europe. Feld calls accelerators "an intense focused period of time where you have an opportunity to learn by doing" and likens them to immersive education programs that are usually found in colleges and universities.[17] Feld differentiated accelerators from business incubators, which gained traction in the 1990s from their origins in the middle of the twentieth century.

"Part of the power of an accelerator is that it's a constrained period of time," said Feld. "You're trying to accelerate time in the life of your learning of your company. You're not trying to incubate your business, you're trying to accelerate time."[18]

Accelerators and incubators, on the surface, seem like reasonable replacements for shuttered schools. Even with a decline in Wilkinsburg's school-age population, the town still needs educational services for children and adults. In addition, Wilkinsburg's overall development could be assisted by business growth. In particular, the town needs Black-owned businesses to grow to the point where they can generate wealth, hire community members, and innovate products. Theoretically, incubators can fill an acute professional development need through business support that's not being offered or not accessible to locals. However, because incubators and accelerators have historically been shown to promote a "bro" culture that mirrors the pale male tech industry, we should think twice about what kind of incubator lands in a Black neighborhood.[19] The wrong one could make matters worse for Black residents who've already been made vulnerable to tech booms and other new market explosions that increase housing costs and displace residents.[20]

WHAT TO DO WITH THE GROWING NUMBER OF VACANT SCHOOLS

The inventory of school facilities in the United States has followed population trends. Total enrollment in public and private elementary and secondary schools (pre-kindergarten through grade twelve) grew rapidly during the baby boom of the 1950s and 1960s, reaching a peak in 1971 at around 50 million students, according to a 2018 National Center for Education Statistics (NCES) report.[21] After creating new schools to sustain that period of growth, enrollment in elementary and secondary schools dropped between 1971 and 1984. Fewer people had fewer babies. Then enrollment rebounded through 2006, followed by a seven-year decline, until 2013 when enrollments restored 2006 levels. Presently, NCES predicts that overall enrollment will increase approximately 2 percent each year until 2026, when total enrollment is expected to reach 56.8 million.

But the overall growth in school-age population is distributed unevenly. Many metropolitan areas are realizing steady increases (such as Dallas, Texas, and Washington, D.C.), but others are growing slowly or even shrinking (for example, Dayton and Toledo, Ohio). Additionally, both regional and local migration trends can affect the constituent population of a particular school, with the growth of the Sunbelt and the return of White families to inner cities posing unique challenges for Black-majority areas. If current trends hold, White transplants will increase the demand for slots in certain urban, Black-majority school districts, as is already happening in Washington, D.C. and Chicago. However, outward migration from Black-majority inner- and outer-ring suburbs will force many districts in those areas to close schools.

SCHOOLS ARE ECONOMIC AND SOCIAL ASSETS

Schools facilitate economic growth. Most discussions of economic growth attributed to schools focus on the productivity generated by the skills gained (or not) from schools. These studies tend to examine economic growth of a state or country relative to the skills of its workforce. Teachers College economist Henry Levin and his colleagues produced one of the seminal articles on the subject in 2007 and found unequivocally that a high school degree outweighs the costs society incurs to produce graduates.[22] They found that "the net economic benefit to the public is $127,000 per student, 2.5 times greater than the costs." Consequently, improving education by cutting the number of students who drop out not only helps individuals but also benefits society as a whole.

Without question, schools generally add value to kids' lives. Schools are second homes for children. Students in the United States spend about six hours a day in school, not including before- or aftercare services, according to analysis from the research and policy analysis nonprofit the National Center on Education and the Economy.[23] Most states require children to attend school 175 to 180 days a year, with 900 to 1,000 instructional hours annually. Aside from boosting students' future earnings, a high performing school affirms students' and teachers' sense that they are valued. Schools that have drinking fountains that give clean water, proper climate controls, comfortable seating, up-to-date technology, and a solid roof send a firm statement about how much a community cares. Conversely, when the roof leaks and classrooms are inadequately heated, a community senses they aren't valued.

Understanding the full economic impact of schools also requires us to view schools as places of industry. Schools hire workers, procure contracts, and produce intellectual property—student and faculty work. Gas stations and bodegas animate the local economy when nearby schools operate. Schools are, indeed, businesses, but they are not analogous to factories. As a former charter school manager, I'd have fits when traditionalists would resist likening schools to any kind of business for fear students would be viewed as products. Actually, students receive services that schools provide. However, I'd also cringe when reformers, in their attempts to discredit traditionalists for focusing on labor issues, said things like, "Schools aren't human resources offices," meaning that schools were more about the adults than the kids. But the fact is that a lot of teaching *is* about the adults. Kids can't teach themselves so districts do have significant H.R. offices that must account for everyone, from the teachers to the lunch ladies in the cafeteria. Schools employ a significant portion of the middle class, the general standard for the percentage in society living a quality life. To discount the benefits that schools create from simply operating is to miss how important an economic asset they are to communities.

There are findings that highlight the correlation between property values and school quality. Economists estimate that in suburban neighborhoods nationwide, a 5 percent increase in academic performance can lift home prices by 2.5 percent.[24] While it's somewhat complicated to parse out how school quality increases home values, it's much easier to see what happens when a school isn't open for business. Vacant school properties are typically indicative of inequitable financing, academic failure, district dysfunction, chronic deferred maintenance problems, and population loss, none of which increases home prices in the surrounding area.[25]

To compensate for the inevitable loss of revenue that results from closing a school, cities raise taxes on their residents. Places like Wilkinsburg are put in a "tax trap," caught between raising taxes and/or cutting services, and this has given the Black-majority, predominantly low-income residents of Wilkinsburg the highest tax rate in Allegheny County for much of the 2010s.[26]

Vacant schools present a slew of other problems. They take up space that could be generating tax revenue for the city. They pose a danger for local residents; unoccupied properties have been shown to increase health risks and attract violence. In addition, districts must spend resources to keep up unused schools so they don't become a hazard to the neighboring community. It's clear; vacant schools extract significant value from neighborhoods. But what is lost in the economic discussion is the cost closed schools extract from social capital—the connections between people and groups that can be leveraged for growth. The violence, economic hardship, and academic underachievement that have beset Wilkinsburg are partially the result of a lost social connection that schools once provided.

Since I attended Johnston as a student, four of nine schools in Wilkinsburg have shut down. Without the social cohesion that schools help provide, it's less likely communities can see value in their assets and themselves. There's an esprit de corps that comes with class reunions and election days. There is a byproduct of togetherness from parent-teacher association meetings. The community bonds that come from rooting on the sports teams are immeasurable. People in struggling towns need victories for their collective self-esteem any way they can get it, whether it's football, basketball, or track and field.

Districts have options when it comes to what to do with a closed facility. They can mothball it, meaning keep the school empty but service it to prevent deterioration and decay. They can lease it to another school operator, nonprofit, or business. Districts can sell the property at or below market rate. In addition, vacant buildings can be repurposed or demolished.

A 2013 Pew Charitable Trust report examined the impact of shuttered schools across the country on communities and the factors that go into a district's decision on what to do with them. The report presents a series of recommendations for school districts when closing a school. In general, Pew finds that the faster a district can execute the closure, the better. It's very costly for districts and cities to hold on to empty buildings. Districts that ostensibly couldn't afford to keep the building open can barely afford to pay for the necessary maintenance, security, and insurance to keep it vacant as they search for a new occupant or wait until the school-age population rises. Leasing is difficult because the costs of renovation are often cost prohibitive. For every dollar spent on upkeep, a dollar is lost in profit in a potential sale. In places where the demand for real estate is high, like present-day Washington, D.C., districts can sell vacant properties quickly, maximizing their sale value. However, declines in the school-going population often correspond with an overall population decline, which doesn't bode well for demand. Larger buildings are harder to sell because, typically, there are fewer groups in the area able to buy them or use them in another form. In Washington, D.C., the overall population is increasing, which makes it easier to sell or convert properties to meet community needs.

However, location of the building is a significant factor in the marketability of a school. "Some larger structures tucked into residential neighborhoods would be better candidates for commercial or institutional conversion if they were on busy roads or commercial corridors," the Pew report states.[27] Among the twelve cities in the study, taking on a charter school tenant was the most popular use for vacant public schools, at 42 percent. Government/nonprofit came in second at 22 percent, followed by other educational (12 percent), residential (10 percent), to be determined (9 percent), and other (5 percent).

Black-majority cities looking to develop economically and socially must have a plan to address imminent or existing vacant school properties. And if outside investors don't see the opportunities in the assets that have potential, then municipalities must create the opportunities themselves.

INCUBATING FIRMS FOR COMMUNITY GROWTH

In some ways, Michael Skirpan, cofounder of Community Forge, is what people think of as the personification of a gentrifier. He's a thirty-something White guy, dressed grungy, seemingly in need of a haircut. He studied philosophy and physics as an undergraduate and possesses a Ph.D. in computer science. He looks like the kind of person about whom residents would say, "What's this White guy doing here?"

Skirpan was reared not too far away, in the Mon Valley, an area composed of small, rusted out steel towns along the banks of the Monongahela River approximately thirty miles south of downtown Pittsburgh. Not dissimilar in size and substance from Wilkinsburg, the Mon Valley towns of Donora, Belle Vernon, Monessen, and Braddock also have proud histories of economic vitality and self-sufficiency. They have current and former residents who brag about the towns' heydays in the 1940s and 1950s when traffic was as thick as the smoke that poured out the stacks from the steel production. Now, abandoned brick buildings stand as monuments to a bygone era. Skirpan probably feels somewhat at home in Johnston School.

Skirpan's grandfather was a labor organizer in the 1960s who successfully fought for higher wages and better conditions, after a period in the 1940s and 1950s when workers gave their blood, sweat, and tears to supply steel during wartime. But the industry didn't keep pace with their overseas competitors' technological advancements, and, therefore, the mills began to lay off workers and shut down operations.

"While steelmakers in Europe and Japan invested in the newer technologies, steelmakers at home doubled down and reinvested in the old ways," went a 2014 NPR profile of the Mon Valley.[28] American companies didn't adapt. Communities bore the brunt of waning competitiveness and productivity, and the towns withered alongside the mills. Skirpan embodies this history. The need for innovation and adaptability, as well as a penchant to organize people, is in Skirpan's blood.

According to its mission statement, Community Forge seeks to "grow an inclusive Community Space dedicated to creating opportunities for Wilkinsburg by supporting small business, promoting learning, contributing to neighborhood wellbeing, and cultivating regional partnerships." Initially, Skirpan, along with his wife and friends, conceived of a space to host educational, cultural, and civic activities, but they eventually decided to turn Community Forge into an incubator that seeks social as well as business returns on his investment. "What we're incubating here is not just about money," he told me. It is also about "incubating community."[29]

So in 2017, Skirpan went door-to-door and hosted a cookout, asking residents what kind of offerings they wanted to see in the shutdown Johnston Elementary. Not surprising, most residents wanted more activities for children, to fill the void created when the school closed. However, Wilkinsburg also needs businesses to grow at a scale such that they can hire local residents and boost the economy as well as offer hope to aspiring entrepreneurs. So Skirpan set out to meet that need by acquiring Johnston School to host a unique kind of incubator: one that blended business and community development.

Being Wilkinsburg, there were a few potholes in the road. Initially, Skirpan was unable to secure a loan to purchase the building. That's when XPogo, an extreme pogo sticking company, entered the picture. (If you're wondering what extreme pogo sticking is, let alone what it has to do with Wilkinsburg, you're not alone. Let's just say these rocket-like, tricked out pogo sticks aren't the childhood staple I may have played with on Johnston's playground as a child.)

XPogo was also interested in purchasing the building: the big playground we played kickball and basketball on would make for an eye-catching, outdoor showroom for an extreme sport company. But nothing says gentrification like an extreme pogo sticking business in the middle of the 'hood. So XPogo backed away from purchasing the building. However, members of its board decided to partner with Skirpan by joining Community Forge's board of directors, enabling Skirpan to secure a loan to purchase the property in July 2017. As a bonus, Community Forge also secured the kind of highflying tenant (pun intended) that could help pay the mortgage. XPogo has a space in the building.

Soon thereafter, the local nonprofit Gwen's Girls, an organization dedicated to girls' empowerment, approached Skirpan about using the space for some of their programming efforts in the area.[30] Gwen's Girls provides after-school and summer programming, career planning services, as well as science, technology, engineering, and math (STEM) enrichment to girls in the area. So its leadership looked at the building and vetted Skirpan to make sure he was committed to community and to make sure the building could accommodate the organization's basic needs. The 900-square-foot classrooms, along with all the security features the school offered, met their expectations. After meeting with Skirpan, Gwen's Girls committed to leasing two spaces even before Community Forge officially opened its doors in January 2018. In XPogo, a national organization in need of a headquarters, and Gwen's Girls, a locally respected organization with a history of serving Black communities, Community Forge had secured two very different tenants who could attract other tenants to the building to help pay the bills, which immediately came into view.

"This building is expensive to run because of heating and our interest rate," Skirpan told me. Erected in 1922, Johnston School isn't a model of architectural efficiency. The energy and maintenance costs the school district struggled to pay now lay in Skirpan's hands. Remember, incubators are businesses. The business model literally banks on tenants generating revenue for the space. But he and his board wanted to make sure low-income residents had access to the opportunity—as they should.

"We looked at the numbers and we were like, we could actually give about a third of our tenants some kind of subsidy, and we were able to give a $400 a month subsidy," he told me.

Over the course of a year, Community Forge signed on twenty-four tenant businesses, about half of which are individual owners who share a space. The other half operates in full classrooms. As word got around town of the price break, more prospective tenants applied. More than half of the lessees receive some kind of subsidy to rent space, which costs Community Forge more than they originally had budgeted for. The occupants' current rents may sustain the costs of the building and the one full-time and one half-time employee Community Forge has on the payroll, but that comes at the expense of the owners' livelihoods.

"In some way, we're not sustainable because we [Skirpan and his wife Jacqueline Cameron] give so much volunteer labor. I've never been paid on this project." Skirpan gets by as an adjunct faculty member at Carnegie Mellon University. While in-kind services is part of their business model, admittedly the arrangement is not good for his own bottom line. This puts pressure on tenants to generate revenues so they can pay full freight or even invest back into the incubator.

THE BUSINESSES

The businesses Community Forge incubates or houses are diverse. In addition to XPogo and Gwen's Girls, Community Forge incubates GoPhleb, LLC, a mobile phlebotomy company; Barrels to Beethoven, a music school dedicated to preserving steel pan instruction; Pittsburgh Housing Development Association, an organization that helps low- and moderate-income residents purchase a home; Treelady Studios, a music studio; Steel City Indie, a comprehensive media company specializing in films, documentaries, web services, and special events; Pittsburgh Democratic Socialists of America, a chapter of the national Democratic Socialists of America that does local political organizing; and Global Human Performance, which offers athletic training, among other things There are also several individual artists specializing in visual, conceptual, and therapeutic artwork. In total, two dozen ethnically diverse entrepreneurs and business owners have signed leases.

Johnston's conversion from a school to an incubator is still very much under construction. Cans of putty and paint litter the gritty hallways. Semblances of the old school are everywhere. The signs of transformation remain in many of the classrooms. Each room has a different look and feel, depending on the needs and the character of the business owner. In my old first-grade classroom, now Barrels to Beethoven, an assortment of steel drums are meticulously ordered in rows from the front to the back of the classroom. The sunlight glistens on the silver drums, giving the room an almost magical ambiance. In stark contrast, Treelady Studios feels like a warm, private home studio, minus the fireplace, of a famous producer. (The company does have a Grammy award on its résumé.) Audio boards and computers surround a single seat in the center of the room. Speakers are hung neatly from the ceiling, giving a decorative feel to an otherwise functional space.

Enter the room of the K-Theatre Dance Complex on the second floor and you'll see the black vinyl laminate flooring that you typically find in dance studios. Standalone barres line the windows looking outward toward speeding cars whisking along the nearby highway down below. Mirrors line one of the walls where chalkboards used to be, held up by the gutters that once held chalk. The original chalkboards on an adjacent wall were preserved, revealing a list of dance exercises for the day. Above the mirrors and chalkboards and assorted images of the Alvin Ailey American Dance Theater, images of Misty Copeland and other dance greats are plastered randomly over the white walls, photographed at every turn, twist, and arabesque. You get a sense that the pictures project the dreams and inspirations of owner and operator Kontara Morphis.

A Pittsburgh native, Morphis attended the Pittsburgh High School for the Creative and Performing Arts, locally referred to as CAPA. There, she studied dance, she says, learning the basics of ballet, jazz, modern, and tap. After graduation, she took master classes with the Alvin Ailey Dance Theater, the Dayton Contemporary Dance Company, and the cast of *The Lion King* Broadway musical, and performed under the direction of Norma Jean Barnes and Staycee Pearl with Xpressions Dance Academy, a world-renowned dance company. As founder and artistic director of K-Theatre, Morphis teaches ballet, jazz, modern, hip-hop, tap, and theatre to students age seven to seventeen. Morphis says Community Forge has supported her business from the day she became a tenant in January 2018, by placing her in funding networks, assisting in grant applications, and connecting her to other people and resources in the building.

Morphis says she treats her classroom studio like a conservatory, in that she teaches theory and history in addition to dance. But she is very open to teaching youth who don't yet consider themselves dancers. "I'm really into working with students who don't really know that they have the ability to dance," she told me. "I know the outcomes that occur when children are exposed to dance."[31] Morphis enjoys teaching students who need opportunities to develop and mature in other aspects of their lives besides dance.

"It's just like a family environment, so once you're at K-Theatre it's like home," said Calina Womack, one of her former students, now the director's assistant. "I learned how to come out of my shell more . . . We tend to stay out of the spotlight for fear of being shunned for being Black," said Womack.[32] Children need stages to dance and shine on in spite of the outside world that doesn't see value in them.

Still, just like every other business in the region, tenants must connect to other customers, revenue sources, and broader economic forces in the region to grow. Morphis charges $60 per month per child for tuition. With less than two years in operation, it's hard to envision the scale at which her firm can grow. Because many of Community Forge's less-established firms are community-facing service organizations, their growth is somewhat constrained by residents' abilities to pay.

CREATING A NEW KIND OF SCHOOL

"Every time I come back to this building, I have a flood of memories," Erin Perry (no relation) told me.[33] Perry is the executive director of the Legacy Arts Project in Pittsburgh. She rented a space for one of her art programs in Community Forge during its first summer of operations. Like me, she also attended kindergarten in room 5, but a decade later, when a married Ms. Hogan still presided but under her married name of Mrs. Smith.

Perry has fond memories of her unusual accomplishments while at Johnston. "I have to humbly admit that I was the stunts champion," Perry crowed. As a child, Perry took gymnastics lessons, and in gym class at school, Perry showed off to her peers' and teachers' delight. "I had my picture on the wall that said I was the stunts champion," she says, beaming.

She is still performing for Johnston. In the summer of 2018, Community Forge hosted her summer arts program that brought approximately fifty children to her old stomping grounds. As an art administrator, she finds creative ways to forge positive memories and build community. "Art is life. It might sound clichéd," Perry says, "but art is the act of creating. Every moment we have the opportunity to create something."

Maybe we should look at Community Forge as a different kind of school, one that demands state, federal, and local funding. Leaders in cities like Wilkinsburg must address the adult educational and workforce development needs that include workforce and business training. In addition, families still need educational services close by, so they work while their children get access to enrichment activities. We're in an era of lifelong learning. From a public policy perspective, what we consider a school must change to meet the demands of local communities. Community Forge can offer other municipalities with shuttered schools a model.

Communities may not be able to afford to keep elementary schools open, but they also can't afford to have schools sitting dormant, waiting for outsiders to recognize their assets. Sure, there are other possibilities: grocery stores, job training centers, drug counseling centers, manufacturing plants, art galleries, and more. I even wonder if Community Forge can better take advantage of the traffic that continues to stream by at rush hour. Nevertheless, incubators can help innovate how cities repurpose valuable community assets to meet the economic, education, and social infrastructure needs of the city.

"Are arts for other people, or can arts exist without an audience?" Perry asks, sharing a question she's constantly grappling with. However, her reflections also inform why we must think carefully about repurposing schools.

"I'm of the mind that art does exist without an audience, that it doesn't always have to be for someone else," she says, adding that, for children, we need to create spaces that convey that "who they are is enough."

A school can exist without an abundance of children. Perry sees the need for Community Forge. The people of Wilkinsburg need a safe place to grow, heal, and develop. Community-focused incubators can become part of the social infrastructure that's needed in Black-majority cities.

5

The Apologies We Owe to Students and Teachers

The walls of the dean's conference room at the University of New Orleans College of Education and Human Development displayed framed black-and-white photographs of African American children. Some looked out of the frames with curious gazes, others with blissful smiles or serious stares. Their images were reminders for the decisionmakers in the room that our choices have a real-world impact on children. I attended many meetings in that room as a professor and administrator but, somehow, over time, I stopped thinking of the faces of the children in the photographs. They blended into the walls, unnoticed. However, one day in spring 2008, I stared pensively in their faces as I questioned what had led me there that day.

Outside the building, the waters of Hurricane Katrina had long since receded, but the watermarks that stained nearby homes remained like scabs, covering the healing underneath. In the Gentilly neighborhood, where the university and three of the four charter schools it managed were based, darkish yellow lines were etched nine feet up the walls of many homes. Beige and white trailers, temporary shelters provided by the Federal Emergency Management Agency, littered the neighborhood. Some of our teachers lived in those trailers, waiting for the state to process loans through a federal program designed to fund people's rebuilding efforts.

There is never a good time to terminate someone, but doing so in the aftermath of Katrina seemed particularly bad. School employees and students, struggling to find their footing, had just begun to settle in. And yet, with the faces of those children looking down on us, I was about to fire the leaders of our school.

"Do you think the leaders we have in the schools are the ones who will move us forward?" It was a serious question the dean of the college, James Meza, posed to the executive team of our charter management organization—the Capital One-University of New Orleans Charter Network.

In the room with us were Vera Triplett, our chief operating officer, and Patrick Nedd, the financial officer. Together, we decided that the principals and assistant principals of three of the four schools we managed needed to be let go. In doing so, we dealt one more blow to New Orleans' teachers, especially its Black teachers.

The education sector in New Orleans had already been buffeted by waves of firings. In December 2005, the Orleans Parish School Board (OPSB) terminated approximately 7,500 employees from the Orleans Parish School District, of which roughly 4,300 were teachers. Seventy-one percent of those teachers were Black, and 78 percent were women, according to a report by the education think tank the Education Research Alliance.[1] Some of OPSB's former employees had eventually found jobs in our charter network. Our decision to fire our schools' leaders peeled off the scab from a wound the city had yet to recover from. Of the six principals we planned to terminate, five were women and all were Black.

On three separate occasions, I waited nervously in that conference room with our operations officer to tell the leadership pairs of our three elementary schools—Pierre A. Capdau, Medard H. Nelson, and Gentilly Terrace—that their annual contracts would not be renewed. Each time, we first met the principal, then the assistant principal. The proceedings mimicked case studies I had read in education leadership classes back in graduate school. We parroted a script that explained why we were meeting: "As part of our annual review . . ." Like a metronome, I repeated to each person, "We will not be renewing your contract."

We opened the discussion for questions, but we didn't need to show cause when deciding not to renew an annual contract, and we exercised that right, so there wasn't much room for a rebuttal. For the most part, the principals didn't offer any. They knew the drill. The individual meetings felt horribly long but, in reality, they were no more than five, maybe ten, minutes.

Five, maybe ten, minutes.

When the city eventually reopened for business after Hurricane Katrina, returning residents tried to resuscitate basic institutions, like schools. One of those residents was Wylene Sorapuru, who spent days and weeks cleaning up the Capdau and Nelson elementary schools.

"We were in [Capdau]; no lights, no electricity, so you were freezing cold," Sorapuru told me.

A few weeks before Katrina made landfall, the University of New Orleans (UNO) hired Sorapuru to serve as the assistant principal for Nelson Elementary. She was already a member of the UNO family, taking classes in our doctoral program. Prior to that when she came to our charter schools, she was a decorated teacher and administrator in the New Orleans public schools. Her mother served as a principal in the district. Her sister was an assistant principal. Given our circumstances, we were lucky to have her experience.

Capdau Elementary didn't get flooded, but it had been a refuge of last resort during and after the storm. "There were people living in the Capdau building during Hurricane Katrina so there were old clothes, there was feces on walls. There was trash everywhere," Sorapuru recalled. "Our first order of business was to help clean this place up."

Thanks in part to Sorapuru's hard work and leadership, Capdau opened in January 2006. Immediately after, Sorapuru and her colleagues had just one month to prepare Nelson Elementary—the school she had been hired to lead before the storm—to open in a temporary location. She helped locate the teachers who had originally been set to start the academic year, checking to see who could return to the city; many teachers still didn't have homes to return to. At the same time, she and her staff had to interview teacher candidates to fill vacated slots and register parents to enroll children. Nelson opened on schedule at the temporary site, and then in its original location six months later.

Staff, including leadership in our charter school network, doubled in those first two years after Katrina to approximately 100 people, and we bonded quickly as we put ourselves and our schools back together again. Just as my mother had knitted us into a family out of difficult circumstances, the leadership of the university and our schools became family after Katrina.

Before and immediately after the storm, I was an assistant professor with limited contact with the schools, but over time I became more involved. Before the storm, I helped analyze academic performance data. I led professional development sessions and spoke at graduation ceremonies. After the storm, I helped write the charter applications that landed the university Gentilly Terrace and Early College High School, and I worked with the dean to apply for funding for the schools. I genuinely felt invested in our small school network. My contributions eventually landed me the fancy title of CEO of the Capital One-UNO Charter Network.

If the pictures of the children on the walls of that university conference room could talk, they would have censured us. Before we fired our teachers, we had bragged to funders about how Capdau

Elementary essentially doubled its school performance score since we took it on as a charter. The executive team regularly touted the success of our interventions, pointing to the fact that Capdau and Nelson were moved off the state's list of failing schools. We plugged the stat that our charter, Early College High School, ranked in the top ten (8/21) in 2008 among all public high schools in the city, including those that were test-in (schools that select students based on a test score), selective-admission schools.

But behind the scenes, Timothy Ryan, our board chair (and president of the University of New Orleans) started openly questioning the rate of our progress in board meetings. If those pictures of Black children could talk, they would repeat the number of times Ryan asked, "Why can't we be more like KIPP?" The Knowledge is Power Program, commonly referred to as KIPP, is a national charter network that also had a presence in New Orleans. It regularly outperformed other networks, including ours. If you consider education a competition, as we did at the time, KIPP schools were the ones to beat. We wrongly put ourselves in a make-believe horserace.

I spent restless nights back then waiting for the *Times-Picayune*, New Orleans's daily paper at the time, to report the next day on citywide test scores on the state exams. I remember jumping out of bed as soon as I heard plastic wrapping slap the concrete porch steps, the sound of the morning paper being delivered. My anticipation didn't stem from wanting to know our scores. The state department of education had already privately delivered them to us weeks prior. I rushed to see where exactly we ranked among other schools, whether or not our schools fell above or below the fold. The position on the newspaper's page set the tone in our school board meetings and established a pecking order among our peers at gatherings. In the charter world, ranking, as much as test scores, determined our authority, reputation, and overall standing.

After the state restarted collecting data after the storm, our schools sat without fanfare in the middle of the list for two years in a row, after languishing in the bottom for years prior. So, supposedly on behalf of Black children, we decided that the leaders who had raised our test scores from the bottom to the middle; helped locate and hire teachers, clean buildings, recruit students, and restart schools in the wake of Hurricane Katrina were incapable of leading us forward.

I still remember the shame I felt in 2008 when Sorapuru walked into that conference room. "You could barely look me in the face," she said to me in an interview for this book. Sorapuru didn't know I was looking into the faces of the Black children on the walls.

But the leaders we fired survived and flourished. People moved from one institution to the next so quickly in the years after Katrina. Other school networks immediately picked up all our former leaders. Sorapuru would go on to blossom as the chief academic officer for one of the most successful charter organizations in the city.

Meanwhile, the Capital One-UNO Charter Network team struggled. I resigned a few years later, along with my dean. Within five years of the firings, none of the members of the executive team remained. And the schools dropped in the rankings.

We had justified our decisions, in part, as supported by data. We constantly called ourselves *data-driven* decisionmakers, a go-to catchphrase at the time, suggesting that growth was the only thing we should be concerned about. To justify the upending of schools and pre-Katrina educators, reformers will rattle off the same numbers. In 2005, Orleans Parish ranked sixty-seventh of sixty-eight Louisiana parishes in student achievement. With the exception of a few high-performing selective admissions schools where White and middle-class students were concentrated, most public schools in the decade before Katrina were low-performing schools.[2] In the 2004–2005 school year, 64 percent of public schools in New Orleans were deemed "academically unacceptable" by Louisiana accountability standards; the figure was 8 percent for public schools in Louisiana overall. In the same year, the city's public schools had a twelfth-grade dropout rate of 16.8 percent while the statewide rate was 7.6 percent.

But many of us who posted these numbers did so in a vacuum, ignoring the racism that certainly influenced those numbers. For centuries, schools were used as a conduit to fund White people and their institutions. University of Wisconsin-Madison professor and New Orleans native Walter Stern documented in his book *Race and Education in New Orleans: Creating the Segregated City* how schools were used as urban planning and economic development tools. By placing schools reserved for White families in places that were not developed, the board used facilities for the public toward the settlement of White people.[3] On behalf of their constituents, White district leaders neglected Black schools in Black neighborhoods for much of the twentieth century. Stern explained how those practices created real economic benefits for Whites and burdens for Blacks that are manifested in the test scores we use to justify reforms. Stern said in an interview with the New Orleans' NPR affiliate, WWNO 89.9:

> The resources and protections that followed the creation of White schools meant that the surrounding houses increased in property value. And with Black neighborhoods, often identified as such because they had Black schools, property values did not increase, or even declined. So this created obstacles that we still see today in terms of persistent wealth gaps between White people and African American people, particularly since owning a home is often the greatest source of a person's wealth.[4]

The context of racism in Norman Rockwell's painting of six-year-old Ruby Bridges, who integrated all-White, public William Frantz Elementary school in the face of death threats and teacher boycotts, is the setting in which academic performances should be gauged. Current reformers must be placed in this same history. When they speak of performance absent of a racist context that devalues schools, it's to further devalue the work of educators, leaders, parents, and children to seize greater control and power.

I'm clear that we didn't base our decision to fire the principals only on children's test scores. Yes, our pride and embarrassment motivated us, but there was something much more insidious at play that our leaders suffered for. We fired Black people, and particularly Black women, partly because we couldn't value them as part of a solution moving forward. And we weren't the only ones. Education reformers' vision for a future New Orleans didn't include Black women, and their decline in the teaching corps showed it. In the end, it was this exclusion that hurt New Orleans's children the most, and it is this for which we must account.

PROOF OF RACISM: THE DECLINE IN THE NUMBER OF BLACK TEACHERS AFTER KATRINA

In 2018, Roy Wood Jr., a correspondent on the news satire program *The Daily Show with Trevor Noah*, addressed the debate around whether or not President Donald Trump had used the N-word in the White House and/or on the set of his reality show, *The Apprentice*. After playing audio of the many racist things Trump has said in public, Wood exclaimed, "I don't need footage of [former wrestler/ action movie star] the Rock in the gym to know if he works out! Have you seen his arms?"[5]

But just as the Trump administration's press secretary Sarah Huckabee Sanders deflected reporters' questions about her boss's racist remarks by denying the president is racist, education reformers deny their distrust of Black people, and Black women in particular.

Few people will actually confess to being racist—or even recognize that prejudice lies at the heart of their actions. But actions speak louder than words. The dramatic disappearance of Black folk from the teaching workforce in New Orleans reveals that education reformers categorically blamed them for underachieving kids and exposes an underlying and unacknowledged racism in the reform movement. A workforce 7,500-strong, including 3,000 Black teachers, was summarily fired in the months after the storm waters receded.

"They were saying how poor a job we [teachers] did," Billie Dolce, a New Orleans teacher who was fired after the storm, told MSNBC in a 2015 documentary.[6] "This was an opportunity for the schools and the students in Orleans Parish to make some progress. . . . This is—what I thought—the state's opportunity to wipe out everything and start anew."

If there was ever a time New Orleans and members of its Black community needed teachers to have job security, it was after Hurricane Katrina. The city desperately needed evacuees to return to help jump-start the recovery, principally by working. The unemployment rate is an essential indicator of economic fitness. Available jobs motivate evacuees to return to the city; without work, they may be forced to take up employment elsewhere to make ends meet. Finding a way to rehire the pre-Katrina teachers would have been in the city's best interest. As city and state officials worked together in the aftermath of Katrina, it became clear that leaders didn't see value in New Orleans educators.

As Florida Woods, then principal of Paul L. Dunbar Elementary School, told the education newspaper *Education Week* in September 2005, "The people who were there should be the ones given the opportunity to rebuild. . . . We know the history, we know the culture of the city, the district, and the people."[7] The firing of the teachers signaled they weren't welcomed back to the city.

The reformers' eventual replacements for the predominately Black, female workforce revealed who we really wanted in the city—young White people with little to no teaching experience. In the 2004–2005 academic year, the year before Katrina, 17 percent of the teachers in New Orleans public schools had less than three years of experience, according to the data collected by the Cowen Institute, an education think tank at Tulane University. By 2009–2010, that number had more than doubled, to 39 percent. The percentage of Black teachers dropped from 71 percent to 49 percent from 2005 to 2014, which was equivalent to about 4 percent of the entire African American working-age population of New Orleans at the time, according to the Education Research Alliance report.[8] That precipitous decline could not have happened without deliberate efforts to bring in a new, Whiter workforce. Reformers were more than willing to rebuild without Black women, the largest demographic among the fired employees.

Louella Givens had served as a member of the Louisiana State Board of Elementary and Secondary Education before, during, and after Katrina. In the documentary film *A Perfect Storm*, she made her beliefs about the mass layoffs known: "While people in New Orleans Parish was still underwater and on rooftops, there was a plan being formed to take away the schools in Orleans Parish."[9] That plan included a state takeover of district schools and a strategy to convert those state-managed schools to charters, which are not subject to union rules, do not require teachers to be certified, and where, most important, the principals have the right to hire and fire whomever they please.

Before Hurricane Katrina, the University of New Orleans managed two of the six charter schools that existed under the state entity the Recovery School District (RSD). Contrary to what the name now suggests, the RSD existed prior to the storm as part of a 2003 state constitutional amendment to allow state takeover of repeatedly failing public schools. Schools that didn't show adequate progress over a number of years could be taken over by the state entity. The RSD's mission in 2003 was "to provide the supports and interventions necessary to put academically struggling schools on a path toward success."[10] Converting district schools into charters became one of its primary interventions.

In November 2005, the state legislature passed Act 35, which lowered the bar for what it meant to be an academically unacceptable school, dramatically expanding the RSD post-Katrina. Policymakers tailored Act 35 to enable the appropriation of all but sixteen of 126 public schools in New Orleans. In addition to granting the RSD authority to manage the schools, the legislature also gave it say-so over the land and buildings occupied by the schools. In every sense, the legislative action was a takeover of New Orleans public schools.

The move essentially eliminated the New Orleans school district's power to oversee hiring and firing in public schools and shredded a critical professional network Black people had forged over the years. The charter school era was predicated on the notion of breaking up the monopoly that unions have on schools. Collective bargaining agreements, aka union contracts, had a stranglehold on schools, reformers cried. It was impossible to get rid of bad teachers, they argued. They linked student outcomes solely to teacher performance and got rid of the teachers they deemed ineffective. Charter schools are concentrated in districts that are majority Black. This caused upheaval to municipal workforces nationally in Black communities, which are disproportionately represented in public sector union jobs. (According to the Bureau of Labor Statistics, the share of Black workers in unions, at 12.5 percent, is the highest among the major racial groups.[11] Education services professions represent the second-highest unionization rate among all occupations.) By laying blame for underachievement at the feet of Black teachers, the Black community lost discrimination protections the public education often provides.

Black teachers represented the majority of teachers in the pre-Katrina context also because they had professional and social ties to it. The Sorapuru professional family tree reflected a Black legacy of access. Many of the new charter organizations utilized out-of-town teacher-training and recruitment organizations, which limited the pathways locals had to middle-class teaching jobs.

The stated philosophy behind charter school reform included the view that the administrative structures of traditional school districts were a drag on educational growth. Many reformers claimed these structures stifled innovation and tied leaders' hands with red tape. As time passed, it became clear that many in the charter community associated the Black workforce with the old structure and sought to rid the new schools of this weight.

Despite the reformers' negative view of the traditional school districts, in the years after the storm, Blacks still dominated the pool of prospective teachers in New Orleans. That was only natural, as Blacks were more than 60 percent of the adult population in the city. However, the devaluation of Black talent was reflected in their decline in the workforce. This devaluation was also reflected in the belief that charter schools needed to recruit from elsewhere to succeed.

In December 2007, the Bill & Melinda Gates Foundation, the Doris and Donald Fisher Fund, and the Eli and Edythe Broad Foundation, all prominent philanthropic organizations in education reform, announced their plans to provide several grants to New Schools for New Orleans, a pro-reform nonprofit support organization; New Leaders for New Schools, a nonprofit educational leadership training program; and Teach for America of Greater New Orleans, a nonprofit teacher placement organization. All these groups aimed to increase and develop new talent for charter schools. Researcher Sarah Reckhow of Michigan State University and Megan Tompkins-Stange of the University of Michigan found in a 2015 Michigan State University study that, beginning in 2008, the Gates and Broad foundations, in particular, shifted their philanthropic investments "from local education groups to national advocacy organizations and from discrete project-based initiatives to systemic reform efforts."[12] That shift from local to national amounted to pulling investments from residents with deep local roots and transferring them to organizations without native ties to Black communities. Concurrent with these philanthropic trends, the proportion of White teachers from outside New Orleans rose significantly.

If you follow philanthropic giving in New Orleans, as Reckhow and Tompkins-Stange did, you'll see that it literally paid to avoid seeing Black folk as part of the solution to the schools' problems. Reckhow and Tompkins-Stange's 2015 study found that although the Gates and Broad foundations generally consider their role in funding efforts to be apolitical, the lion's share of their grants cultivated a pro-reform, mostly White network. On the ground, I could see that grantees in New Orleans had little to no links to Black communities, teachers, and social networks.

The resulting small orbit of academics, advocacy groups, and think tanks that received funding amplified the preferred policy approaches to education reform. The Gates and Broad foundations were just two stars in a constellation of funders and education groups that were aligned. In their study, Reckhow and Tompkins-Stange quoted a Gates official who explained, "Anybody who cares to look would find very quickly that all of these organizations [are] suddenly singing from the same hymnbook."

The Recovery School District and many independent charter leaders limited their hiring pools to predominately White organizations and colleges, which, in New Orleans, had a disparate impact on Black women. No White reformers are on record saying they don't believe in Black teachers. But the proof is in the pudding: Consenting to institutional choices that single out one group for preferment at the expense of other racial and ethnic groups is the very definition of institutional racism. No one ever had to admit to not wanting to hire Black New Orleanians when the institutions and the reform-minded charter leaders did the weeding out for you. The message was clear: New Orleans teachers need not apply.

"Nobody was clamoring to give me a job," former teacher Katrena Ndang told *Education Week*. "Everywhere else in the city, they brought their people back, no matter where you worked. For me, it was like the school system telling me I didn't matter. They wanted anybody but the teachers who were there before."[13]

By fall 2007, about half of the terminated teachers had returned to Louisiana public schools. However, only 37 percent were re-employed by 2013, including 15 percent who worked in other parishes. The other 13 percent moved out of education. A decade later, in 2017, nearly two-thirds of the teachers who had worked in New Orleans before Katrina were no longer in the field. The Education Research Alliance, a New Orleans-based research center at Tulane University, found that the reforms significantly reduced the number of pre-Katrina teachers in the system.

"Overall, our best estimate is that the combined effects of dismissal and reform, separate from the hurricane effect, reduced the 2007 education employment of pre-Katrina New Orleans teachers by at least 16 percentage points," the Education Research Alliance study says.[14]

In a 2012 *Washington Post* editorial, Jo-Ann Armao, an editor at the newspaper, wrote, "The horrors of Katrina created a blank sheet that is (thankfully) absent in other cities."[15] But 80 percent of the teaching cohort of 2004–2005 in other school parishes—also affected by the storm—was still employed in 2007–2008, which is 30 percentage points higher than in New Orleans. Armao's editorial ignored the manmade disasters in the wake of the storm. The hurricane didn't create a blank sheet; reformers devalued and erased Black teachers from the charter teaching corps.

WHY BLACK TEACHERS MATTER

If I proposed to a governor or a school board that they replace a significant portion of a majority-White teaching corps with Black teachers after a natural disaster decimated a city because doing so would potentially confer educational and social benefits I'd probably be denounced as a racist and publicly excoriated.

Even a cursory reading of the literature on Black teachers should have given politicians and reformers pause before forcing their mass exit, but alas, even the research has apparently been devalued. For years, researchers such as Gloria Ladson-Billings, Pedro Noguera, Lisa Delpit, Adrienne Dixson, Christopher Emdin, and James A. Banks—all people of color—validated the need for Black women teachers in New Orleans schools through their studies on teachers of color. Their scholarship serves as the foundation for inquiries like one by Stanford University researcher Thomas Dee who, the year before Katrina, found that Black students of both sexes who had a Black teacher scored 3 to 6 percentile points higher on standardized tests in reading than those who did not. [16] Dee found a similar increase in the math scores of Black students taught by a Black teacher.

In a 2017 study published by the Institute of Labor Economics, researchers found that low-income Black male elementary school students who were paired with a Black teacher in the third, fourth, or fifth grades were 39 percent less likely to drop out of high school.[17] The researchers also found that matching low-income Black students of both sexes with at least one Black teacher between the third and fifth grades increased their aspirations to attend a four-year college by 19 percent.

In addition to academic gains, Black students taught by Black teachers exhibited better behavioral outcomes. According to 2015 research by Adam C. Wright, a professor of economics at Western Washington University, behavioral assessments of Black students in the classroom significantly improve when they have a Black teacher rather than a White teacher.[18] Wright found that as Black students receive instruction from a greater number of Black teachers, the probability of suspension decreases. In a 2017 study, Wright and his team showed that students of color placed with a teacher of color were less likely to argue or act out than minority students placed with White teachers.[19]

The research suggests that a focus on Black teacher recruitment and retention post-Katrina could have helped prevent educators from using excessive suspension and expulsion, which was certainly a problem prior to Katrina. However, reformers instituted "zero-tolerance" policies that became fashionable at the time, criminalizing mundane school infractions. School leaders were told to "sweat the little things," such as uniform infractions, walking out of line, and unsanctioned verbal communication.[20] "In 2007–8, if a student had a stripe on their sock or a mark on a shoe, there was a consequence," Ben Kleban, then CEO of the charter network College Prep told the *Atlantic* in 2014.[21] Multiple violations culminated in out-of-school suspensions. While reformers didn't create discipline disparities between White and Black students, reform didn't help reverse those injustices. Isn't that what reform is supposed to do—correct injustices? Instead, evidence suggests there was an increase in expulsions in the years just after the reforms with the increase of White teachers.[22]

Having brown skin doesn't make you a better teacher. However, there's something about living in brown skin that gives you a different set of expectations for your Black students than your White peers.

"I didn't' need a trick to get kids to be respectful and sit down and take their education seriously," said Amanda Aiken, a former teacher and administrator for College Prep who happened to be one of the few Black staff members in her school. It didn't take long for White teachers to lean on Amanda beyond her official role as an academic coach. They began seeking her out to discipline and manage specific students. White teachers asked, "Oh, Ms. Aiken, can you talk to this child because he won't sit down," Aiken said. She'd walk in the classroom, look at the child and ask, "Are we going to do this today?" Aiken explained that the student would sit down as he or she did in Amanda's classroom. "When you are one of the only Black people in a school, you also end up being the disciplinarian," she said. The advantage Black teachers bring to schools goes beyond a reduction in the number of Black kids who are suspended to an increase in the number of Black kids who go on to college.

American University economics professor Seth Gershenson and his colleagues examined, in a 2016 study, how racial lenses color teacher expectations.[23] They found that when White teachers and

Black teachers assessed the same African American students, White teachers were 40 percent less likely to predict that their Black students would complete high school, and 30 percent less likely to believe they would graduate from a four-year college program. Black female teachers were more likely than any other demographic group to believe that their Black male students would graduate from high school. The researchers argued that the low expectations many teachers have of their Black students could negatively affect these students' school performances and goals for the future. Therefore, an increase in Black teachers could positively affect the goals and expectations that Black students set for themselves. It makes sense that if teachers instill high expectations in their students, said students will be more likely to believe they can grow up to be a teacher than those who don't believe in themselves. Why return to a place that brings you down?

According to research conducted by a team of education researchers led by Betty Achinstein, increasing diversity in teaching is also important because teachers of color are more likely to teach and stay at schools that are considered "hard to staff."[24] Urban schools with higher minority and low-income populations often suffer from higher levels of teacher turnover. Retaining minority teachers in these hard-to-staff schools may allow for increased stability in urban schools. Education reforms that decrease the number of Black teachers hurt their own cause in the long run. Especially in Black-majority cities where there are higher percentages of both Black students and teachers, reducing the number of Black teachers can be detrimental to students' social mobility, their future professional opportunities in teaching, and the local economy.

Black students aren't the only ones who benefit from efforts to increase the percentage of Black teachers in schools. In their research on the impact of minority teachers in the classroom, University researchers Alice Quiocho and Francisco Rios argue that having a teacher of color is beneficial to students of all races.[25] Because of the lived experience that comes with being a person of color, minority teachers are able to identify and deconstruct the racial and cultural biases present in school systems, making it more likely that classroom discussions include a social justice orientation. Reducing the number of Black teachers also robs White students of the opportunity to form critical relationships that could disrupt how racism is passed on to the next generation. Racist children become racist adults. Black teachers can help end the cycle. Alas, this was the lens that was clearly needed in New Orleans after the storm, when, instead, education reform negatively affected Black workforces.

Black teachers are assets. If the purpose of education reform is to boost students' academic outcomes, reduce suspensions, raise expectations, and even recruit (less racist) teachers into the profession, research suggests that increasing the number of Black teachers should be part of any serious strategy. Any reform that reduces the number of Black women teaching in our schools isn't a reform; it's the same old repression Black communities have dealt with for generations, wrapped in a different garb. But the narrative of the charter school experiment puts its racist effect in the sheep's clothing of academic improvement.

HIDING VIOLENCE WITH NUMBERS

Neerav Kingsland served as the chief strategy officer for New Schools for New Orleans, a nonprofit intermediary that takes private, philanthropic, and government dollars and relays them to schools and other nonprofits as a form of advocacy for education reform. Kingsland recounted a story that I've heard him, and many other education reformers, use dozens of times as an opening salvo against the New Orleans Public Schools (NOPS) district. It's the story of Bridget Green, a Black New Orleans student who earned the honor of valedictorian of her 2003 class but wasn't allowed to walk the stage, give the graduation speech, or enjoy many of the other privileges that go along with that distinction. Jo-Ann Armao, in her 2012 *Washington Post* editorial on the educational landscape in the aftermath of Katrina profiled Kingsland, and she repeated the oft-used talking point[26]: Louisiana education law would not allow her to graduate because, even after five attempts, she couldn't pass the math competency section of the graduation exit examination—hence the system was a failure. Kingsland and other reformers made Green the poster child for a system that, according to Armao, had "no chance for sustainable improvement, given the enormity of its dysfunction."[27] Armao wrote: "Green's story is emblematic of the hopelessness that used to mark New Orleans's schools."

What was truly emblematic of New Orleans post-storm was the media and funders' unapologetic exploitation of Green. Reformers introduced the tale of Green's failures to funders and policymakers, using it to argue for education reform and charter schools. The repeated use of Green's name in presentations, editorials, documentaries, and speeches embroidered a narrative into the city's fabric that was used to shame a Black-majority school board and district. "Neerav Kingsland lives and breathes numbers," wrote Armao in her editorial.[28] Reformers were about facts as much as they were about narrative.

While the focal point of the Bridget Green tale involved the numbers and data on a standardized test, the shaming of Bridget Green had nothing to do with numbers or data; it was completely narrative driven. Tying standardized tests to potential success disadvantages Black students. Even among high achievers, Black students tend to score lower than White students on standardized tests for various reasons, including less access to test-prep services and self-defeating fears of reinforcing stereotypes.[29] Plus, standardized test scores are a poor predictor of college success. The National Association for College Admission Counseling released a research report in 2012 that revealed students with strong high school GPAs and low standardized-test scores generally performed well in college, while students with low high school GPAs and high test scores generally performed poorly.[30]

Since 2001, when a bipartisan Congress passed the federal education law No Child Left Behind (NCLB), which established measurable academic achievement goals and mandated that states report disaggregated educational outcomes by race, educators have reflexively used data-driven expressions to demonstrate their accountability for academic goals and to rationalize their decisions. By forcing states and districts to generate, show, and measure data, NCLB advanced education to the modern era.

Prior to NCLB, many districts didn't look at outcomes by race. Educators often haphazardly used intuition, professional judgment, and bias to make decisions. Being data-driven was a novel approach at the time. Education leaders began using data to determine how to address students' educational plans, hire and promote personnel, budget, enroll students, and coordinate transportation. As a school administrator after the passage of the NCLB Act, it's hard for me to see how district and school administrators were able to make key academic decisions without having access to critical, basic school, district, and statewide data. However, it's foolish to assume that data-driven decisions are morally sound ones and that numbers aren't used for unjust means.

While data is valuable, it should never have become the be-all. In my leadership role at UNO, experts and laypeople constantly asked, "What's the fastest way to close the Black-White achievement gap?" I often responded sarcastically, "Stop educating White people."

Most can see how ludicrous and mean that approach and reproach to closing the gap is. It would be data-driven but horribly wrong. Yet, my snarky response was no better, and no less preposterous, than firing teachers en masse, suspending and expelling Black children in droves, and forcing children to walk on White lines like they were in jail (all of which happened), to close a numerical gap. No, you shouldn't be data-driven; decisions in education should be community-driven, with data being used as a tool for uplift. New Orleans post-Katrina became a place where test score growth became the ultimate excuse to ignore community and ethical considerations.

Around 2011, I wanted to see how and where Bridget Green had landed. In about an hour-long conversation, I learned a few things that I can share. She told me she became too ashamed to live in New Orleans, meaning we humiliated her out of New Orleans. Green couldn't take seeing her name in print or in video reports. But I did learn in that conversation that she is doing well professionally and socially outside the city, in spite of her performance on those standardized tests. I also learned that no one in public policy should be data-driven only. Schools and school districts certainly need reform and change, but we should all be community-driven and use data to help uplift the public.

IN SERVICE OF HIGHER TEST SCORES

Almost immediately after Katrina, parents of special-needs students (and their lawyers) officially filed complaints to local, state, and federal authorities on behalf of children who were not being served by the new schools. Because schools are held accountable for test scores, they have an incentive to attract and keep high-scoring students; special education students, with low scores, become especially vulnerable to exclusionary practices. Students with special needs also come with a higher price tag; specialized services are more expensive for charter schools to offer, as they can't leverage the economies of scale available to intermediate school districts. So, in the wake of Katrina, many charters simply decided not to serve students with special needs.

It's impossible to get an exact count of how many families were denied services en route to charter schools' pursuit of higher test scores. But plaintiffs in a 2010 federal class action lawsuit filed by the Southern Poverty Law Center (SPLC) against the Louisiana

Department of Education attested to representing a class of nearly 4,500 New Orleans students with disabilities (both diagnosed and unidentified). Some families were told the school could not serve their children's particular needs. Other students with special needs were "counseled out"; that is, encouraged to leave the school. An innumerable number were suspended or expelled. According to a report on New Orleans schools on the tenth anniversary of Katrina, 21 percent of all Black students were suspended or expelled in 2008, compared to 9 percent of White students.[31] (I coauthored the report, published by The Data Center, a nonprofit research outfit.)

In the 2010 lawsuit, SPLC claimed that New Orleans students with special needs were denied legally mandated services; that schools failed to apply consistent policies to identify and evaluate students' needs; and that schools failed to develop adequate review processes for students' records. All ten plaintiffs attended charter schools or schools in the Recovery School District. There was no mention in the lawsuit of the Orleans Parish School Board. When the suit was filed, students with disabilities made up 12.6 percent of students in schools directly run by the RSD, but in New Orleans' charter schools, only 7.8 percent of students were identified as having a disability, with eleven schools reporting demographics of 5 percent or less. Clearly, there were bad school leaders who refused to educate students with special needs.

In the face of mounting pressure from nonprofit organizations such as Families and Friends of Louisiana's Incarcerated Children, the Juvenile Justice Project, and Southern Poverty Law Center, and from individual families and advocacy groups, the RSD, NOPS, and a large number of school management organizations came together and agreed on a set of policies aimed at combating school discipline problems. As a result, the RSD and NOPS created a centralized expulsion process for the 2012–2013 school year to ensure all students received fair and consistent treatment. In December 2014, the Louisiana Department of Education reached a settlement agreement with SPLC by consent decree, meaning that the state agreed to allow its schools to be closely monitored to ensure they were making the necessary improvements.[32] Officials also implemented a school monitoring process to improve identification, location, and evaluation of students who may have special needs. Since the filing of the lawsuit, special needs services as well as suspension and expulsion rates have improved; test scores have as well. However, education activists who railed against blatant inequities should receive much more credit for those improvements. Lawsuits pushed equity when independent schools were slow to act.

Around the same time the SPLC filed its lawsuit in 2010, U.S. Secretary of Education Arne Duncan called Hurricane Katrina "the best thing that happened to the education system in New Orleans," a statement that projected the sense that he accepted the tradeoff of trauma inflicted on public school families.[33] He later apologized.

The truth of the matter is that Duncan wasn't the only person to disregard the harm inflicted on Black people in favor of test-score growth. When you don't see anything worth building on, you'll take a "start from scratch" approach. After Hurricane Katrina, many talked about New Orleans schools as a "clean sheet of paper."[34] People bandied around phrases such as "starting from scratch" and "wipe the slate clean"—anything that allowed them to treat teachers, students, and parents as if they were as easily erased as drawings on an Etch A Sketch.[35] It seems that many considered public schools' employees collateral damage in the "grand experiment" (another worn-out phrase).[36] And some folks in other parts of the country openly wished for a storm to do what Katrina did to New Orleans, wipe out the old and justify starting over.

"I find myself wishing for a storm in Chicago—an unpredictable, haughty, devastating swirl of fury," wrote Chicago-based opinion writer Kristen McQueary on the tenth anniversary of Katrina.[37] She added, "That's what it took to hit the reset button in New Orleans. Chaos. Tragedy. Heartbreak." On numerous occasions,

I've had people say to me, "I wish we had a Hurricane Katrina." People's thoughts do drive actions, and McQueary's revealed that people are capable of creating man-made storms to unleash the reforms they want.

Neerav Kingsland currently oversees education giving at the Laura and John Arnold Foundation, a private foundation focused on criminal justice, health, education, and public finance. In July 2018, he announced the creation of a nonprofit named The City Fund to expand reforms in New Orleans as well as in places like Washington, D.C. and Denver, where charters have also taken root.[38] The education news outlet Chalkbeat reported The City Fund raised $200 million that same month. "Although the group is likely to start in a small number of cities," the news outlet stated, "that presentation [announcing the nonprofit's creation] also made its ambitions clear: it aspires to eventually be in 'every city in America.'"[39] As long as New Orleans' education reform is viewed as a success, there will be those who will replicate its failures.

Jonathan Chait, columnist for *New York Magazine*, is one of many journalists to take a before-and-after view of New Orleans schools in the aftermath of Katrina. Chait wrote, "Before the reforms, New Orleans students . . . lagged far behind more affluent students. Since the reforms, the achievement gap has nearly closed. The proportion of New Orleans students performing at grade level, once half the rate of the rest of the state, now trails by just 6 percent. . . . The results have vindicated the strategy."[40]

Academic achievement scores have improved 11 to 16 percentage points, depending on the subject and method of analysis, according to economists Doug Harris and Matthew Larsen in their study on post-Katrina school reforms.[41] They also attributed a 4 percent to 7 percent increase in the college persistence rate and a 3 percent to 5 percent improvement in the college graduation rate to the reforms. What's missing from most analyses is an effort to seek noneducational value that reforms added or did not add to individuals and communities. No person would wish to replicate what happened in New Orleans among their own communities, children, colleagues, and neighbors. The loss of jobs, civic representation, and dignity must be added to the examinations.

Chait didn't cite the high-flying graft charter schools were supposed to eliminate but, instead, perpetuated: Kelly Thompson, former business manager of Langston Hughes Academy, was busted pilfering almost $675,000 in 2010. A Lusher Charter School employee embezzled $25,000 in the 2011–2012 school year. Darrell K. Sims, fifty-five, formerly with the New Orleans Military and Maritime Academy, was charged with theft by fraudulent checks in the amount of $31,000 in 2013.[42] Auditors found that an employee of KIPP New Orleans misappropriated two checks totaling almost $70,000 in 2014. These charges mirrored past crimes in the traditional district committed by people like Ellenese Brooks-Simms, the New Orleans School Board member who accepted bribes of approximately $140,000 in 2010.[43] Worse, Chait made no mention of the battles fought by the SPLC, activists, and local families that were responsible for improving practices that led to more authentic academic outcomes. And let's be clear, Blacks have made gains in spite of the education they've received. Give parents some credit.

Like others who report on the New Orleans educational system, Chait essentially gives a hall pass to reformers for academic gains in spite of the harm and trauma we've caused to Black people. By failing to include metrics of performance besides standardized test scores, reformers enabled behaviors that can be detrimental to Black families. Saying school reforms worked because scores on statewide exams increased can be like boasting that a person lost weight while getting sick. Investments in education work, and certainly New Orleans students benefit from billions spent on education. But what would the return on investments be without the drag of racism on our community. What if the billions spent on post-Katrina reform went primarily to Black-led school boards, educational service providers, and contractors? How excellent would our communities and schools be if we trusted Black people with community investments.

LOOKING AHEAD

"I'm going from place to place to place having the same conversations about how to recruit teachers of color," Travis Bristol, assistant professor at Boston University, told me. Bristol, who examines national, state, and local education policies that affect the recruitment and retention of teachers of color in schools, regularly talks to state and district leaders about his research across the country. He continued, "Recognition of the need is certainly there." Nationally, the majority of students in public schools are minorities, but as of 2017 only 18 percent of teachers are people of color. And that number is in decline.[44]

You can't help but sense Bristol's frustration with saying the same thing over and over yet being unable to get traction. The conversations about recruitment and retention of Black teachers are scattershot: They're not connected; many of the people driving them aren't linked to communities of color, let alone to Black teacher preparation programs at minority-serving institutions (MSIs), which include historically Black colleges and universities (HBCUs) and Hispanic-serving institutions (HSIs).

Discussions on how to increase the percentage of teachers of color should emanate from the campuses of MSIs, which conferred 16 percent of all degrees in 2014 and account for 27.9 percent of all degrees conferred to Asian-American students, 44 percent to Hispanic students, and 33 percent of all degrees awarded to Black students. If we want more teachers of color, we should go to institutions where they excel.[45]

When I managed charter schools in New Orleans post-Katrina, I often heard White educators say the "color of the teacher doesn't matter." This statement clearly reflected wide-held views; shortly later, the number of Black teachers declined by about 20 percent. Then, when it became painfully obvious that schools with a majority of Black and Hispanic students needed teachers of color, the questions became, "Where did all the Black teachers go?"[46] and "Where are the teachers of color?"[47] These ill-informed op-eds get one thing right: They suggest that color-blind educators have finally reached a point where they can admit that improving educational outcomes demands that we recruit more Black and Hispanic teachers and keep existing ones in the profession. As the saying goes, absence makes the heart grow fonder.

Those who are finally seeing that race matters in teaching must also accept that officials at MSIs and their teacher preparation programs have to take the lead in these discussions, on their turf, by their rules. Just as we need more teachers of color, we need more Black and Hispanic leaders to change the system.

"Foundations and even the federal government look to HBCUs because our social and human capital produces innovation," explains Deena Khalil, assistant professor at Howard University, a school colloquially referred to as the mecca of Black education in the United States. "But," she added, "funders aren't giving money to HBCUs at the same levels as predominately White institutions." In 2015, a U.S. Department of Education official noted that "any one of [the major research institutions] received more than all of the Black colleges combined. And that's including Howard University. That's a disconnect."[48]

The same deficit perspective funders have of children—as needing to be fixed—is the same viewpoint they have when considering HBCUs. So, funders look to the White organizations that may have helped create the pipeline problem to solve issues that Black and Hispanic organizations already have solutions for.

After more than ten years of working to build national pipelines to fill school leadership and teaching positions, the leadership of

New Schools for New Orleans provided seed funding to establish the Norman C. Francis Teacher Residency program at Xavier University in New Orleans to support local workers. The program prepares aspiring Black educators for a career in teaching with two years of coursework and a yearlong, classroom-based apprenticeship. While students don't have to be from New Orleans to participate, it's encouraging that an anchor institution, Xavier University, is a principal actor. It's a novel approach, pairing an HBCU with five charter management organizations based out of New Orleans (Choice Foundation Schools, FirstLine Schools, InspireNOLA, KIPP New Orleans, and New Orleans College Prep) to train between twenty-five and forty new Black teachers every year by placing them in schools. In 2017, the residency program was given $3 million as a part of a nearly $13 million grant from the U.S. Department of Education to train some 900 new and diverse teachers for New Orleans.[49] Twenty-five percent of the grant is expected to be matched by private dollars over the next three years. Loyola University received $1 million to fund its Master of Arts in Teaching program, and the remainder was distributed among four local education nonprofits: Relay Graduate School of Education, Teach for America Greater New Orleans, teachNOLA, and Kingsland's former organization New Schools for New Orleans.

"Research is finding that children perform better when they have teachers in front of them that know about their history, that know about their culture, that look like them," said Renee Akbar, chair of the Division of Education and Counseling at Xavier. "And we want to put those kinds of teachers back into the classrooms here in New Orleans."

But there's a flaw in the program: the use of a middleman like KIPP, TFA, and teachNOLA to distribute the funds. On the surface, the partnership seems like a novel way to increase the number of Black collegians who go into teaching. However, there is nothing innovative about putting money in White institutions' hands to improve Black people or their institutions. HBCUs don't need a middleman or intermediary. They need the funds to help them build back the capacity lost in the New Orleans school takeover.

Khalil, the assistant professor at Howard, says that MSIs are in competition with the very alternative-route teaching certificate programs, Relay and TFA, that have been able to attract investments that historically Black institutions have found elusive. Referred to as "fast track" programs because they require fewer credits, these programs receive millions from state and federal governments as well as philanthropic foundations. Many alt-cert programs, by design, place teachers in communities in which they are outsiders. Although the Norman Francis Residency encourages students who have at least committed to a local institution to go into teaching, national organizations siphon off funds that HBCUs need to thwart the larger problem of devaluation.

"School and district leaders tell us they need a grow-your-own strategy to recruiting teachers of color," said Khalil, who explained that going local makes it less likely teachers will have a deficit perspective—negative presumptions about particular socioeconomic, racial, and ethnic groups. "HBCUs are essential to a grow-your-own approach because we train people from surrounding areas to teach in there."

However, the cost of tuition to become a teacher is a deterrent for Black and Hispanic students, especially those who decide to attend a private institution. Nearly three-quarters of students who attend HBCUs are eligible for the federal Pell grant, meaning they've demonstrated financial hardship. Many of these students believe they can't afford to be teachers. This is the chicken of structural racism coming home to roost. People in places like New Orleans who hoarded wealth at the expense of Black students' academic performance and Black neighborhoods also made it more difficult to develop future teachers who happen to live in devalued communities. If we want more Black teachers, we need scholarships and job guarantees to attract Black candidates. Knocking down the financial barriers to entering the profession is the first step toward respecting them once they land the job. Investing in Black college students acknowledges their value and shows that a career in teaching is valued.

In spite of all the "discovering" of HBCUs by White reformers, there's no news here for Black and Hispanic folk, who have been concerned about recruitment and retention issues for some time— all people had to do was listen, read existing research, and invest in Black people and institutions.[50]

But one thing is clear: The reduction in the number of Black women who teach can never lead to academic success for Black children and cannot be considered a success. The ability to hold on to Black women in the teaching profession must be included as an essential indicator of school improvement.

In 2015, the Albert Shanker Institute's report *The State of Teacher Diversity in American Education* essentially made the same claim, asserting that more must be done to improve working conditions and help retain teachers of color. In the Black districts where charter schools are highly concentrated, improving teachers' work conditions benefits students and also improves the conditions for Black women in urban schools, which leads to a better community overall.

We cannot allow whiteness to get in the way of authentic education reform. Financing structures concretized by a district system funded by property taxes, curricula that ignore slavery and other significant components of American history, low pay, a severe underrepresentation of teachers of color, limited work-based learning options and afterschool programs, as well as the school-to-prison pipeline and poor services for special needs students have existed for decades. These are the issues that deserve disruption. To blame school boards and teachers while ignoring structural inequality is to blame Black people.

I know of no reform sector that has embraced the questions presented in the introduction of this book quite like education reform: *Why can't you be more like White people? Why can't you get married and act like "normal" middle-class White families (without the leg up that federal policies have given White people over the decades)? Why can't you achieve academically like White people?* This is why I often say the education reform movement is too White to do any good.[51] No Black student can be saved with reforms that leave White supremacy unchecked. To be clear, there is nothing inherently wrong with charter schools or alternative teacher certification programs. Charter schools and other reforms have been mostly used as a weapon of White supremacy, evidenced by the New Orleans story. If there ever was a place that should have seen an increase of Black leaders and teachers alongside a corresponding rise in test scores, it should have been New Orleans.

In New Orleans in 2015, I attended a W. K. Kellogg Foundation America Healing event to promote racial reconciliation and healing. Listening to a keynote speech given by James Joseph, ambassador to South Africa under President Bill Clinton, I was struck by a particular sentence in his remarks: "Forgiveness empowers the victim and disarms the enemy."

One of the biggest mistakes I made as a school leader was to summarily fire many of my principals and assistant principals. To them, I say, I am sorry. I didn't include you in my vision for future improvement and I am guilty of the same actions as Kingsland, Duncan, Armao, and Chait. Our collective lack of support for NOPS teachers facilitated more layoffs than budget shortfalls or legislative changes ever could.

There's no way to turn back the clock, but we can apologize and promise to do better. With all the talk about innovation in education, we have to remind ourselves there is nothing more innovative than care. And we all should apologize for not caring enough.

Now I know that improving conditions for students starts with improving the conditions of the people closest to them. We can't improve schools despite the community. We can't fire our way to success. What is the benefit of reform when our mothers, fathers, and friends are hurt by it? I've learned from my mistakes by figuring out ways to encourage innovation in schools while keeping Black women gainfully employed. I also have learned that I must uplift our children as examples of what makes us great, not for what makes us weak.

I am sorry, Bridget Green.

6

Having Babies Like
White People

Few individuals will admit they value people based on skin color, but our appraisals of racial groups comes out in the wash, in home prices; the stripping of political representation through the takeover of our boards and schools; the terrorism inflicted upon our cities and towns; as well as birthing outcomes, including infant and maternal mortality. From a research perspective, it's easier to pinpoint racial bias in housing prices than to quantify the impacts other manifestations of bigotry have on our physical being. Few metrics capture the intersectional nature of devaluation like infant and maternal mortality rates. According to the Centers for Disease Control (CDC), in 2016, a higher percentage of Black babies died before their first birthday than all other racial categories, 11.5 deaths per 1,000 live births compared to 9.4 for American Indian/Alaska Native, 7.4 for Native Hawaiian/Pacific Islanders, 5.0 for Hispanics, 4.9 for Whites, and 3.6 for Asians.[1] Mortality rates among Black mothers also tells a horrifying story of racism. Each year, approximately 700 women die in the United States from causes related to pregnancy or childbirth.[2]

The death rate for Black women is three times higher than the rate for White women. And most maternal deaths are preventable (60 percent).

Because values of assets are associated with the race of the residents who are close in proximity, we can expect housing prices to rise when Black women achieve a semblance of reproductive justice. For Black-majority cities to matter, Black lives must matter.

"All fertile persons and persons who reproduce and become parents require a safe and dignified context for . . . fundamental human experience," wrote researcher, activist, and founding mother of the reproductive justice movement Loretta Ross. According to the nonprofit organization Ross founded, SisterSong, reproductive justice is "the human right to maintain personal bodily autonomy, have children, not have children, and parent the children we have in safe and sustainable communities."[3]

The first time I was introduced to the concept of reproductive justice is when Mom and Karen agreed that my brothers and I would live in a home and community that was sustainable. If only federal policy would have backed them up. For too long, policymakers thought they could add value to Black women's lives by eliminating unplanned pregnancies as a way to encourage assimilation, economic mobility, and longevity. Essentially, Black women are told to restrict their family options through family planning. Black women should be offered the opposite.

Adding value to Black communities demands policies that ensure that Black mothers and children, regardless of their family structure, have as good a chance at living a year after giving birth as anyone else. Browbeating Black women, telling them they should wait till marriage to have a child, won't remove policies and structures that are taking the lives of Black women and their babies. Talking about marriage without mention of wealth, as family planning advocates typically do, obfuscates one of marriage's significant functions—wealth transfer (for White people). Wealth correlates with marriage, especially when you have it. Yet you seldom hear family planners advocate for policies that promote Black wealth to incentivize marriage. Nonetheless, when we shift blame from mothers to policy, we begin to understand how to improve the contexts in which mothers give birth and children are born into. I learned this firsthand during the multiple attempts my wife and I made to expand our own family.

"Push, push, push, Mama; push," my wife Joia implored. Quiana, angled upright on the birthing bed, replied with grunts of effort. Que's husband Dooley offered his support from where he stood at the head of the bed. In that quaint labor and delivery room in Touro Infirmary in New Orleans, I learned that being an obstetrician includes being a cheerleader. It was my first time seeing my wife in action as a gowned and gloved OB/GYN. The way she rooted for Que, as friends call her, I could tell Joia had started practicing for the job when she was still a cheerleader in high school. "He's almost here—push, Mama."

Joia, Que, and Dooley had all been in this position before. Joia had delivered three of their six children, in a different hospital. This time was different. I stood on the other side of the bed, opposite Dooley. Joia sat on a rolling stool between Que's legs, which were hoisted in stirrups. The attending physician stood behind Joia, who repeated the same exhortation to push that was nearly a chant: "Push, push, push, Mama; push." I couldn't see the particulars for the draping gown, but I watched in amazement as Que birthed Robeson Perry, my biological son with Joia. My wife had assisted in the birthing of her own son by Que, our surrogate. Technically, Que was a gestational carrier, meaning she supported Joia and my genetics (assets) to build something none of us could do separately. After years of fertility treatment, our last frozen embryo, of thirteen, had finally arrived.

Joia caught Roby, a nickname I began using almost immediately, and pressed him against her breast. She desperately wanted to create the skin-to-skin bond that physicians say is important for a child's development.[4] Joia then presented Roby to Que to hold and touch. Finally, it was my turn.

"I will always remember the look on your face when you first held Roby," says Joia now. "I could see you thinking to yourself, 'This is me.'"

Joia was right, but when I look back on the events leading to Roby's birth, it's not just our story I see but also the life-threatening racism that imperils Black women and their newborns in cities across the country.

There is something going on in America that endangers all women who give birth. "More women die in the US from pregnancy-related complications than in any other developed country. The US is the only industrialized nation with a rising maternal mortality rate, and between 2000 and 2014, there was a 26 percent increase in the maternal mortality rate," according to an analysis of 2018 CDC data by the American College of Obstetricians and Gynecologists, a membership organization of physicians.[5] However, "Black women are three to four times more likely to die from a pregnancy-related complication than non-Hispanic White women."

And Black women can't seem to buy or educate their way to better outcomes, as mortality disparities exist even after controlling for variables of income and education. Black women, specifically, are endangered, but much of the research and advocacy around improving outcomes for Black women and their babies avoids discussion of racism by focusing, instead, on individual behaviors, particularly policing the behavior of mothers. Smoking, drinking, prenatal care, sleeping practices (safe sleep), and obesity receive a significant amount of policy attention, shaping medical providers' practices and attitudes. However, research also shows that the institutions that govern medicine—state and hospital boards, accreditation agencies—as well as lackluster care can also generate negative outcomes. Introducing the concept of structural racism into the discourse on birth outcomes should shift the focus of medical practice from blaming the patient to reconsidering taken-for-granted policies, social practices, and attitudes that perpetuate racial inequality and disparities.[6]

In their article "Structural Racism and Health Inequity," UCLA professors of public health Gilbert Gee and Chandra Ford write that "structural racism is defined as the macro level systems, social forces, institutions, ideologies, and processes that interact with one another to generate and reinforce inequities among racial and ethnic groups."[7] Structural racism refers to how society's policies and practices serve to aid White families in building wealth and limit Black families from accessing similar opportunities.[8] Structural racism negatively affects Black patients as well as the Black administrators and physicians who are part of the system. My wife knows this too well.

THE LONG ROAD OF HAVING A CHILD

It took us three years of trying to have a baby to get to that labor and delivery room in Touro Infirmary. After a year of marriage trying to but not getting pregnant, Joia and I decided we needed a little help. So we went to see Peter Lu, a fertility doctor. He was widely regarded as the best reproductive endocrinologist in New Orleans, but more important, Lu had trained Joia in medical school at Louisiana State University.

After an initial evaluation, we made three attempts at intrauterine inseminations, placing sperm inside her uterus with, more-or-less, a turkey baster. But that didn't work. So we decided to take a much bigger step by undergoing in vitro fertilization, in which an extracted egg is fertilized with sperm to produce an embryo, which is then transferred to the uterus. It's a time-consuming, involved, and expensive procedure, but we had the means, the commitment, and the connections to try it.

To start, I had to give Joia fertility shots, which helped Joia produce more eggs, which would be introduced to my sperm to generate the embryos. The shots also helped make her uterine lining more conducive for the fertilized egg to stick. It needed to be like a shaggy carpet, but Joia would say, "My lining is more like a throw rug." So every morning for weeks, I'd hear Joia call out in her cheerleader voice, "Time for my shot." Up to that point, I had never given anyone a shot. But I told myself I had to be able to do much more than that if I wanted a child. Joia enjoyed having me take care of her, but this couldn't have been pleasurable for her.

We developed a little routine. After I gave her a morning shot in our bedroom, we went to the fertility clinic to have her blood drawn at 7 a.m. every day or two. I got used to giving shots. I doubt she got used to receiving them.

Not long after the first insertion of the embryo, Joia tested positive for pregnancy. To minimize her activity levels and reduce the risk of miscarriage, we spent a lot of time talking in our bedroom. To pass the time, we dreamed out loud, talking about the possibilities of having a boy.

"What do you think about naming your child after yourself and having a junior?" Joia asked during one of those morning sessions.

"I don't want to burden my child with my name. It has too much baggage," I replied. "Besides, there are so many names of people who are really worthy to be named after."

I offered the name Amistad, after the ship in which enslaved Africans staged a successful mutiny in 1839. But the name felt too heavy for a child to carry. I tossed around the name Stargell, after one of my favorite baseball players, Willie Stargell of the Pittsburgh Pirates. Then, Joia suggested, brilliantly, "What about Robeson? Isn't your favorite civil rights leader, Paul Robeson? You talk about him all the time."

She was right. I often say Paul Robeson is the most under-appreciated—and devalued—civil rights leader of his era. The name Robeson had meaning, and it sounded good. And the historic figure's nickname was Robey, which I always thought was pretty cool. (We dropped the "e".) The name stuck.

One of those mornings in our bedroom, while we discussed our hopes and dreams, Joia began spotting. She didn't seem too worried. A little spotting is normal, she explained. But not long after, she got a phone call from the clinic to update us on the blood work: The pregnancy had failed. She had had a miscarriage within the first month. Joia relayed the bad news to me as caringly as a good physician would, attempting to let me (and, I thought, herself) down easy.

We still fell hard. That day, silence immediately replaced the chatter of possibilities. We lay in bed, staring at the ceiling well into the night. I hurt for me and for her. Joia didn't cry during our many attempts, even after the first miscarriage, and she didn't shed a tear (at least in front of me) after the second. For me, each of the three failed pregnancies after IVF felt worse than the last. The elation the next time the embryo took wasn't as high, but the sorrow of receiving the call confirming a miscarriage lasted longer than before. Joia stayed positive and matter-of-fact—till the next abbreviated pregnancy.

It was 2009. It was warm, but not hot. They say there are only two seasons in New Orleans: Mardi Gras and Saints football. I think it was Mardi Gras season when Joia decided to get a myomectomy—a surgical procedure to remove uterine fibroids, which are benign tumors of muscle and did not need to be removed. "I did it out of desperation," she says. "I knew it wouldn't help me get pregnant. There's no data to support it would. But I needed to do something."

I went with her to all the appointments. I took care of her before and after the procedure. We watched the video of the surgery like a Will Smith movie, seeing the grapefruit-sized fibroid being removed from her body. After allowing for adequate recovery time, the embryos were inserted for a third time and we got pregnant again. This time, however, we reserved all expectations.

The pregnancy extended past a month, and our hopes started to pick up. Around the sixth week, Dr. Lu asked us to come to the office to give us the results of our regular blood work. "You're no longer pregnant," Lu said.

Joia burst into tears.

Dr. Lu and I look at each other, somewhat stunned. "I don't think either of you expected that," Joia said. She hadn't cried during the other failures, from our natural efforts to IVF. "All I could think is, I had done everything." And Joia did do everything. I, on the other hand, had not.

Before Roby's birth, there were many days I did not give or receive love. After a little more than a year with no child, I began scrutinizing her. I started asking, "Why are you drinking?" and "Can you exercise some more?" With almost no medical knowledge, and a wife whose professional life was all about pregnancy and giving birth, I made incorrect and mean-spirited assertions about the causes of her infertility. Quite simply, I blamed Joia for us not getting pregnant.

I had internalized the racism that finds fault with Black women. Frustration and resentment wove their tentacles around our love. When she cried in Dr. Lu's office, I could see the residue of the stress I had imposed on her in every tear.

We returned to our bedroom to talk. We only had two embryos left. I suggested adoption. But when we were married, I had gained two children through Joia, from her first marriage, Jade and Carlos—a girl and a boy.

"You'd say, 'I don't have to have genetic links to members of my family,'" she recalled. "You'd say, 'A blended family was all that I knew.'" I believed those statements when I made them, but she knew I had resigned myself into thinking that we were not going to have a biological child together.

"That's when I decided to call Que," Joia said.

WOMEN AGAINST THE MACHINE: HOW STRUCTURAL RACISM HURTS WOMEN AND BIRTHING OUTCOMES

During the same time Joia was trying to have a baby, she was under considerable professional strain. It was on a different level of magnitude than difficult patients and a pressed husband; from 2004 to

2015, local and state hospital officials were actively seeking to revoke her medical privileges.

In 2001, Joia began her private practice in what was then called Baptist Memorial Medical Center, a hospital originally founded by the Southern Baptist Convention in 1926. Her father, also a physician, who lived directly across the street from the hospital in a house on Claiborne Avenue, warned Joia against setting up shop there.

"My father told me, 'They don't let Colored doctors over there,'" Joia recalled. But growing up seeing the hospital every day gave Joia a different perspective. "I saw it as the beautiful, old, New Orleans hospital. In my mind, we were New Orleans, too, and should be there." Joia soon became the first Black obstetrician in private practice at Baptist.

Soon after she opened her doors, clear signs of racism arose. "An older, White physician who shared office space with me strongly encouraged me to not see Medicaid patients because, I [read: he and the hospital] 'didn't want that type of clientele.'" Because of the high poverty rate in New Orleans, Medicaid is the primary insurance for a large proportion of births, including many Black patients. Seeing Black patients isn't just a moral imperative; it's a financial one. In a Black-majority city, Black physicians have a clear numerical and financial advantage, because they can convert their social networks— which include low-income patients—into customers. The older physician suggested that Joia needed to "protect" her [read: his] patients who had private insurance by not seeing poor people on Medicaid. Like schools, hospitals are segregated.[9] Joia made a sound ethical and business decision to ignore his advice. But her decision came at a steep price.

In 2004, seven Baptist OB/GYN doctors formed an ad hoc committee to review all Joia's cases for a "pattern of questionable judgment as well as an unacceptable delay in treating obstetrical patients," according to records provided by Joia. None of the reviews were spurred by patient complaints. Still, the committee issued a report based on their perceived pattern that recommended suspending Joia's obstetrical privileges at Baptist Hospital, which led to a series of appeals over the course of a year. Around the same time, I met Joia at the birthday party of a local New Orleans news anchor in February 2005. The same year, on Monday, August 29, Hurricane Katrina upended our lives.

At the time Hurricane Katrina was barreling across the Gulf of Mexico, Joia and I had just begun to consider ourselves a couple. We had been spending considerable time together, but we became closer as the massive storm approached. As someone who had lived in New Orleans for only a little more than a year, the evacuation process threw me for a loop. I shadowed Joia's movements as much as I could.

We were both working at our jobs two days before Katrina made landfall: Joia in her private practice, me at the University of New Orleans. Joia had patients she needed to take care of, so she stayed in the city as long as possible, giving them detailed contingency plans if they entered labor during evacuation. A cousin had already transported Jade and Carlos north to the Black majority city of Grambling, Louisiana, to join their grandmother. Having lived a significant part of her childhood in Grambling, hurricane evacuations presented opportunities for Joia to go home. I received word on the 27th, during a class I was teaching, that Mayor Ray Nagin had called for a mandatory evacuation. After I disbanded the students, I went straight to Joia's house to make our escape.

All my possessions that were in Joia's house could fit in a duffle bag, so packing for me was easy. We expected to get out of harm's way and relax for a few days. In New Orleans, we call these trips "evacu-cations." We finally left, less than twenty-four hours before Hurricane Katrina made landfall.

Those few days of our planned getaway turned into weeks. We had to put Jade and Carlos in school in Grambling. I worked remotely at Grambling University, which provided me an office, teaching my courses online. But Joia needed to work. It became clear that we needed to make a living away from New Orleans for at least a few months.

After the waters subsided and city officials permitted residents to return in late September, Joia made more appeals, including hiring lawyers, to clear her name and to find work. None of the OB/GYNs from the ad hoc committee returned to Baptist Hospital in the first two years following Hurricane Katrina. Baptist's CEO, Renee Goux, informed Joia there was no way to complete the appeal process with committee members scattered across the country in the aftermath of the storm. Having had her obstetrical privileges suspended at Baptist, Joia began doing deliveries in the one suburban hospital that had not flooded. The conditions of her suspension still allowed Joia to provide gynecological services to patients. Joia could not participate in deliveries, but she continued to see patients for gynecological services.

I fell in love with Joia because I saw up close how she fought for what was right rather than what was convenient. Regarding relationships forged during Hurricane Katrina, people say that the storm either brought you together or tore you apart. In December 2006, Joia and I jumped the broom at the African American Museum in the historic New Orleans neighborhood of Tremé, where free people of color fought for liberty and justice, in front of about 150 friends and family.

One day in 2008, while Joia and I were walking in Lakeside Mall after attending the birth of a child, Thomas Ryan, the original chair of the ad hoc committee saw Joia wearing scrubs, and he looked visibly angry. Ryan communicated with the state medical board to ask if Joia or the hospital had reported the results of his ad hoc committee's review. When he was told no, the state engaged in a full-blown investigation into whether or not the hospital had sanctioned her and if her efforts to work were in violation of those restrictions. Although Baptist realized no consequences for their failure to disclose, it led to years of hearings and legal fees for Joia to prove she was, indeed, able to practice under the stipulations provided.

Joia had to make a decision that Black folk have to make regularly. Do we accept an overreaching punishment, in this case one that restricted her license beyond Baptist, in recognition to power? Or do we resist? We resisted, fighting every step of the way. But Joia (and I) lost opportunities to build wealth because of the financial costs of battling a systemic effort to punish her. We knew our price, but nevertheless, the board stained her professional reputation and sapped our energy.

Almost two years later, in the midst of us trying to get pregnant, Joia and the Louisiana State Board of Medical Examiners mutually agreed that, for her to continue practicing medicine, she must have her license suspended for six months and stay on probation for three years. It was a settlement that was supposed to put the elongated ordeal behind us. There were conditions around her suspension that a board-certified OB/GYN would find humiliating, but she accepted them. It was time to move on.

"The ultimate unfairness of the Board's decision has its origins on the inherent unfairness of the peer review system affording fellow physicians the vehicle to advance marginal claims with worrying about being sued for their biased actions," Joia's lawyer Jerome Pellerin wrote me in an email. "Coupled with an investigative staff, the Board had unilateral authority to sanction. Justice is not blind."

I can't prove her professional trials contributed to our difficulties having a child, but they certainly didn't help. The risk of miscarriage is significantly higher in women with a history of exposure to psychological stress, according to research. A review of multiple studies—meta-analysis—found that "psychological factors can increase the risk [of pregnancy loss] by approximately 42 percent," according to a 2017 study published by *Scientific Reports*.[10]

"I was tired and was hopeful this was a pathway forward. Many docs who lose their license are not able to return," Joia said. "Signing the consent decree was my opportunity to rebuild. But I knew it wasn't over."

When she couldn't see patients, Joia leveraged her medical knowledge to become a public health expert. Joia became the director of clinical services for the New Orleans Health Department while she worked as a medical director for a clinic in the neighborhood of Tremé, serving mostly people without insurance. She began working with city and state government officials on plans to improve infant and maternal mortality rates. Her impact caught the attention of then mayor-elect Mitch Landrieu, who, in February 2010, appointed Joia to his transition team as a member of his health committee. I also served on the transition team, as an education cochair. We learned of Que's pregnancy with Roby when Joia was on the dais at Landrieu's inauguration.

Landrieu eventually named Joia the interim health director to serve under his administration, a job that did not require a medical license. Fully aware of the status of her license, Landrieu originally stood by Joia's candidacy. But the medical community that restricted her practice put pressure on Landrieu to fire Joia, releasing records of her license status to the media. Landrieu originally rebuffed the calls from the medical community and the media reports, but the demands for her ouster grew louder. When the news about her license broke, we were lying in our bedroom watching her professional life unravel before our eyes. Tears rolled down her cheeks, soaking the comforter she had wrapped herself in.

The anger I felt when Hotsy wanted to kick me out of my house as a child was the same anger that filled my gut while watching the reporting of her story. I immediately drove Joia to a hotel in Mobile, Alabama, to get her away from the local news cycle, but upon my return I felt a deep shame. This was not supposed to happen to us. I blamed everyone: Baptist hospital brass, the mayor, as well as Joia. I wanted to leave New Orleans behind.

Joia was forced to resign in May 2010. She didn't work and barely enjoyed any leisure for three months. We renewed the long bedroom talks we'd had when trying to get pregnant. We never talked about deliberately letting go of the past, but sometimes the future is really all you have. We both had Roby to look forward to. Joia attended all Que's appointments. I earned enough money to support the family. We waited for our horizon.

Eventually, Joia landed a job at a health center, three months after resigning from the city. And although I wore my anger, resentment, and bitterness on my sleeve, so much pent-up anger and frustration dissipated when I saw Roby's precious face that December.

At the writing of this book, Roby is a healthy nine-year-old in the third grade, and Joia's license is unrestricted. Now I have an opportunity to atone and a platform to do so publicly. I apologize to Joia for the stress I caused. Through her work on maternal mortality, I've learned not to doubt Black women's accounts of racism but, rather, to trust them. Joia's story is indicative of what Black women go through. Her ordeal is what systemic racism and sexism looks and feels like. And although New Orleans posts some of the lowest infant mortality rates among Black-majority cities, Black babies still die at more than twice the rate of Whites (6.82 to 2.94). And Black women die at three to four times the rate of White women. This is not a coincidence.

FOCUSING ON STRUCTURAL RACISM

The parable of the babies in the river is often used when talking about structural racism and birthing outcomes. There are many variations, but the tale goes something like this: A group of campers set up along a river bend sees a baby floating in a basket caught in a vigorous current. Someone dives in, braves the rushing water, and brings the baby back to shore, rescuing the baby. A day later, another baby is sighted floating down the river. And another camper jumps in to save the baby. The event repeats itself until someone decides to go upriver to see the source of the problem. The parable ends on a cliffhanger to ask an important question, "Who will go upriver to solve in-your-face problems?"

Researchers owe all women a trip upriver. In addition to the individual behavior of the mother, research also points to stress from environmental factors, including structural racism, as causal factors of negative birth outcomes. At best, strictly dealing with individual behaviors around infant and maternal mortality is akin to jumping in the river to save babies without tackling the underlying problem. By avoiding structural racism, physicians and policymakers never get to see what's putting Black women, fetuses, and babies at risk. At worst, ignoring racism is a backhanded way to blame Black women.

Structural racism involves the governance structures as well as private associations and systems (education, health, market, etc.) that are built and organized to distribute social goods to benefit White people. Structural racism restricts people of color from having access to health-promoting institutions. White people have benefited over time from the social goods of greater political power, better-paying jobs, exclusive wealth-building opportunities, quality policing, higher-performing schools, and more access to quality healthcare, which explain why Whites, in the aggregate, post better health outcomes, including higher life expectancy.[11]

Evidence clearly demonstrates that structural racism and discrimination negatively impact health: Black infant mortality rates as well as life expectancy significantly improved in the South after the passage of the Civil Rights Act, until 1980.[12] Harvard researcher Nancy Krieger explained in 2011 in the *American Journal of Public Health* why Black outcomes improved during that period but then regressed. "The period encompassed the passage of the Civil Rights Act, the policies of the War on Poverty, and the establishment of Medicare, Medicaid, the Occupational Safety and Health Administration, and the Environmental Protection Agency; thereafter, in reaction, subsequent administrations curbed both government regulations and initiatives promoting equity."[13]

Addressing past discrimination affects health outcomes positively or negatively, as Ronald Reagan's presidency shows. The health gains that ended in the 1980s were concurrent with Reagan's War on Drugs. The war on drugs "had little to do with drug crime and nearly everything to do with racial politics," according to Krieger. Reagan used the war on drugs as an ideology that pushed against the beliefs undergirding the War on Poverty legislation, which had been introduced by Democrat Lyndon Johnson in 1964. A Republican, Reagan's history of disagreement with the War on Poverty can be traced back to the 1968 Republican National Convention, when he famously said, "We must reject the idea that every time a law's broken, society is guilty rather than the lawbreaker. It is time to restore the American precept that each individual is accountable for his actions."

But who holds society accountable for structural racism? Using death records from 2010 to 2013 in the study "Separate and Unequal: Structural Racism and Infant Mortality in the US," Tulane University researcher Maeve Wallace and Joia, her coauthor, found that degrees of racial inequality in educational attainment, median household income, unemployment, occupation, imprisonment, and juvenile custody showed harmful effects on Black infant mortality, while White rates remained unaffected by those factors.[14] Across the states, when racial inequality in unemployment increased, Black infant mortality increased by 5 percent. A decrease in inequality in education by 13 percent was correlated with a decrease in Black infant mortality by 8 percent. Changes in these disparities did not impact White infant mortality—positively or negatively. Aside from reduced inequality, an increase in the median household income for the total population also was significantly associated with a decrease in Black infant mortality rate, with a $12,641 increase leading to a decrease in Black infant deaths by 17 percent. There was no other association between improvement in the total population's well-being and reduction in the Black infant mortality rate.

The results of my wife's study also revealed areas of persisting inequality. The rate of Black imprisonment nationwide was an average of 6.2 times higher than of Whites. In states where a greater share of Blacks had college degrees, employment in professional or managerial positions, and a higher median household income, Black infant mortality was lower. However, the Black population has less access to all these opportunities compared to Whites, which is a product of structural inequality.

STRUCTURAL RACISM PLAGUES BLACK-MAJORITY PLACES

"Your zip code is a stronger predictor of your health than your genetic code." Harvard researcher David Williams used his catchphrase at a 2013 lecture at the University of Missouri. Williams' statement is backed by his extensive research on the social determinants of health—the neighborhood conditions that are detrimental to residents' life expectancy. Poverty, crime, inferior schools and healthcare providers, as well as other negative predictors of health resulting from policy choices tend to cluster in Black neighborhoods. Life expectancy can vary by as much as twenty years between Black and White neighborhoods that are separated by only a few city blocks.[15] Social determinants are considered by many experts as the root causes of health disparities among racial groups, and they can easily be mapped.[16]

Jim Crow and racist housing laws strongly influence our presence in specific places. However, people with common interests and histories tend to congregate to protect their culture, resources, and livelihoods. I'm inclined to think racism follows Black people wherever we settle. School districts, neighborhoods, and entire cities become magnets or targets for racist policies. Defined geographic areas hold people, and these locales contain the social determinants that influence health outcomes. I presume that communities' outcomes differ based on differing abilities to respond to the negative factors. This is why we must take an asset approach to studying cities. Looking at strength can lead us to finding solutions some communities have used to combat racism.

There are different ways researchers evaluate the concentration of class and race in an area to help identify the presence of the structural racism that underlies racial health disparities. The Index on Concentrations at the Extremes (ICE), which is a methodological tool that quantifies how persons in a specified area are concentrated in a specified societal distribution, is used regularly to study neighborhood composition.[17] A value of −1 on the ICE index means that 100 percent of the population is deprived, and a value of 1 means that 100 percent is privileged. A score of 0 represents an essentially even distribution of socioeconomic classes.

In a 2018 study, University of California researcher Brittany Chambers and her team employed the ICE index to study preterm birth (PTB) and infant mortality in California.[18] The researchers controlled for factors including age, education, country of origin, insurance coverage, prenatal visits, pregnancy, body fat, cigarette use, alcohol and drug use, infection, diabetes, hypertension, depression, and previous PTB. The lowest quintile of the race, income, and combined ICE value had the highest percent of preterm birth and the highest infant mortality rate. People and the places in which they live are inextricably linked. There was a more significant difference in the percentage of preterm births than in the infant mortality rates. Black women were more likely to reside in a deprived neighborhood as measured across the indices. Further, the odds of Black women living in these neighborhoods were comparable to those of Black women in neighborhoods with comparable ICE scores in Boston and New York City, the only other cities in which such a study has been performed.

BLACK WOMEN CAN'T BUY THEIR WAY
TO BETTER HEALTH OUTCOMES

The racism that comes along with gaining a middle- or upper middle-class job can be so stressful that it leads to negative health outcomes. Public health researcher Alicia Lukachko and colleagues at Columbia University examined the impact of structural racism on cardiovascular health.[19] To measure structural racism, the researchers explored disparities in four areas: political participation, employment, educational attainment, and incarceration in the United States. "Results indicated that Blacks living in states with high levels of structural racism were generally more likely to report past-year myocardial infarction than Blacks living in low-structural racism states." But the researchers also found that Whites living in states with high levels of structural racism experienced insignificant or lower odds of myocardial infarction compared to Whites living in low-structural racism states. The researchers, therefore, argue that "structural racism may not only harm the targets of stigma but also benefit those who wield the power to enact stigma and discrimination."[20]

Individual risk factors (for example, age, income, medical insurance, etc.) did not mitigate the harms of structural racism on Blacks. In fact, Blacks with higher status positions were at increased risk for heart attack. Racism puts people at risk at different socioeconomic levels. The stress of Black women climbing the social ladder takes its toll on those who have achieved some level of professional success. Joia's experience with her hospital should not be considered an isolated case between labor and management. It must also be placed in a context in which middle- and upper-class Black women are wanting for workplaces void of racial harassment and micro-aggressions. The racism stemming from OB/GYN departments and state boards hurts Black physicians and their Black patients.

In a damning investigation of New Orleans hospitals and their high rates of maternal death and morbidity, *USA TODAY* found "a complicated mix of misdiagnoses, delayed care and a failure to follow safety measures" in the same hospital Roby was born in, Touro Infirmary.[21] The paper examined billing records from 7 million births in thirteen states across the country.[22] These kinds of life-threatening childbirth complications are happening at Touro more often than at most hospitals. Touro is one of 120 hospitals in the database where mothers were more than twice as likely to have had blood transfusions, hysterectomies, seizures, heart attacks, strokes, or other "indicators that their deliveries turned deadly."

In a statement to *USA TODAY*, a Touro spokesperson said the hospital serves "medically vulnerable" patients, placing all the blame squarely on the patients rather than the care they received. "Lifestyle diseases, the high cost of healthcare, delaying or noncompliance with medical treatment, limited care coordination, poor health, high rates of poverty and high rates of morbidity are all realities of our State and community," the spokesperson continued.

We should never forget that hospitals, healthcare systems, and medical researchers have a long history of blatant racism, including not seeing patients, harmful experimentation, and severe malpractice.[23] However, much of the structural racism that correlates with negative health outcomes referenced in this chapter are also indicative of harmful macro environment. For instance, White physicians don't recognize Black women's pain, literally or figuratively. Black women are subsequently blamed partly because they are systematically undertreated for pain.[24] Researchers at the University of Virginia found "that a substantial number of White laypeople and medical students and residents hold false beliefs about biological differences between Blacks and Whites." These differences predict racial bias in pain perception and treatment.[25] This research is predicated on earlier findings that Blacks are less likely to receive analgesics—painkillers.

"When Black patients say that they are in pain, they are less likely to be both believed, evaluated and treated for their pain," said Joia. "This belief that Black patients have a higher tolerance for pain and at the same time are more likely to be drug seekers, causes illnesses to be missed and can even have deadly consequences."

So we shouldn't be surprised to hear about near-death experiences, even among Black women who have greater access to quality healthcare. Professional, educational, and economic advancement don't unhinge negative perceptions that come along with being a Black person. Giving birth is already fraught with danger for all women. The social disease of racism makes medical maladies worse.

"First, everyone—from doctors to the media to the public—needs to stop blaming women for their own deaths," wrote professor and researcher Monica McLemore in an article in *Scientific American*.[26] "Instead we should focus on better understanding the underlying contributing factors. These include a lack of data; not educating patients about signs and symptoms—and not believing them when they speak up; errors made by health care providers; and poor communication among different health care teams."

Dismantling the structures that create health disparities is not an impossible undertaking. It means significantly reducing the prison population, like New Orleans did when its 2010 headcount of 3,400 prisoners went down to 1,600 in 2016.[27] Undoing racism looks like the inclusionary housing policy Minneapolis adopted in 2018, which ensures that "affordable housing is provided in new residential or mixed-use developments," countering the single-family zoning practices that fueled segregation.[28] Undoing structural racism translates to moving away from geographically-based school funding systems that privilege wealthy neighborhoods to one that gives poorer districts the revenues they need.[29] Deconstructing racism means we establish universal healthcare benefits through a government-run program— what some refer to as a single-payer system.[30] It means making sure every community, large or small, urban or rural, rich or poor, has equal broadband access. These are practical, achievable goals we can work toward to dismantle structural racism—but first we must stop identifying race as the risk factor and point the finger at structural racism and racist public policy instead. McLemore also recommends interventions, as "wider access to midwifery, group prenatal care, and social and doula support are effective in improving maternal health outcomes."

We have little choice but to use our collective strength to deconstruct structural racism. We must use the power of our social connections to do so.

THE ASSET OF OUR SOCIAL CONNECTIONS

One day in the fall before Roby was born, I attended a family gathering attended by dozens of my relatives. During one of the many moments of laughter and revelry, I shared the story of how Joia and I had hired a surrogate and that we were having a baby in December. After my family let out oohs and aahs, the room became silent.

Then one of my cousins shouted, "Andre has made it! They're having babies like White people now." Laughter erupted. I thought to myself, she's kind of right.

Every person, regardless of race, should have the opportunity to have and raise a child. The American Society for Reproductive Medicine proclaims that creating a family is a basic human right.[31] Structural racism, a lack of wealth, and limited job opportunities limit our ability to have children. Instead of restricting our options, the focus of federal policy should be on creating conditions that make way for Black women to expand the ways they choose to make family. In the United Kingdom, three rounds of IVF are included in the public insurance.

"Joia and I have always been close," Que, our gestational carrier, told me when I asked her why she agreed to have our child. "She delivered three of my babies. I'd have my child in five or ten minutes—easy."

After Joia and I married, we weren't the only ones worried about us getting pregnant. Many of Joia's patients, including Que, did, too. Que politely asked for updates on whether or not Joia was expecting a child. "If you ever need a surrogate, call me," Que recalled saying then. "It didn't take me 24 hours to call Joia back. I'm one of those people who loves giving back."

Facilitating life is a big way to give back. Que told me her husband was fine with her being a gestational carrier. None of her friends or family members objected. Que became very excited about the prospect. She didn't know anyone who had been a gestational carrier.

Que and Joia's story is unique, in a way. Black women have greater need for assisted reproductive treatment and are less likely to receive it.[32] Cost and a lack of information are barriers to treatment. But Black people's communities, their loving networks, are our most powerful asset. We have to leverage that love the way Joia did with Que. Que was a high-risk patient in that she already had several children, which puts the mother in danger of delivering early. Que carried Roby for Joia out of love.

In 2015, Joia attended a convening of advocates and policy experts who focus on the advancement of reproductive rights for Black women. Monica Simpson of SisterSong, Katrina Anderson of the Center for Reproductive Rights, and columnist Elizabeth Dawes invited approximately two dozen people, including Joia, to discuss the state of Black maternal health. That meeting birthed the nonprofit Black Mamas Matter. According to its website, "We center Black mamas to advocate, drive research, build power, and shift culture for Black maternal health, rights, and justice."[33] Since the organization's founding, it has held the first ever Capitol Hill briefing on Black maternal health, created a Black maternal health week in April, and hosted a conference attended by more than 300 people. The group authored a "Black paper" titled "Setting the Standard for Holistic Care of and for Black Women," which is used nationally by health care providers and public health officials to guide medical standards in hospital.³⁴ Black Mamas Matter models how the rest of us can deconstruct racism.

As memorable as holding my son for the first time was, and seeing hints of me in him, was the love that filled that labor and delivery room. I absorbed the magnitude of how Joia's former patient had become the surrogate for our child, and how accepting Dooley, her husband, was of Que's decision. I thought about the sacrifice Mom made for me and how Roby would someday understand his connection to her. I was glad to see how happy Dooley was for Joia and me, and how relieved he was that Que made it through alive. Dooley stood by Que's side through the pregnancy and birth. I wanted to love and support my wife that way. The physician, Jenny Lapeyrolerie, a dear friend, a Black woman, and Joia's colleague, took care of us along the journey. And all our families supported Joia and me along the way. Love definitely brought Roby into the world. I'm hoping that love can help him live out a normal life course.

If Black lives are to matter, we must be willing to trust in the manner Que trusted Joia. Meaning, Black women must be trusted to have children and raise a family in a manner they see fit. And we must be willing to invest in the potential of lives we have yet to see. One of the most effective ways to invest collectively is through political organizing, getting representation in legislative halls at the local, state, and national levels. There is nothing wrong with Black people that ending racism can't solve. Consequently, we're not going to get reproductive justice or equitable cities without engaging in electoral politics, chiefly getting Black women into more seats at the legislative tables.

7

For the Sake of America, Elect a Black Woman President

Adding value to Black-majority cities requires federal investments in housing, education, business development, and healthcare. It's unlikely, with the current makeup, that a predominately White U.S. Senate and House will vote for legislation that will prioritize adding value to Black neighborhoods. Appeals to lawmakers for this kind of progressive policy haven't worked so far. Adding value to Black-majority places requires that we replace misaligned lawmakers with those who represent our interests.

There is hope on this front. Our votes and voters are some of our greatest assets. Investments toward uplifting the Black electorate and Black women candidates can help shift a legislative environment that leans away from one that blames Black communities toward one that offers policy solutions. From school board to the president of the United States, investments toward getting Black women elected are down payments for inclusive, progressive change.

Three days before Keisha Lance Bottoms was officially sworn in as the new mayor of Atlanta in 2018, an exuberant crowd waited to receive her at an invite-only appreciation day-party at an upscale restaurant located in the neighborhood of Buckhead. I was in Atlanta at the time for an unrelated visit, and a friend of the mayor invited my wife and me to join the crowd of roughly 300 friends and family members. The party stopped two mouths with one morsel: Lance Bottoms was thanking her supporters for grinding out a difficult campaign, but it was also her birthday. A table filled with birthday-inspired pastries and cakes greeted us at the front of the room. The joy of new beginnings filled the place.

The mayor-elect had yet to arrive, but many took advantage of the late afternoon lighting and took selfies on the balcony. On a stage in the back, a DJ played hip-hop and R&B hits at a volume loud enough to draw people to the dance floor but low enough to hear yourself and others talk.

"My mayor's name is Keisha," echoed over beats, affirming the enjoyment in having a mayor with a distinctively Black name.

As soon as the crowd recognized the song the DJ played, "Started from the Bottom," by rap artist Drake—an obvious play on the mayor-elect's name—all the side activities came to an abrupt halt. The DJ turned up the volume, indicating that Lance Bottoms was somewhere in the building. Her fans shuffled toward the front to better give her a boisterous welcome.

Lance Bottoms defeated her rival, Mary Norwood, a White independent, by a mere 832 votes in a battle waged across racial lines. Norwood had hoped to become the first White mayor of Atlanta since 1973. Polls showed that Norwood garnered 80 percent of the White vote. Lance Bottoms earned more than 75 percent of the Black vote. With almost 450,000 people in Atlanta proper and a Black population of 54 percent, Atlanta is the fourth-largest Black-majority city in the country. That 5 percent difference in "other" voters made the difference.

Since 1990, Atlanta as a whole has been growing, especially in its non-Black population. However, from 2000–2010, Atlanta proper realized a 7 percent drop in Black population, much of which was due to Black middle-class flight to the suburbs (figure 7-1). With racial majorities strongly influencing outcomes, demographic changes opened a window of opportunity for a White candidate. The playing field was pretty much even. Both candidates had to chew into their opponent's base of supporters to win.

Lance Bottoms received a better share of non-Black voters than Norwood got from the non-White electorate. Winners in future Atlanta mayoral elections will have to do the same. However, this strategy bodes well in particular for Black women, whose personal and professional narratives seem to resonate with a diverse electorate.

"Unfortunately, Black women sit at the nexus of a lot of the racial and gender disparities that are present in our country," Associated Press reporter and Atlanta native Erin Whack told me. Whack covered the Atlanta mayoral election. "They are uniquely positioned to talk about a lot of the kitchen table issues because they are directly and disproportionately affected by them." Black women's experiences

FIGURE 7-1. ATLANTA'S CHANGING DEMOGRAPHICS, 1970–2017.

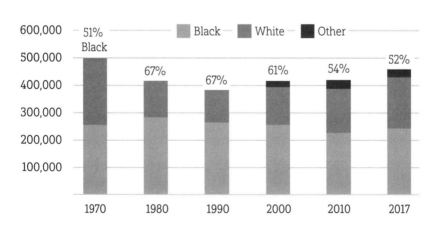

SOURCE: Decennial Census records and American Community Survey U.S. Census Bureau estimates.

are relatable to different classes and racial groups, giving them a unique vantage point on things like education, income inequality, healthcare, and incarceration. More and more Black women have walked in the shoes of corporate executives, professors, and other upwardly mobile professions, following the footsteps of food stamp recipients and mothers of an incarcerated children.

As the DJ's use of the Drake song, "Started from the Bottom," suggests, Lance Bottoms does come from humble beginnings. Mayor Lance Bottoms knows the travails of poverty because Keisha is not that far removed from those struggles. When she was eight, Lance Bottoms came home to find her father, the late R&B singer Major Lance, in handcuffs, arrested for cocaine distribution. Her father once had a promising singing career. He even opened for the Beatles on their first U.S. tour in 1964. However, he came up on hard times thereafter, struggling as a professional artist to pay bills. Eventually, her father resorted to selling drugs as a source of income.

After the arrest, life as she knew it dramatically shifted. Saturdays didn't include just Fat Albert, Scooby Doo, and Fantastic Four cartoons. Little Keisha now made regular visits to various prisons to see her father while he served his three-year sentence, according to her campaign video.[1] "I spent every weekend visiting my dad in prisons across the state," said Lance Bottoms.[2] To make ends meet and feed the family, Lance Bottoms' mother, Sylvia Robinson, went back to cosmetology school at night so she could acquire the skills to land a job. Robinson provided an example to her daughter of how people respond to major life changes. Lance Bottoms followed in her mother footsteps and pursued an education to get ahead. She attended Florida Agricultural and Mechanical University (FAMU), the historically Black university in Tallahassee, for her bachelor's degree in communications and Georgia State University in Atlanta for her law degree. Her father died in 1994, the same year she received her J.D. and the same year she married businessman Derek Bottoms. Lance Bottoms says in the campaign video that she has four children "born of her heart," meaning she adopted her children, who she and her husband raise in the city.

Mayor Bottoms doesn't tell the usual rags-to-riches story. Hers is not a tale of individual endurance *despite* the odds; she highlights the strengths of her family members rather than pointing out those whose faults she needed to overcome. Hers isn't an *I made it in spite of my family* story. "What I saw [in my mother] is someone determined to do whatever she had to do to make sure we still stayed afloat," Lance Bottoms said in the video. As an adult, Lance Bottoms served as a county judge and city council member before running for mayor. She credits a supportive network for carrying her on the path toward the mayor's office.

The rallying cry, "My mayor's name is Keisha," on social media isn't just an avowal of victory among Lance Bottoms' backers; it's an affirmation of Black social, political, and economic power. It also projects the empowering message that everyday women can rise to positions of power. Being Black and a woman didn't put Lance Bottoms or others like her at a disadvantage in her campaign, as evidenced by the results of several elections since. She didn't have to sanitize her blackness to make a connection to others. Black women who represent our community's values and traditions are running on platforms that address Black people's needs while also garnering votes from different races—a blueprint for the future anywhere, not just Black-majority cities.

BLACK WOMEN'S EXPERIENCE IS AN ASSET IN POLITICS

In 2018, the Brookings Institution and the Higher Heights Leadership Fund, a nonprofit organization dedicated to getting Black women elected, collaborated to pinpoint predictors of electoral success among Black women candidates. Much of the data in this chapter comes from what we found.[3] We discovered, not surprising, that Black women are underrepresented among elected officials at local, state, and national levels of government. Black women are more likely to hold state house, state senate, and U.S. House of Representative seats in places where the Black share of the voting-age population is greater. As a result, there is a higher concentration of Black women holding elected office in the Southeast. There have been only two Black women elected to the U.S. Senate in the history of the country. The first was Carol Moseley Braun, who represented Illinois from 1993 to 1999, and former 2020 presidential candidate Senator Kamala Harris of California.

Even though Black women are practically tied in percentage rates within race with White women in voter registration and turnout, they are more likely to be discouraged from running for office than White women and men as well as Black men.[4] When Black women do run for office, they are less likely to receive the early dollars and endorsements that help establish campaigns. This is the structural racism *and* sexism that Black women must contend with when thinking about running for office. Because of these structural hurdles, Black women often lack access to candidate training to help them translate their experience into effective campaign strategies. Support for Black women on the campaign trail often comes not when they desperately need it but when their impact can no longer be ignored.

For generations, Black, mostly male, elected officials came from Black-majority districts. Black people voted other Black people, mostly men, into power. Before the 2018 mid-term election, there were nineteen Black women and thirty Black men serving in Congress, as well as two non-voting delegates. After the January 2018 swearing-in ceremony, there were twenty-three Black women in Congress—twenty-two of whom are now serving in the House—and thirty-two Black men. There is a majority of men despite the fact that there are many more Black women eligible to vote than Black men in Black-majority cities, underlining the underrepresentation of Black women in leadership positions.

The gender differences in the Black electorate are stark and distressing. Highlighting a few cities as examples, estimates from the American Community Survey show there are 22 percent more Black women who are eligible to vote than men in Southfield, Michigan. In Gary, Indiana, there is an 18.5 percent difference in favor of women, and in East Orange, New Jersey, it's 19 percent. Across the country, Black women significantly outnumber men.[5]

However, there is a wave of Black women collectively forging new pathways into public office and breaking glass ceilings we seldom talk about—those in Black-majority cities. Muriel Bowser of Washington, D.C., in 2014, Catherine Pugh of Baltimore in 2016 (no longer in office), Sharon Weston Broome of Baton Rouge in 2016, LaToya Cantrell of New Orleans in 2017, and, of course, Lance Bottoms in 2018 all won in districts with significant Black populations. Black women differ from their Black male predecessors historically by embracing their cultural heritage to attract non-Black voters in places where Blacks are the racial minority.

"Can a Congresswoman wear her hair in braids?" In 2018, Ayanna Pressley lobbed that loaded question to the crowded assembly hall during her victory speech on Election Day.[6] Pressley won the Democratic primary and became the first woman of color elected to Congress from the commonwealth of Massachusetts, besting the ten-term Democratic incumbent, Michael Capuano, with her seventeen-point win.[7] The throng cheered in response.

Also in the 2018 midterms, Jahana Hayes won Connecticut's 5th District; Lucy McBath claimed Georgia's 6th, and Lauren Underwood Illinois' 14th—all Black women who won in similar fashion, by not shying away from their Blackness, in White-majority places. Although GOP Representative Ludmya "Mia" Love of Utah lost her bid for reelection in 2018, she held her more-than-90 percent White district in Utah for two terms. At the municipal level, Vi Lyles's victory in Charlotte in 2017 and London Breed in San Francisco in 2018—both Black women in White-majority cities—were predictive for Lori Lightfoot to win in Chicago in 2019, the largest city today to elect a Black person mayor. Pressley and other Black women in public office are bucking the directive that you have to sanitize yourself and your political agenda for fear of it being "too Black" to garner White votes.

"Those young people are demanding and expecting more from me. And I owe it to them," said Pressley at a private donor meeting in December, as reported by BuzzFeed News.[8] "I ran to fight for the ignored, the left out, and the left behind."

On her official campaign website, Pressley listed several policy issues she hopes to tackle in Congress, including public health, economic development, environment, housing, and criminal justice. According to *Newsweek* reporting, Pressley's platform included "supporting Medicare for all, stricter gun control laws, including a ban on assault weapons, and expanding rent subsidies for low-income families."[9] Apparently, these issues were enough to unseat a ten-term House incumbent to become the first Black woman elected to Congress in the commonwealth. While many of these issues seem like the boilerplate Democratic platform now, it's an agenda that resonates with the social, economic, and political realities that Black women face. Pundits talk about the Democratic Party shifting left; but the party could stand to move toward Black women's agenda. On the surface, the Democratic platform includes many of the items that cross over to a Black women's agenda. However, there are points of emphasis and priority that distinguish a Black women's agenda from a Democratic one.

AMERICA NEEDS A BLACK WOMEN'S AGENDA

If Black women don't raise key issues, such as voting rights and maternal mortality, which are central to the health of our democracy and our people, it's unlikely either political party will make them a serious priority.

The 2018 American Values Survey (AVS) explores overall political attitudes and how increased diversity among elected officials could impact the country. On the question of what issues are the most important, Black women cited racial inequality as most critical, at 29 percent, followed by health care at 21 percent, and the growing gap between the rich and poor at 18 percent. The economy ranked as the fourth-most important issue, at 11 percent; if combined with the wealth gap, it would tie with racial inequality as the top issue for Black women.

Stacey Abrams may have lost her high-profile bid to become the governor of Georgia, but her campaign helped define an element of racial inequality worth pursuing in 2020: voter suppression. The winner of that gubernatorial race, former Georgia Secretary of State Brian Kemp, oversaw an election process that included voting roll purges and strict registration rules known to negatively impact minority voters. Abrams identified these tactics as voter suppression, "warning about right-wing efforts to strategically reduce voter turnout in areas likely to vote blue," according to *The Ringer*.[10]

The national discourse on voter suppression focuses on voter ID laws, equitable accessibility to the voting booth, including expanded polling hours and days, voter purges, and blatant intimidation. However, nothing suppresses votes like incarceration and early death, which together account for most of the disparity between Black women and men in the electorate. Higher rates of incarceration and premature death are primarily caused by a biased criminal justice system tilted against Black men and violence that stems from a lack of opportunity. Discussion of voter suppression should not exclude these issues that take thousands of Black men off the voting rolls.

Yet on the American Values Survey, racial inequality ranked among the least important issues for White men and women (only lesbian, gay, bisexual, and transgender issues were lower). This means that ending voter suppression wasn't likely be a significant focus for either the Democratic or Republican parties; not until Black candidates campaigned and lobbied for it. When Stacey Abrams lost the election, we lost the opportunity for a governor to bring the issue directly to the forefront in a Deep South state with plenty of history of voter repression. However, Abrams and her supporters refused to take a loss—for an issue that probably cost her the election—in vain. Abrams' political rise forced Democrats to raise voter suppression higher on their national agenda. In 2019, during the 116th Congress, Maryland Representative John Sarbanes introduced the For the People Act—H.R. 1. This act includes provisions of voter registration modernization, which, if enacted, would make suppression more difficult.[11] The bill passed the House; however, the Senate won't bring it up. Nevertheless, Abrams presence increases the likelihood that future candidates, including presidential, will bring voter suppression to the forefront of the party platform. Thank you, Stacey Abrams.

Similarly, in April 2019, Representatives Alma Adams of North Carolina and Lauren Underwood of Illinois put an unambiguous Black women's issue on the national agenda. The congresswomen created the first Black Maternal Health Caucus in an effort to reverse the rising mortality rates of women who give birth, which are significantly higher for Black women than White women. The caucus gained thirty members soon after Adams and Underwood, both Black women, introduced it. "This year, we decided enough is enough," said Adams at a press conference, according to reporting by ThinkProgress.[12] Adams and Underwood are backed by Black maternal health practitioners, researchers, and advocates. Organizations such as Black Mamas Matter have been vigorously petitioning Congress in recent years to respond to the disproportionate number of Black women dying in childbirth. And now that representatives who are looking out for their interests are in the halls of power, those demands have a much greater likelihood of turning into policy.

DEVALUATION OF BLACK VOTERS

The 2017 special election for the Alabama U.S. Senate seat vacated by former Attorney General Jeff Sessions accentuates how both major political parties devalue Black women and illustrates why they are underrepresented in Congress. High Black voter turnout in Alabama's Black-majority cities of Birmingham, Montgomery, and Mobile, particularly among Black women, made the difference in the special election for the Senate seat in 2017, granting Democrat Doug Jones a historic victory over the controversial Republican Roy Moore. Moore is a twice-expelled judge who has been accused by multiple women of sexual harassment, including pedophilia. Jones endeared himself to the Black community by prosecuting two Ku Klux Klan members for the 1963 church bombing in Birmingham that killed four Black girls.

In Alabama, a whopping 68 percent of White voters supported Moore, who, upon being asked when was the last time America was "great," had replied at a September 2017 campaign rally, "I think it was great at the time when families were united—even though we had slavery—they cared for one another. . . . Our families were strong, our country had a direction."[13] Black voters within Black cities prevented Moore from bringing his toxic masculinity, homophobia, and multiple charges of sexual harassment to the Senate.[14]

Jones beat Moore by only 1.5 percent, meaning he needed every vote he mustered. All but 4 percent of African-Americans who cast ballots voted for Jones. Blacks accounted for roughly 30 percent of the Alabama electorate, according to a CNN exit poll.[15] And 98 percent of Black women (17 percent of the electorate) cast ballots for Jones. Certainly, Jones needed each vote—but if Moore had courted just a sliver of the Black electorate, he could have won by a landslide.

Prior to the election, many Black voting rights activists criticized the Democratic Party's last-minute get out the vote effort in the state's Black-majority districts. The *New York Times* reported that the Democratic Party cautioned against a late investment in advertising because "spending any money . . . would stir up the Republican base." Meaning, the Democratic National Committee didn't deploy resources into on-the-ground efforts, many of which are managed and staffed by Black women, in Black-majority areas—not exactly an astute assessment of value.[16]

Black women have been saving the Democratic Party, which is not doing very much to uphold its promises to the Black community. There have always been charges from Democrats and Republicans that the Democratic Party takes advantage of—devalues—the Black vote. From replacing Black leadership in the party to woo White suburban voters, not putting financial support behind Black candidates to not investing in the Black "get out the vote" (GOTV) organizations in cities, the Democratic Party seemingly has not delivered policy to reciprocate the Black vote.[17]

Son of Alabama and basketball great Charles Barkley, a noted Republican who campaigned for Jones, offered poignant commentary on the devaluing of Black and poor people. In the minutes after outlets projected Jones as the victor, Barkley said, "This is a wake-up call for Democrats . . . It's time for them to get off their ass and start making life better for Black folks and people who are poor." "Getting off their asses" translates into investments in Black women voters and candidates.

It's very conceivable that Doug Jones' victory could have gone to a Black woman; maybe, it should have. Still, Black women are underrepresented nationally among candidates, making up only 2 percent of challengers to incumbents. Given their recent success in White-majority districts in the north, running more Black women in all localities more than likely will increase those percentages. In 2018, Stacey Abrams became the first Black female major-party gubernatorial nominee in U.S. history. There should be more Black women in the running for statewide offices.

For all intents and purposes, Black women carry the Black electorate in Black-majority cities. Meaning, they are the majority of voters and greater share of the GOTV infrastructure in Black-majority cities. Investments in Black women can yield sizable gains, as evidenced in the Alabama special election. Black men are present and voting at higher rates in recent years. However, our lower numbers in the electorate emphasize why Black women's votes, voices, and leadership are critical. If they are not in positions of power, Black communities lose even more of our collective voice. Make no mistake, Black women value themselves and may very well walk away from the Democratic Party if their votes are taken for granted.

Shirley Chisholm, the first Black woman elected to Congress (1968) and the first woman and African American to seek the nomination for president of the United States from one of the two major political parties (1972), famously said, "If they don't give you a seat at the table, bring a folding chair." A vanguard for women's political leadership, Chisholm tactfully pushed for inclusion throughout the political process, but as her quote suggests, if conventional democratic processes fail, then you have to take matters into you own hands. The party that Keisha Lance Bottoms and other Black women host for their constituents can become the basis for a political party if the two-party system continues to fall short on their investments to our community.

We owe a tremendous amount of gratitude to Chisholm for representing Blacks and women in public office. But it's impossible to thank Chisholm enough for opening our collective eyes to our deeply flawed beliefs about who should be a leader in America. The fact that all but one president in the history of the United States has been a White man would be completely unbelievable if the American psyche didn't see leadership as equating to that one demographic. Representation matters to our political mental health. Chisholm is the spiritual mother of the Black women elected officials who are not only representing people but also remedying the sick American psyche with every chair they bring to the table.

BLACK WOMEN ARE POWERFUL BUT NOT PROTECTED

Growing up in Black America during the 1970s, the portraits of MLK, JFK, and Jesus hung on many Black families' walls. Today, the new trinity of Oprah, Beyoncé, and Michelle Obama could almost replace them. The successes of the movies *Girls Trip* and *Hidden Figures* and the economic and cultural power of the Essence Music Festival in New Orleans are testaments to the economic power and cultural strength of Black women.

The might of Serena Williams; the political leadership of the women behind the Women's March; the public intellectualism of Melissa Harris-Perry, Janet Mock, and Brittany Cooper equal or exceed their counterparts. A higher proportion of Black women enrolled in college between 2009 and 2012 (9.7 percent) than Asian women (8.7 percent), White women (7.1 percent), and even White men (6.1 percent).[18] And Black women are rising in the ranks of elected office. Without question, Black women are standard-bearers who transcend race and class. But we should be clear: The growing educational and cultural influence of Black women doesn't equal protection.

For instance, more Black women may be getting into college, but the route to a postsecondary degree is still beset with harassment. Black girls endure daily threats in school hallways, with butt touches, verbal harassment, and catcalls.[19] And schools fail to intervene, contributing to the girls' insecurity.[20] That may be because school leaders also aren't the best equipped to treat Black girls with respect. Schools also are guilty of harassment. Nationally, Black girls accounted for 45 percent of all girls who were suspended and for 42 percent of girls expelled from K-12 public schools between 2011 and 2012, the highest among all racial/ethnic groups, according to one University of Pennsylvania study.[21]

When girls do get out of school and into the workforce, they have to work more than sixty-six years to earn what a White man earns in forty.[22] Black women have lower earnings than Black men, as well as White men and women (figure 7-2). And while Alicia Garza, Patrisse Khan-Cullors, Opal Tometi, and other Black women coined the phrase *Black lives matter*, U.S. women's maternal mortality rates are the highest in the industrialized world, largely because of racism in the healthcare system as well as physical violence inflicted upon Black women.[23]

We know that Black Girls Rock[24] and Black Girls Run,[25] and yes, they do it with Black girl magic. But I would be lying if I said my stress levels weren't as high for my daughter as they are for my sons. The data shows that she is constantly in danger.

We all should be applauding this era of the Black woman. I'm just not sure men know how. What men may think of as compliments are really catcalls. Harassment, physical abuse, discrimination, and exploitation must stop. A T-shirt I once saw sums it up perfectly: "Black girls are magic but they are also real."

FIGURE 7-2. EARNING DIFFERENCE ALONG RACE AND GENDER. MEDIAN INCOME FOR FULL-TIME WORKERS.

SOURCE: American Community Survey U.S. Census Bureau for 2017.

In a democracy, having the ability to legislate laws, run governments, and shape public policy is the primary way to gain protection, not only for Black women but the country as a whole. For Black lives to matter, Black women must be represented in legislative halls at every level in the United States.

"The most disrespected person in America is the Black woman. The most unprotected person in America is the Black woman. The most neglected person in America is the Black woman," Malcolm X said in a 1962 speech.[26]

When we elect to support and protect Black women, we begin to chip away the culture of physical violence that is normalized in policy in America. Suspensions and expulsions, physical violence, political underrepresentation, and lower pay all reflect a culture of American violence and devaluation. Black women's experiences give them a unique perspective that can shed light on how racism and sexism help stratify groups.

There can be no real, sustainable protection in a democracy without citizenship. Our quality of life and even our existence is tied to the assumptions of who is an official member of the country. Our lack of protection signals a second-class status. Yet there is no more important power that can change that standing in the life of a citizen than the right to vote. Ending racism may solve many of Black people's problems, but electing a Black woman to the highest offices in the land may save America from itself. Exercising our right to vote is the first line of defense against being pushed from our homes and communities.

8

"This city will be chocolate at the end of the day."

In the battles for control and space in Black-majority cities, Black culture is one of the biggest targets for removal. Our shared customs, social habits, traditions, heroes and heroines, music, food, and family practices are often synonymous with the character of cities, and those cultural elements represent much of their attraction. A popular snarky T-shirt in New Orleans reads, "Everything you like about New Orleans was created by Black people." Black-majority cities that realized an influx of new White residents, like New Orleans and Washington, D.C., are more likely to produce these kinds of novelty T-shirts. If you don't live in a Black-majority city, you may miss the context. The T-shirt rightly fires back at transplants who move inside urban cores, sometimes for their cultural "authenticity," only to later police and scrub neighborhood traditions and other signifiers that happen to be the ties that hold the Black community together. Making cities great again for some means making them less Black.

Black culture has proven to be a formidable opponent. Efforts to remove music, street and school names, gathering places, and individuals have been thwarted by the people using the culture that gentrifiers wish to eradicate. Without question, demographic shifts and the scrubbing of Black culture from neighborhoods is influencing the makeup of cities. Our numerical representation in cities is changing as a result. However, Black-majority cities aren't going away. Gentrification, displacement, and migration are creating more Black-majority cities. With the future of a democracy at stake, how Black-majority cities grow will forecast our growth of an increasingly multiracial country. Blacks will continue to pursue economic and social growth wherever we reside. Will racist policies continue to cut off the country's nose to spite its face by excluding, discriminating against, and devaluing Black assets? When Black lives matter so, too, will our democracy.

Since 1995, pulsating percussions, majestic horns, and raspy rap, distinctive of the go-go genre of music, have resounded from speakers in front of the MetroPCS retail phone store located at the intersection of 7th Street and Florida Avenue in the Shaw neighborhood of Washington, D.C. Indigenous to the city, go-go gave rhythm to an otherwise frenetic corner that saw harried college students, busy residents, and rushed workers shuffling to and from their destinations. Over time, the music became the defining feature of the block, if not the city. If you wanted to hear and feel what D.C. represented, you went to that corner.

Howard University professor and author Natalie Hopkinson made a point to walk to that corner on occasion to reminisce about how she came to love D.C. when she arrived in 1994 as a first-year student at nearby Howard. The historically Black university anchors the neighborhood of Shaw, but it's also a stronghold for the Black community nationwide. Referred to as "the Mecca," a tribute to the numerous leaders it has produced, Howard University was founded two years after the Civil War ended in 1867 and evolved to become a preeminent Black college. It has nurtured the minds of Supreme Court Justice Thurgood Marshall, Democratic Senator Kamala Harris, writer Toni Morrison, actor Chadwick Boseman, Professor Hopkinson, and numerous others.

I met Hopkinson in New Orleans in 2007 when she was a reporter for the *Washington Post* covering post-Katrina race relations and the recovery. We've been in conversation about gentrification ever since. When I arrived in D.C. in 2017, she became one of my ambassadors to the city. Born in Canada to Guyanese parents, Hopkinson became a member of the American community partly by living and going to school in D.C. But she also absorbed the music of the neighborhood and city, making that specific aspect of the culture a significant part of her overall identity. There was certainly a return on that investment. The signature D.C. sounds emanating from that block validate her Black existence in D.C. as other cultural cues rapidly disappear. "I walk past that corner to remind myself of D.C. culture, the culture that made the city distinctive and alive," Hopkinson told me. Her 2012 book *Go-Go Live: The Musical Life and Death of a Chocolate City* is a tribute, testimonial, and manifestation of her commitment to the city and its culture. And it was prescient in its analysis of D.C.'s transformation. Since arriving at Howard as an undergraduate, Hopkinson has witnessed a swapping out of population from Black to White in the Shaw neighborhood and throughout the entire city.

In 1970, the Black population in Washington, D.C., stood at approximately 71 percent, according to Decennial Census data. The Black count dropped slightly in 1990, to 66 percent. Then the Black populace took a precipitous dive between 2000 and 2010, tumbling from 60 percent to 51 percent in that ten-year span. The demographic changes in the Shaw neighborhood are more pronounced than those in the city overall, in which the margin of Blacks sat at 48 percent in the 2017 counts, but that rate is in decline. Not surprising, so, too, is the homeownership rate in D.C. Some of that decline is due to our move to the suburbs (highlighted later in this chapter), but the fall also tracks decreasing national numbers (figure 8-1).

After nearly a quarter century of distinctive go-go being played and heard on the corner, the music became conspicuous by its absence in March 2019. The owner of the store, Donald Campbell, told a local city paper, *DCist*, that he cut the music after receiving repeated complaints from new residents of The Shay, a mixed-use housing development located close by. Campbell says he heard virtually no grievances for almost twenty years. In the last five, police and fire officials have visited him roughly twenty to twenty-five times. Officials never issued Campbell a citation because the music was played within the city's decibel restrictions. So, The Shay's residents tried a new tactic to stop the music. They reached out to MetroPCS' corporate

FIGURE 8-1. BLACK HOMEOWNERSHIP IN
WASHINGTON, D.C., 2005–2017.

SOURCE: U.S. Census Bureau.

offices. T-Mobile (which acquired MetroPCS in 2012) capitulated to the objections and ordered Campbell to turn off the music.

When Howard University student Julien Broomfield heard of the music ban, she became angry and sent out a 1:44 a.m. tweet on April 7, 2019.[1]

"I'm not a fan of gogo but the dudes down at Metro PCS on Georgia have stopped playing their music," tweeted Broomfield. "Apparently, the new [whitey] neighbors were complaining about the 'noise.' Simply saying gentrification is sickening is an understatement."

Frustration moved Broomfield to organize. In a tweet during normal business hours, Broomfield wrote, "Use the hashtag #DontMuteDC when you tweet about this! We have to start somewhere!"

The tweet and the hashtag went viral, prompting Hopkinson and go-go music promoter Ronald Moten to start a petition. Within days, more than 80,000 people signed it. Masses descended upon the corner. Go-go musicians joined in and made the protest look like a go-go (party scene). The petition also received support from local elected officials. City councilwoman Brianne Nadeau, who represented the neighborhood, hitched a wagon to the campaign by writing a letter to T-Mobile officials, asking them to intervene.

"Go-Go is a blend of funk, hip-hop, Latin, and other genres that emerged in the '60s and '70s. It is a unique product of D.C. and its Black residents. To this day, it is the indisputable sound of D.C. and its suburbs," Nadeau wrote in her letter. "This corner is often where many hear go-go for the first time. The music that has played there since at least 1995—and the CDs sold next door—have kept this cultural spirit alive."

Two days later, John Legere, president of TMobile, the parent company of MetroPCS, tweeted out that the music would continue.[2] A go-go uprising brought back its music to a Whiter Washington, D.C.

Hopkinson was clear about what was behind the attempts to remove go-go from the corner. "It's an erasure of the cultural remnants of Black D.C.," she explained. "Gentrifiers don't recognize the culture and brilliance of go-go or Black culture."

Mostly White Shay campaigners saw Black culture as a threat to their rental community—not to say that renters shouldn't have a claim on communities. However, the music and phone store have proven to be long-term residents, committed to the city. We should assume that go-go on the block, which predated The Shay, is one of the reasons the area is realizing growth. It's dishonest to say that the volume from the music, which was played at allowable levels, caused the anger toward the MetroPCS store when you live on one of the busiest streets in Washington D.C. In addition, Black culture has always played a role in creating vibrant communities. Commodified versions of Black culture have long been accepted in controlled, limited entertainment corridors, such as Bourbon Street in New Orleans and Beale Street in Memphis. White people obviously enjoy our culture on a basketball court or in a jazz club. The financial success and cultural impact of the film *Black Panther* and the critical acclaim of the drama *12 Years a Slave* show how White people can take Black culture in doses at the movies. However, residing next to said culture in its living, breathing form incites antagonistic responses from people who associate urban decline with Black people.

But what happens when a historically Black university is in the neighborhood? The entire university wouldn't become a nuisance, would it? A university, which is charged with developing minds and producing research and service that uplifts places wouldn't be devalued, would it? The entitlement revealed in attempts to erase culture also shows itself in antagonistic behaviors toward Black institutions of higher education.

Along with an increase of White people in the Shaw neighborhood came an escalation in tensions between White residents and Howard students. The university's main quadrangle, affectionately known as "The Yard," is where Howard's traditions are displayed and celebrated. It's an area in which historic fraternities and sororities

stroll and where thousands gather for homecoming. Being a historically Black university, Howard's campus provides students with a
safe, sacred, culturally enriching space in a city where such spaces
are disappearing. Blackness is on full display on The Yard as a result
of that sense of security. But the Shaw neighborhood's White residents increasingly felt more comfortable using The Yard—private,
university property—conspicuously to exercise, take their dogs for
walks, and lay out picnics.

There have always been "town and gown" issues between university students and local residents in what has historically been a Black
neighborhood. Questions of who belongs on a campus arise at every
college, especially urban campuses. But Shaw locals' recent use of
the campus as an outdoor space for their pets to relieve themselves is
emblematic of how White privilege makes no qualms about defiling
Black spaces. In regard to using The Yard as a dog park, local resident
Sean Grubbs-Robishaw had the audacity to tell local television station
Fox5 News on April 18, 2018, that if students were so unhappy with
residents' presence, they should move the campus.[3] "They're in part
of D.C., so they have to work within D.C. . . . . It's our community,
and that's how it should be."

The comment understandably sparked citywide outrage among
Black D.C. residents across various social media channels and helped
fuel even more go-go-inspired protests across the city. On April 24,
thousands took to the streets in the historic area of 14th and U streets
in the Northwest quadrant of the city. Go-go bands provided the
soundtrack as people danced, celebrated, and shouted chants using
the mantra #DontMuteDC. Black folk took our political battles to
the streets.

To view the cultural articles of Black people as harbingers of
decline or to devalue anchor institutions that happen to be Black-led
is to believe growth comes only from an environment that is anti-
Black. A legacy of the Home Owners' Loan Corporation's redlining
maps is that it has ingrained in people's minds that Black people

are hazardous. From Wilkinsburg to Washington, D.C., blackness is considered risky, inspiring an illogical antagonism toward Black assets. The suggestion that Howard University, an esteemed institution of higher learning, should simply move out of D.C. exemplifies the very real attacks on institutions, researchers, and people that are situated to produce inclusion. For Whites, to live in a Black city is to be in an inferior one.

FEAR OF A CHOCOLATE CITY

"We as Black people, it's time, it's time for us to come together," proclaimed New Orleans Mayor Ray Nagin on Martin Luther King Jr. Day in 2006—approximately four months after Hurricane Katrina made landfall in the city on August 29, 2005. "It's time for us to rebuild a New Orleans, the one that should be a chocolate New Orleans," Nagin added. "And I don't care what people are saying Uptown or wherever they are. This city will be chocolate at the end of the day." You know Nagin was trying to preach to a Black choir when he closed out his speech with, "It's the way God wants it to be."

I was a professor at the University of New Orleans before and after Katrina, and was in the city when Nagin made his chocolate city comments. Less than half the city had returned from where they had evacuated to at that point. I returned to work on the city's recovery efforts as soon as officials allowed residents to come back in the city. Neighborhoods in which kids had played openly in the streets and old folks had played spades on porches looked like ghost towns.

The Black population was especially slow to return. Black, low-income evacuees lacked the financial resources to come back to the city and rebuild their homes. Many were forced to remain where they had evacuated to until city, state, and federal authorities figured out ways to dispense disaster recovery funds to individual families. But word travels fast and far. From a distance, many learned that the city's leaders, including Nagin, plotted to keep Black residents out.[4] Indeed, in December 2005, the Urban Land Institute recommended to Nagin's Bring New Orleans Back commission that New Orleans shrink its footprint, converting certain residential areas to green space or have them return to wetlands. Prioritizing razing property even for environmental concerns is a losing proposition in any situation, but it's extremely unfavorable for a Black mayor who goes along with recommendations of leveling Black communities and homes.

A few months later, in 2006, the commission unveiled maps with green dots that indicated the specific residential areas that urban planners thought it would be wise to convert.[5] Many evacuees could not immediately move back to their residences because of the damage, but they still considered their neighborhood home. Naturally, the commission's initial recommendations raised the ire of all residents, but the dots particularly covered the Black areas of the city that struggled mightily to repopulate: the Lower Ninth Ward, Gentilly, Hollygrove, and parts of New Orleans East. Nagin's chocolate city speech was an attempt to apply a political salve to the real concerns that Blacks weren't protected. However, he introduced a phrase that gets to the core of White fears.

As a Black resident of New Orleans, I didn't find Nagin's comments particularly antagonistic or divisive. Made popular by the funk band Parliament Funkadelic, the 1975 song "Chocolate City" is an ode to Washington, D.C. and the DJs who originally coined the phrase. The song solidified the term as the colloquial saying for a Black-majority place. When P-Funk sang, "Hey, uh, we didn't get our forty acres and a mule, But we did get you, CC, heh, yeah," they trumpeted Black people's gains in spite of the U.S. federal government's broken promise to redistribute land after the Civil War.[6] In word and in melody, the song claims spaces that White people abandoned for the suburbs in the sixties and seventies. The song is not about erasing White culture. Parliament dedicated the song to

Washington, D.C., but it's an anthem to all Black-majority cities, of which P-Funk named a few: Newark, New Jersey; Gary, Indiana; "and we workin on Atlanta." (For the moment, we got Hotlanta.)

In the song "Chocolate City," there's certainly some playful jabbing going on with the colloquial use of the pronoun "ya," in the *gainin on ya* refrain. It's not a threatening omen for White people to watch their backs. We're certainly not trying to take White people's (like those in The Shay) place in oppressing others. It's also not meant to say we're catching up to White communities. Our pursuit of life, liberty, and happiness won't end with White parity, or with integration, for that matter. Redress for historical racial discrimination will have more to do with that. We've been craving more than a simple majority. Since English colonists brought Africans to Virginia in 1619, we've been on a quest to claim space that affirms our cultural heritage and customs and secures basic needs like safety, employment, and housing—to simply be.

Nagin gave an inherently political speech, placating Black residents on MLK Day. It was a less eloquent "Black Lives Matter," a demand for our right to exist. Nagin's use of "chocolate city" certainly wasn't jarring—at least for many of us who commonly use it. However, many White residents took offense. Resident Alex Gerhold told CNN that Nagin's remarks were "stupid" and "pitiful."[7] Gerhold continued, "He used the wrong dairy product to describe us. We're more Neapolitan, not chocolate." Another White resident who spoke to CNN, Ann McKendrick, was much more pointed: "You can't reunite a city if your comments are going to divide a city."

The backlash from White residents was so strong that Nagin issued an apology two days later. "I'm really sorry that some people took that the way they did, and that was not my intention," the mayor said. CNN reported that Nagin said he never should have used the term "chocolate." In a way, his chocolate city speech was a distraction from the city's muckety-mucks plotting to raze homes, which Nagin should have been apologizing for. Instead of addressing the plan to erase communities, his apology reinforced the notion that a Black-majority city isn't a good one.

Racist agendas and policies strongly influence the concentration of Blacks in cities and towns, and we should strive to eliminate those inherent biases and structural inequities. But we should not assume that racism is the main ingredient in the social glue that bonds Black folk. Black people won't necessarily disperse or disappear with the eradication of racism. The social, human, and cultural capital as well as other assets that have Black people sticking together in the presence of racial injustice will continue to hold people in cities and towns even in the absence of racism.

BLACK CITIES AREN'T GOING ANYWHERE

American cities in which the share of the Black population is greater than 50 percent are on the rise. They include the core cities of metropolitan areas such as Detroit, Baltimore, and Memphis, as well as smaller suburban municipalities like East Cleveland, Ohio, Wilkinsburg, Pennsylvania, and Ferguson, Missouri. Black-majority cities (which I take to include Census-designated places such as cities, towns, and townships) numbered 460 in the 1970 census, and had gone up to 1,148 by the 2010 census. And, as of the latest census estimates in 2017, there are now 1,262 Black-majority cities, an increase of more than 100 during this decade alone (figure 8-2).

The last fifty years have given rise to a large, varied class of Black-majority cities—both urban and rural, new and old. However, the rise in the number of Black-majority cities isn't because the country is becoming significantly Blacker (the share of Blacks in the country has increased only by 1.5 percentage points since 1970). There are more Black cities because of shifts within and between regions and metropolitan areas.

My broader exploration of Black cities is really a quest for op-

FIGURE 8-2. BLACK-MAJORITY CITIES IN THE UNITED STATES, 2017.

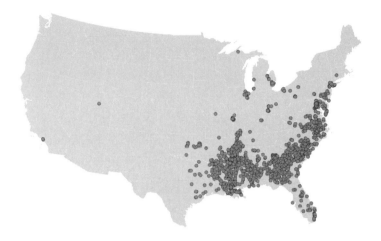

SOURCE: American Community Survey U.S. Census Bureau estimates.

portunity, sustainability, and investment. Where Blacks congregate says a lot about where they don't, and how Black people live in Black-majority cities foretells how other racial/ethnic groups will progress as more cities become minority-White in the future. Therefore, the development and growth of Black-majority cities presents an opportunity. Recognizing the worth of Black-majority cities will test our nation's ability to build upon the strengths that diverse communities provide, so we can all grow positively into our inevitable, collective future.

Among today's Black-majority cities, most Black people live in large ones (54 percent). However, almost half of chocolate city residents are in medium-sized cities (41 percent) and small towns (5 percent). Most of the Black-majority cities are clustered in the South, and they are home to the overwhelming majority of Black people. In fact, there hasn't been a moment in American history when the majority of Black people hasn't lived in the South. From the epicenter in the South, the cities line the Atlantic Coast up through New York State.

The Black populations in the Midwest and Northeast are about equal in total, but there are far more Black cities in the Midwest, and far more Blacks living in Black cities in the Midwest (table 8-1). This is largely due to big metro areas like Chicago, Detroit, and St. Louis having many Black-majority suburbs, which is less common in the Northeast. From 1970 to 2010, the total number of Census-recognized cities grew by nearly 50 percent. But most of today's Black-majority cities—more than 800 of the 1,148 in 2010—already existed in some form in 1970. Moreover, the Black share of the U.S. population rose only slightly over this period, from 11.1 percent in 1970 to 12.6 percent in 2010. Therefore, more than anything else, the emergence of Black-majority cities reflects a changing demographic landscape *between* and *within* cities. A new great migration and intra-metropolitan movement has reshaped urban, suburban, and rural communities, facilitating the rise of today's Black-majority cities.[8]

My colleague David Harshbarger and I categorized the ways Black cities came to be since 1970. Cities generally became Black-majority in one of four ways since 1970. There are *Boomtowns* that gained both Black and non-Black population from 1970 to 2010: cities such as Waldorf, Maryland, De Soto, Texas, and Valdosta, Georgia. There are *White Flight* cities that gained Black population but experienced a decrease in non-Black (largely White) population: places like Wilkinsburg, Birmingham, and Memphis. There are *Suburbanized* Black cities that lost both Black and non-Black population to surrounding suburbs: Detroit, Atlanta, and St. Louis. And there are those cities that have been *Gentrified* in that they've lost Black population but gained non-Black population. This trajectory describes Washington, D.C. as well as Western cities such as Los Angeles, Compton, and East Palo Alto, in which the growing non-Black population is made up almost entirely of Asian and Hispanic newcomers. These are the cities that are realizing the kind of strife occurring in Washington, D.C. However, White angst is clearly not limited to gentrifying cities.

Black-majority cities—chocolate cities—are here to stay. The

TABLE 8-1. BLACK-MAJORITY CITIES AND THEIR BLACK RESIDENTS, BY REGION

	Number of Black-majority cities	Number of Black residents of Black-majority cities	Number of Black residents in the region	Percent of Black residents living in Black-majority cities
South	1,080	6,277,894	24,154,425	26
Midwest	136	1,677,030	7,766,541	22
Northeast	46	613,383	7,366,655	8
West	4	19,293	4,299,572	<1
Total	1,266	8,587,600	43,587,193	20

NOTE: Regional boundaries reflect Census conventions.

SOURCE: 2017 American Community Survey, U.S. Census Bureau.

fight against those who question our existence will continue for the foreseeable future. Black cities have certainly been shaped by racism, but Black communities aren't defined by it. Our pursuit of justice and freedom must continue to rest at the core of our community definition. For inclusive growth to occur, individuals must shift the burden of change from people to policy. There is nothing wrong with Black people that ending racism can't solve.

While Hotsy and Dot implored Mom to place me into foster care from the hallway of my childhood home, Mom remained stalwart, forming a barrier between me and a world that ostensibly would not protect me. She clutched the doorway as if her life depended on it. Afraid and deflated, I sat on the bed behind her in silence.

I began to tune out the lengthy back and forth between Mom and my would-be ousters. Eventually, the footsteps of Hotsy and Dot walking down the stairs caught my attention. I heard echoes of their conversation fade away as they exited the house. Mom released her grip on the doorframe. She turned toward me. I could barely look at Mom for the shame. She sensed my hopelessness and reached for me. Then, Mom held me as tight as I imagine she did the doorframe.

"You're not going anywhere," Mom said gently. "This is your home, and you are my son."

I believed her. I also knew Dot and Hotsy weren't going away either. I avoided them as much as I could for the few years I lived in our house before I went off to college, seldom speaking to either. Hotsy lived with me so I had to learn how to ignore him, pretending he didn't exist. Unfortunately, the practice of closing my eyes to people right in front of me became a coping mechanism that I actively try to dislodge from my psyche today.

People should not be ignored, even those who seek to harm you. That is to say, we should not close our eyes to racists or racism. Devaluation is essentially about lowering value based on false notions of human worth. The correction for devaluation is not indifference or dehumanization.

On July 14, 2019, when President Donald Trump sent his racist tweets asserting that four U.S. congresswomen of color "go back and help fix the totally broken and crime infested places from which they came," many analysts had wrongly declared that his patently vile and illogical statements (three of the congresswomen were born in the United States) were separate and distinct from supposedly real public policy issues and agendas.[9]

One *Washington Post* columnist, Kathleen Parker, stated that the president's motives were clear—to "create chaos, distract the masses, look mad, take care of business." The *Post* columnist is not alone. The four women who Trump targeted, Reps. Alexandria Ocasio-Cortez (D-N.Y.), Ilhan Omar (D-Minn.), Ayanna Pressley (D-Mass.) and Rashida Tlaib (D-Mich.), held a press conference the next day and declared the clearly racist comments a distraction.[10]

Black cities aren't going anywhere; bigotry isn't either. People like Trump will continue to try to erase us from our communities. They will tell us to "go back." Establishing that black, brown, and Asian people don't belong or aren't real Americans is how our democracy ended up with *legal* segregation, internment camps, housing discrimination, and racially biased criminal justice systems and immigration policies. Trump clearly didn't create this practice; he adopted it from his predecessors. Those who study policy and dismiss racism as a distraction aid and abet in its proliferation.

Charging that fellow Americans should "go back" is to say certain people are not real members of a community and can be discriminated against. Telling fellow Americans to "go back" is to signal to others that you espouse a belief in a hierarchy, which obviously flies in the face of democracy. This form of bigotry is here to stay, but we can dislodge the prejudice that's codified into law. Erasing Black culture, imprisoning Black people, taking over Black-led school districts, and denying Black people wealth-building opportunities are ways that policy tells us to "go back." We may not change people's beliefs, but we can change policy.

In 2019 when the #DontMuteDC rallies occurred less than two miles from my office, it became clear to me that facts aren't enough to move policy. Data will help only so much. Solving for devaluation also demands a cultural response—from the people who live it. Bar charts and scatter plots won't necessarily move a crowd toward policy solutions. Research can certainly help. As I stood in the thick of one of the demonstrations, I immediately thought about this book, my role at the Brookings Institution, and the family that raised me in Wilkinsburg. The entire scene felt familiar. Washington, D.C., offered a different backdrop, but my family in Wilkinsburg, Detroit, and New Orleans face similar situations—fighting for dignity and basic services essential to economic and social mobility. I asked myself: Is my scholarship part of the drumbeat of this demonstration? Is it connected to the people we partner with from devalued neighborhoods? Researchers who are invested in inclusion should not distance themselves from Black culture, which continues to have the most effective tools in advancing equity. Fannie Lou Hammer, Martin Luther King Jr., Malcolm X, and Elsie Mae Boyd all understood this. Now I do.

Black-majority cities are home to our brothers and sisters, and although we may not be related genetically, we are connected civically. Knowing your price means understanding the value of family. My mother understood that my family may love me or hate me, they may empower or devalue me, but we as a people aren't going anywhere. The fight to form a civic family that lives under a just, equitable, and loving roof will press on.

Notes

INTRODUCTION

1. Bill Toland, "In Desperate 1983, There Was Nowhere for Pittsburgh's Economy to Go but Up," *Pittsburgh Post-Gazette*, December 23, 2012, www.post-gazette.com/business/businessnews/2012/12/23/In-desperate-1983-there-was-nowhere-for-Pittsburgh-s-economy-to-go-but-up/stories/201212230258.

2. Amy Traub and others, "The Asset Value of Whiteness: Understanding the Racial Wealth Gap," February 6, 2017, Demos, 21, https://www.demos.org/sites/default/files/publications/Asset%20Value%20of%20Whiteness_0.pdf.

3. Andre M. Perry, "Black Incomes Outpace the National Average in 124 Black-Majority Cities: So Where's the Investment?" Brookings, November 15, 2017, www.brookings.edu/blog/the-avenue/2017/11/15/black-incomes-outpace-the-national-average-in-124-Black-majority-cities-so-wheres-the-investment/.

4. Chad Shearer, Isha Shah, Alec Friedhoff, and Alan Berube, "Metro Monitor 2018," Brookings, February 20, 2018, www.brookings.edu/research/metro-monitor-2018/.

5. Gary Deans and others, *Toni Morrison Uncensored* (Princeton, NJ: Films for the Humanities & Sciences, 2003).

6. Andre M. Perry, "Why Does Black Pride Provoke Such Defensiveness?" Hechinger Report, November 20, 2018, https://hechingerreport.org/why-does-pride-in-blackness-provoke-such-defensiveness/.

7. Emily Badger and others, "Extensive Data Shows Punishing Reach of

Racism for Black Boys," *New York Times*, March 19, 2018, www.nytimes.com/
interactive/2018/03/19/upshot/race-class-white-and-black-men.html.

8. Ibid.

9. Dylan Matthews, "The Massive New Study on Race and Economic
Mobility in America, Explained," Vox, March 21, 2018, www.vox.com/policy-
and-politics/2018/3/21/17139300/economic-mobility-study-race-black-white-
women-men-incarceration-income-chetty-hendren-jones-porter.

10. Arindrajit Dube via Twitter: "If you overlay the @nhendren82 (+coauthors)
percentile-percentile plots, it suggests the exceptional mobility is for white men.
This point should be discussed more when hypothesizing explanations for these
patterns," March 23, 2018, https://twitter.com/arindube/status/9771540486536
56064?s=20.

11. Barbara Mackay "The End of an Era in *Two Trains Running*," Theater
Mania, April 6, 2018, www.theatermania.com/washington-dc-theater/reviews/
two-trains-running-arena-stage_84711.html.

12. Philip S. Foner, ed., *The Life and Writings of Frederick Douglass*, vol. 2 (New
York: International Publishers, 1976), p. 437.

CHAPTER 1

1. "Borough of Wilkinsburg, Allegheny County Pennsylvania (PA) 15221,"
Living Places.com, www.livingplaces.com/PA/Allegheny_County/Wilkinsburg_
Borough.html.

2. Ibid.

3. Finnegan Schick, "Wilkinsburg High Graduates Its Last Class," *Pittsburgh
Post-Gazette*, June 4, 2016, www.post-gazette.com/news/education/2016/06/04/
Wilkinsburg-High-graduates-its-last-class/stories/201606040111.

4. "Guide to the Dunning McNair and Dunning Robert McNair Papers,
1793–1857 DAR.1943.01," University Library System Digital Collection of the
University of Pittsburgh, http://digital.library.pitt.edu/islandora/object/pitt:US-
PPiU-dar194301/viewer#ref3.

5. Wilkinsburg Historical Society, *Wilkinsburg* (Mt. Pleasant, NC: Arcadia
Publishing, 2007).

6. Ibid.

7. Damon Young, "Wilkinsburg, The Side of America's 'Most Livable City'
Pittsburgh Doesn't Want You to See," The Root.com, May 10, 2016, https://very
smartbrothas.theroot.com/wilkinsburg-the-side-of-americas-most-livable-city-p
-1822523115.

8. "Students Welcomed to Westinghouse Academy after Merger with Wilkinsburg WPXI," August 29, 2016, www.wpxi.com/news/students-welcomed-to-west
inghouse-academy-after-merger-with-wilkinsburg/431559251.

9. Elizabeth Behrman, "Community Space Planned for Former Johnston
Elementary School," *Pittsburgh Post-Gazette*, June 23, 2017, www.post-gazette.com/

local/east/2017/06/23/Wilkinsburg-Johnston-Elementary-building-purchased/stories/201706230021.

10. Carolyn M. Brown, "Best Accelerators for Entrepreneurs of Color to Get Funding," *Black Enterprise*, August 9, 2016, www.blackenterprise.com/best-accelerators-minority-startups-small-businesses-get-funding/.

11. Brentin Mock, "The Case for Saving the Small Black City," CityLab, August 9, 2017, www.citylab.com/equity/2017/08/saving-the-small-Black-city/536145/.

12. Project for Public Space, "What Is Placemaking?" www.pps.org/article/what-is-placemaking.

13. With the use of millions of lasers, lidar measures how long the beams take to bounce back and uses the data to build a 3-D map that is more precise than radar offers and easier for a computer to understand than a 2-D camera image. See Alex Davies, "What Is a Self-Driving Car? The Complete WIRED Guide," Wired, December 13, 2018, www.wired.com/story/guide-self-driving-cars/.

14. Eugene Kim, "What It's Like to Be Black in Silicon Valley," *Business Insider*, July 22, 2016, www.businessinsider.com/being-black-in-silicon-valley-2016-7.

15. Aaron Aupperlee, "Report: More than $687M Invested in Pittsburgh Tech Companies in 2017," TribLIVE.Com, March 20, 2018, https://archive.triblive.com/business/technology/report-more-than-687m-invested-in-pittsburgh-tech-companies-in-2017/.

16. Greg Fischer, Bruce Katz, and Julie Wagner, "How to Build an Innovation District that Really Works," CityLab, July 5, 2017, www.citylab.com/equity/2017/07/how-mayors-can-drive-inclusive-growth/532569/.

17. Ryan Donahue Joseph Parilla, and Brad McDearman, "Rethinking Cluster Initiatives," Brookings, July 19, 2018, www.brookings.edu/research/rethinking-cluster-initiatives/.

18. Enrico Moretti, *The New Geography of Jobs* (New York, NY: Mariner Books, 2013).

19. Neil Lee and Stephen Clarke, "Do Low-Skilled Workers Gain from High-Tech Employment Growth? High-Technology Multipliers, Employment and Wages in Britain," *Research Policy* 48, no. 9 (November 1, 2019): 103803, https://doi.org/10.1016/j.respol.2019.05.012.

20. "Metro Monitor 2017 Dashboard," Brookings, February 23, 2017, www.brookings.edu/interactives/metro-monitor-2017-dashboard/.

21. Wilkinsburg Historical Society, *Wilkinsburg*.

22. Deana Carpenter, "Wilkinsburg Community Development Corporation Sets $3 Million Goal for Train Station Renewal," *Pittsburgh Post-Gazette*, October 14, 2016, www.post-gazette.com/local/east/2016/10/14/Wilkinsburg-Community-Development-Corporation-sets-3-million-goal-for-train-station-renewal/stories/201610100198. Personnel from the WCDC informed me that an additional $3 million needed to be raised after initial assessments, totaling $6 million.

23. "The Wilkinsburg Train Station Restoration Project," webpage, https://wilkstation.org/.

24. Megan Guza, "A Year Later, Survivor of Wilkinsburg Massacre is Determined to Walk Again" TribLIVE.Com, March 9, 2017, https://archive.triblive.com/local/pittsburgh-allegheny/a-year-later-survivor-of-wilkinsburg-massacre-is-determined-to-walk-again/.

25. Kevin Slane, "A Newscaster Faces Criticism for Using #PittsburghStrong after She Was Fired for Her Facebook Rant about Race," Boston.Com, April 5, 2016, www.boston.com/culture/local-news/2016/04/05/newscaster-faces-criticism-using-pittsburghstrong-fired-facebook-rant-race.

26. Aaron Renn, "When Suburbs Need to Merge," CityLab, September 9, 2017, www.citylab.com/equity/2017/09/suburbs-should-merge/540258/.

27. Eduardo Porter, "Why Big Cities Thrive, and Smaller Ones Are Being Left Behind," *New York Times*, October 10, 2017, sec. Economy, www.nytimes.com/2017/10/10/business/economy/big-cities.html.

CHAPTER 2

1. David Brooks, "Opinion: The Nature of Poverty," *New York Times*, May 1, 2015, www.nytimes.com/2015/05/01/opinion/david-brooks-the-nature-of-poverty.html.

2. Andre M. Perry, Jonathan Rothwell, and David Harshbarger, "The Devaluation of Assets in Black Neighborhoods," Brookings, November 27, 2018, www.brookings.edu/research/devaluation-of-assets-in-black-neighborhoods/.

3. The Notorious B.I.G., "Things Done Changed," www.genius.com/The-notorious-big-things-done-changed-lyrics.

4. djvlad, *DL Hughley: My Home Got Appraised for Less Because of My Black Family Photos (Part 6)*, 2018, www.youtube.com/watch?v=qmVgdwyXHWw.

5. Herb Boyd, *Black Detroit* (New York: Harper Collins, 2017).

6. Joyce Shaw Peterson, "Black Automobile Workers in Detroit, 1910–1930," *Journal of Negro History* 64, no. 3 (1979): 177–90, https://doi.org/10.2307/2717031.

7. Ibid.

8. Boyd, *Black Detroit*, 142.

9. Shaun Gabbidon, *W. E. B. Du Bois on Crime and Justice: Laying the Foundations of Sociological Criminology* (United Kingdom: Routledge, 2016).

10. Gary Kleck and Dylan Jackson, "What Kind of Joblessness Affects Crime? A National Case–Control Study of Serious Property Crime," *Journal of Quantitative Criminology* 32, no. 4 (December 1, 2016): 489–513, https://doi.org/10.1007/s10940-016-9282-0.

11. Boyd, *Black Detroit*, 143–44.

12. David Callahan, "How the GI Bill Left Out African Americans," Demos, November 11, 2013, www.demos.org/blog/11/11/13/how-gi-bill-left-out-african-americans.

13. Ross Eisenbrey, "Detroit's Bankruptcy Reflects a History of Racism," Economic Policy Institute, February 25, 2014, www.epi.org/blog/detroits-bankruptcy-reflects-history-racism/.

14. Robert Allen, "Detroit '67: The Officer Who Led the Raid on the Blind Pig that Ignited the Riot," *Detroit Free Press*, July 22, 2017, www.freep.com/story/news/local/michigan/detroit/2017/07/23/detroit-67-officer-raid-blind-pig-riot/487326001/.

15. "Uprising of 1967," Detroit Historical Society, https://detroithistorical.org/learn/encyclopedia-of-detroit/uprising-1967.

16. Thomas J. Sugrue, "Driving While Black: On the Line," n.d., www.autolife.umd.umich.edu/Race/R_Casestudy/R_Casestudy5.htm.

17. Ibid.

18. Brentin Mock, "Redlining Is Alive and Well—and Evolving," CityLab, September 28, 2015, www.citylab.com/housing/2015/09/redlining-is-alive-and-welland-evolving/407497/; Mary B. Collins, Ian Munoz, and Joseph JaJa, "Linking 'Toxic Outliers' to Environmental Justice Communities," *Environmental Research Letters* 11, no. 1 (January 2016): 015004, https://doi.org/10.1088/1748-9326/11/1/015004; Brentin Mock, "How People of Color Are Zoned for Displacement," CityLab, September 13, 2017, www.citylab.com/equity/2017/09/climate-changes-inevitable-displacement-of-most-vulnerable/539232/.

19. Robert Fairlie, Alicia Robb, and David T. Robinson, "Black and White: Access to Capital among Minority-Owned Startups," SIEPR, February 2017, working paper, https://siepr.stanford.edu/research/publications/black-and-white-access-capital-among-minority-owned-startups.

20. "The NCES Fast Facts Tool Provides Quick Answers to Many Education Questions," National Center for Education Statistics, https://nces.ed.gov/fastfacts/display.asp?id=65.

21. "Hurricane Costs," NOAA Office for Coastal Management, https://coast.noaa.gov/states/fast-facts/hurricane-costs.html.

22. Curtis Florence and others, "The Economic Burden of Prescription Opioid Overdose, Abuse and Dependence in the United States, 2013," *Medical Care* 54, no. 10 (October 2016): 901–06, https://doi.org/10.1097/MLR.0000000000000625.

23. Raj Chetty and others, "Race and Economic Opportunity in the United States: An Intergenerational Perspective," Working Paper, National Bureau of Economic Research (March 2018), https://doi.org/10.3386/w24441.

24. David R. Harris, "'Property Values Drop When Blacks Move in, Because . . .': Racial and Socioeconomic Determinants of Neighborhood Desirability," *American Sociological Review* 64, no. 3 (1999): 461–79, https://doi.org/10.2307/2657496.

25. Caitlin Knowles Myers, "Discrimination and Neighborhood Effects: Understanding Racial Differentials in US Housing Prices," *Journal of Urban Economics* 56 (2004): 279–302.

26. Valerie A. Lewis, Michael O. Emerson, and Stephen L. Klineberg, "Who We'll Live With: Neighborhood Racial Composition Preferences of Whites, Blacks and Latinos," *Social Forces* 89, no. 4 (2011): 1385–1407.

27. Jacob W. Faber and Ingrid Gould Ellen, "Race and the Housing Cycle: Differences in Home Equity Trends among Long-Term Homeowners," *Housing*

Policy Debate 26, no. 3 (May 3, 2016): 456–73, https://doi.org/10.1080/1051148
2.2015.1128959.

28. Ibid.

29. Sun Jung Oh and John Yinger, "What Have We Learned From Paired Testing in Housing Markets?" *Cityscape* 17, no. 3 (2015): 15–60.

30. "A Review of the State of and Barriers to Minority Homeownership," statement of Alanna McCargo, Vice President for Housing Finance Policy, Urban Institute, before the Subcommittee on Housing, Community Development, and Insurance, Committee on Financial Services, United States House of Representatives, May 8, 2019, https://financialservices.house.gov/uploadedfiles/hhrg-116-ba04-wstate-mccargoa-20190508.pdf.

31. Emily Badger, Quoctrung Bui, and Robert Gebeloff, "The Neighborhood Is Mostly Black. The Home Buyers are Mostly White," *New York Times*, April 27, 2019, sec. The Upshot, www.nytimes.com/interactive/2019/04/27/upshot/diversity-housing-maps-raleigh-gentrification.html.

32. University of Richmond, *Mapping Inequality*, https://dsl.richmond.edu/panorama/redlining/.

33. Andre M. Perry and David Harshbarger, "America's Formerly Redlined Neighborhoods Have Changed, and so Must Solutions to Rectify Them," *Brookings* (blog), October 14, 2019, www.brookings.edu/research/americas-formerly-redlines-areas-changed-so-must-solutions/.

34. Ta-Nehisi Coates, "The Case for Reparations," *The Atlantic*, June 2014, www.theatlantic.com/magazine/archive/2014/06/the-case-for-reparations/361631/.

35. Andre M. Perry, "Georgetown University's Students Provide a Blueprint for Reparations," *The Hechinger Report* (blog), April 23, 2019, www.hechingerreport.org/voting-for-reparations-one-institution-at-a-time/.

36. "Can 'Baby Bonds' Eliminate the Racial Wealth Gap in Putative Post-Racial America?—UNC Carolina Population Center," bibliographic entry, www.cpc.unc.edu/research/publications/4896; Matthew Boesler, "'Baby Bonds' Could Help the U.S. Wealth Gap," Bloomberg.Com, April 5, 2019, www.bloomberg.com/news/articles/2019-04-05/-baby-bonds-could-help-the-u-s-wealth-gap.

37. Boesler, "'Baby Bonds' Could Help the U.S. Wealth Gap."

38. "What's Your Home Worth? A Review of the Appraisal Industry," testimony before the Subcommittee on Housing, Community Development, and Insurance of the Financial Services Committee, June 20, 2019, https://financialservices.house.gov/calendar/eventsingle.aspx?EventID=403835.

39. Appraisal Institute, "U.S. Valuation Profession Fact Sheet, December 2017," www.appraisalinstitute.org/assets/1/7/U.S._Appraiser_Demos_3_1_16.pdf.

40. Donald J. Trump via Twitter: "As proven last week during a Congressional tour, the Border is clean, efficient & well run, just very crowded. Cumming District is a disgusting, rat and rodent infested mess. If he spent more time in Baltimore, maybe he could help clean up this very dangerous & filthy place," www.twitter.com/realdonaldtrump/status/1155073965880172544.

41. Ovetta Wiggins, "Md. Lawmaker Apologizes for Allegedly Using N-Word

with Her Colleagues," *Washington Post*, February 25, 2019, sec. Maryland Politics, www.washingtonpost.com/local/md-politics/md-legislative-black-caucus-to-meet-with-lawmaker-accused-of-using-the-n-word/2019/02/25/b66a5850-38fe-11e9-a2cd-307b06d0257b_story.html.

42. Kelly Weill, "GOP Senate Candidate's Spokesperson: Black Cities are 'Sh*tholes,'" July 29, 2018, *Daily Beast*, sec. Politics, www.thedailybeast.com/gop-candidate-corey-stewarts-spokesperson-called-Black-majority-cities-shitholes; Andre M. Perry, "The Evidence Is in on Trump: This MLK Day Brings a Reckoning on Silence," Brookings, January 12, 2018, www.brookings.edu/blog/the-avenue/2018/01/12/the-evidence-is-in-on-trump-mlk-day-bring-reckoning-on-silence/.

43. Andre M. Perry, "Racism Is Not a Distraction: It's Policy," Brookings, July 19, 2019, www.brookings.edu/blog/the-avenue/2019/07/19/racism-is-not-a-distraction-its-policy/.

44. Richard Rothstein, "How Government Policies Cemented the Racism That Reigns in Baltimore," *American Prospect*, April 29, 2015, https://prospect.org/article/how-government-policies-cemented-racism-reigns-baltimore.

45. Andre M. Perry, "Why Is Neighborhood-Based Discrimination Still Acceptable?" GOOD, September 22, 2013, www.good.is/articles/why-is-neighborhood-based-discrimination-still-acceptable.

46. "Factbox—Puerto Rico vs. Detroit: What's Different?" Reuters, May 3, 2017, www.reuters.com/article/us-puertorico-debt-bankruptcy-detroit-fa-idUSKBN 17Z2LT.

47. Eisenbrey, "Detroit's Bankruptcy Reflects a History of Racism."

48. Nicole Brown and Ivan Pereira, "Amazon Won't Build Headquarters in LIC after Pushback," A.M. New York, February 2019, www.amny.com/news/amazon-headquarters-nyc-1.27303323.

49. Brad Plumer, "We Saved the Automakers. How Come That Didn't Save Detroit?" *Washington Post*, July 19, 2013, www.washingtonpost.com/news/wonk/wp/2013/07/19/we-saved-the-automakers-how-come-that-didnt-save-detroit/.

50. Chris Isidore, "Bailout Debate: How the Big 3 Came Apart and How to Fix Them," CNNMoney.com, November 17, 2008," https://money.cnn.com/2008/11/17/news/companies/gm_fixes/index.htm.

51. Todd Zywicki, "'Bankrupt: How Cronyism and Corruption Brought Down Detroit,'" *Washington Post*, February 10, 2014, www.washingtonpost.com/news/volokh-conspiracy/wp/2014/02/10/bankrupt-how-cronyism-and-corruption-brought-down-detroit/.

52. Poppy Harlow and Chris Isidore, "State Set to Takeover Detroit City Government," CNNMoney.com, March 1, 2013, https://money.cnn.com/2013/03/01/news/economy/detroit-takeover/index.html.

53. Gus Burns, "Detroit Released from State Oversight; Expensive Debt and Pension Bills Loom," MLive.com, April 30, 2018, www.mlive.com/news/detroit/index.ssf/2018/04/detroit_exits_financial_oversi.html.

54. Christine Ferretti, "For Detroit Retirees, Pension Cuts become Reality,"

Detroit News, February 27, 2015, www.detroitnews.com/story/news/local/wayne-county/2015/02/27/detroit-retirees-pension-cuts-become-reality/24156301/.

55. "Growing Detroit's African-American Middle Class: The Opportunity for a Prosperous Detroit," Detroit Future City, February 2019, https://detroitfuturecity.com/middleclassreport/documents/DFC_Growing-Detroit%E2%80%99s-African-American-Middle-Class.pdf.

CHAPTER 3

1. Margery Austin Turner, "What Does 'Community Development' Mean to You?" Urban Institute, September 25, 2012, www.urban.org/urban-wire/what-does-community-development-mean-you; Elizabeth A. Duke "Investing in What Works for America's Communities, Foreword: Building Sustainable Communities." Based on a speech delivered by Governor Duke at the National Interagency Community Reinvestment Conference on March 27, 2012 in Seattle, WA. www.whatworksforamerica.org/ideas/foreword-building-sustainable-communities/#.XKYwWPnwaUl.

2. Anne Ruisi, "East Ensley Exodus Shows Population Shift," AL.com, January 15, 2012, http://blog.al.com/spotnews/2012/01/east_ensley_exodus_shows_popul.html.

3. Carol Robinson, "Birmingham Homicides in Danger of Hitting 22-Year High," AL.com, October 10, 2018, www.al.com/news/birmingham/2018/10/birmingham_homicides_2018.html; Carol Robinson, "Magic City Murder 2018: Birmingham's Chilling Homicide Numbers," AL.com, January 2, 2019, www.al.com/expo/news/g66l-2019/01/63973b3b087694/magic-city-murder-2018-birming.html.

4. Marlene Hunt Rikard, "Tennessee Coal, Iron and Railroad (TCI)," Encyclopedia of Alabama, September 16, 2015, www.encyclopediaofalabama.org/article/h-2328.

5. Robert Norrell, "Caste in Steel: Jim Crow Careers in Birmingham, Alabama," *Journal of American History* 73, no. 3 (December 1986): 669–94.

6. Paul Worthman, "Black Workers and Labor Unions in Birmingham, Alabama, 1897–1904," *Labor History* 10, no. 3 (Summer 1969): 375–406, https://doi.org/10.1080/00236566908584085.

7. Alonzo Gaines, transcript of interview with Alonzo Gaines, University of Alabama at Birmingham, UAB Libraries, February 27, 1984, https://uab.contentdm.oclc.org/digital/collection/oralhistory/id/260/.

8. Ibid.

9. David B. Schneider, "Downtown Ensley & Tuxedo Junction" (Main Street Birmingham Inc., 2009).

10. "Tuxedo Junction – Birmingham," Sweet Home Alabama, https://alabama.travel/places-to-go/tuxedo-junction.

11. Ibid.

12. Carolyn M. Brown, "Best Accelerators for Entrepreneurs of Color to

Get Funding," Black Enterprise, August 9, 2016, www.Blackenterprise.com/best-accelerators-minority-startups-small-businesses-get-funding/.

13. Schneider, "Downtown Ensley & Tuxedo Junction."

14. Ibid.

15. Blaine Brownell, "Birmingham, Alabama: New South City in the 1920s," *Journal of Southern History* 38, no. 1 (February 1972): 21–48.

16. Anne Ruisi, "Birmingham Library Friends Preserving 1926 Jim Crow-Era Map that Promoted Racial Zoning," *Birmingham News*, Spot News, September 24, 2012, http://blog.al.com/spotnews/2012/09/birmingham_library_friends_pre.html.

17. Norrell, "Caste in Steel."

18. Ibid.

19. "Birmingham Population, 1880–2000," Birmingham Public Library, www.bplonline.org/resources/government/BirminghamPopulation.aspx.

20. Ibid.

21. Norrell, "Caste in Steel."

22. Ibid.

23. Raymond Arsenault, *Freedom Riders: 1961 and the Struggle for Racial Justice* (Oxford University Press, 2006), http://site.ebrary.com/id/10159272.

24. Jeremy Gray, "Bull Connor Used Fire Hoses, Police Dogs on Protestors (May 3, 1963) (Videos)," AL.com, May 13, 2013, http://blog.al.com/birmingham-news-stories/2013/05/bull_connor_used_fire_hoses_po.html.

25. "Four Black School Girls Killed in Birmingham," History, A&E Television Networks, February 9, 2010 (updated September 9, 2019), https://www.history.com/this-day-in-history/four-black-schoolgirls-killed-in-birmingham.

26. Pub. L. No. 88-352, 78 Stat. 241 (1964).

27. Jon Reed, "How to Grow a Neighborhood: The Revitalization of Ensley," *Birmingham News*, November 6, 2015, www.al.com/news/birmingham/2015/11/how_to_grow_a_neighborhood_the.html.

28. Jordi Oliveres, "Watch: What Is Afrofuturism?" April 20, 2016, www.theroot.com/watch-what-is-afrofuturism-1790855036.

29. Kat Tenbarge, "Why Octavia E. Butler is Referred to as the Mother of Afrofuturism," Inverse, June 22, 2018, www.inverse.com/article/46330-octavia-e-butler-why-she-s-referred-to-as-the-mother-of-afrofuturism.

30. Anya Sotek, "'There Are Black People in the Future' Becomes an Artwork-in-Residence," *Pittsburgh Post-Gazette*, January 11, 2019, www.post-gazette.com/ae/art-architecture/2019/01/11/There-Are-Black-People-in-the-Future-artwork-in-residence-Alisha-Wormsley/stories/201901110081.

31. "Janelle Monáe – Many Moons" (2008), IMVDb, short film directed by Alan Ferguson, https://imvdb.com/video/janelle-monae/many-moons; Alisha Acquaye, "Black to the Future: OkayAfrica's Introduction to Afrofuturism," OkayAfrica, July 10, 2017, www.okayafrica.com/african-future-okayafrica-intro duction-afrofuturism/.

32. Audre Lorde, "Poetry Is Not a Luxury," (1985), https://makinglearning.files.wordpress.com/2014/01/poetry-is-not-a-luxury-audre-lorde.pdf.

33. Ryan Donahue, Joseph Parilla, and Brad McDearman, "Rethinking Cluster Initiatives," *Brookings* (blog), July 19, 2018, www.brookings.edu/research/rethinking-cluster-initiatives/.

34. "Nguzo Saba – The Seven (7) Principles of Kwanzaa: UJAMAA," Prema's Kwanzaa Web, http://www.endarkenment.com/kwanzaa/nguzosaba/ujamaa.htm.

35. Federal Reserve Bank of Cleveland, "2016 Small Business Credit Survey: Report on Minority-Owned Firms," November 2017, www.fedsmallbusiness.org/survey/2017/report-on-minority-owned-firms.

36. Jared Weitz, "Why Minorities Have So Much Trouble Accessing Small Business Loans," Forbes, January 22, 2018, www.forbes.com/sites/forbesfinancecouncil/2018/01/22/why-minorities-have-so-much-trouble-accessing-small-business-loans/.

37. "Report to the Congress on the Availability of Credit to Small Businesses, September 2017," Board of Governors of the Federal Reserve System, www.federalreserve.gov/publications/2017-september-availability-of-credit-to-small-businesses.htm.

38. "The Mortgage Market Is Now Dominated by Non-Bank Lenders," *Washington Post*, February 22, 2017, www.washingtonpost.com/realestate/the-mortgage-market-is-now-dominated-by-nonbank-lenders/2017/02/22/9c6bf5fc-d1f5-11e6-a783-cd3fa950f2fd_story.html.

39. "JPMorgan Chase Expands Entrepreneurs of Color Fund to Drive Inclusive Economic Growth in Chicago's South and West Sides," JPMorgan Chase & Co., July 19, 2018, www.jpmorganchase.com/corporate/news/pr/eocf-economic-growth-chicago-south-and-west-sides.htm.

40. "Wells Fargo Sponsors Gallup Industry Study to Gain Insight into Financial Needs of Diverse-Owned Small Businesses," Wells Fargo Works for Small Business, May 20, 2015, http://wellsfargoworks.com/insights/press-release/financial-needs-of-diverse-owned-small-businesses.

41. "Community Possible Grant Program," US Bank, www.usbank.com/community/community-possible-grant-program.aspx.

42. "Community Development Financial Institution (CDFI) and Community Development (CD) Bank Resource Directory," December 29, 2010, www.occ.gov/topics/community-affairs/resource-directories/cd-bank-and-financial-institution/index-cd-bank-and-financial-institution.html.

43. "CDFI Fund 2018," Community Development Financial Institutions Fund, www.cdfifund.gov/Documents/CDFITO2_YIR18_Final508_20190321.pdf#search=fy%202018%20year%20in%20review.

44. "Impact Performance," Opportunity Finance Network, August 27, 2018, https://ofn.org/impact-performance.

45. Patrick Sisson, "How Opportunity Zones Could Become a Big Catalyst for Inner-City Development," Curbed, April 12, 2018, www.curbed.com/2018/4/12/17227124/investment-opportunity-zones-economic-development.

46. Christopher A. Coes and Tracy Hadden Loh, "National Opportunity Zones Ranking Report," n.d., 72.

47. AfroVirginia, "Jackson Ward Historic District," African American Historic Sites Database, http://afrovirginia.org/items/show/221.

48. "Jackson Ward Historic District," National Park Service, www.nps.gov/nr/travel/richmond/JacksonWardIID.html.

49. AfroVirginia, "Jackson Ward Historic District."

50. Christina Montford, "6 Interesting Things You Didn't Know about 'Black Wall Street,'" *Atlanta Black Star*, December 2, 2014, https://atlantaBlackstar.com/2014/12/02/6-interesting-things-you-didnt-know-about-Black-wall-street/.

51. Ibid.

52. Victor Luckerson, "Black Wall Street: The African American Haven that Burned and Then Rose from the Ashes," *The Ringer*, June 28, 2018, www.theringer.com/2018/6/28/17511818/Black-wall-street-oklahoma-greenwood-destruction-tulsa.

53. Chris M. Messer, "The Tulsa Race Riot of 1921: Toward An Integrative Theory of Collective Violence," *Journal of Social History* 44, no. 4 (2011): 1217–32.

54. "1921 Tulsa Race Massacre," Tulsa Historical Society & Museum, www.tulsahistory.org/exhibit/1921-tulsa-race-massacre/.

55. Montford, "6 Interesting Things You Didn't Know about 'Black Wall Street.'"

56. "Two Whites Dead in Race Riot," *Morning Tulsa Daily World*, June 1, 1921, https://chroniclingamerica.loc.gov/lccn/sn85042345/1921-06-01/ed-1/seq-1/#words=RACE%2BRIOT.

57. Ibid.

58. "Many More Whites Are Shot," *Morning Tulsa Daily World*, June 1, 1921, https://chroniclingamerica.loc.gov/lccn/sn85042345/1921-06-01/ed-3/seq-1/#words=RACE%2BWAR.

59. Kimberly Fain, "The Devastation of Black Wall Street," JSTOR Daily, July 5, 2017, https://daily.jstor.org/the-devastation-of-black-wall-street/.

60. Chris M. Messer and Patricia A. Bell, "Mass Media and Governmental Framing of Riots: The Case of Tulsa, 1921," *Journal of Black Studies* 40, no. 5 (2010): 851–70.

61. Stan Diel, "Fourth Avenue Business District, Booming under Segregation, Still Works to Rebound 50 Years Later (Photos)," AL.com, March 15, 2013 (updated January 14, 2019), www.al.com/business/2013/03/fourth_avenue_business_distric.html.

62. "Upcoming Plans for Fourth Avenue Historic District. Here Are Some," *Birmingham Times*, February 21, 2019, www.birminghamtimes.com/2019/02/changes-coming-to-the-historic-fourth-ave-business-district-here-are-some/.

63. Diel, "Fourth Avenue Business District, Booming under Segregation, Still Works to Rebound 50 Years Later."

64. Reed, "How to Grow a Neighborhood: The Revitalization of Ensley."

65. Schneider, "Downtown Ensley & Tuxedo Junction."

66. Erica Wright, "Notable Birmingham Landmarks Undergoing Preservation," *Birmingham Times*, October 18, 2018, www.birminghamtimes.com/2018/10/notable-birmingham-landmarks-undergoing-preservation/.

67. Stephanie Rebman, "Birmingham Approves Funding for REV Birmingham, BBA and Several Others," *Birmingham Business Journal*, November 21, 2018, www.bizjournals.com/birmingham/news/2018/11/21/birmingham-approves-funding-for-rev-birmingham-bba.html.

68. "Council Approves Contract with REV Birmingham to Push Growth in Downtown Ensley," WBRC FOX 6 News, November 20, 2018, www.wbrc.com/2018/11/21/council-approves-contract-with-rev-birmingham-push-growth-downtown-ensley/.

69. Erin Edgemon, "Birmingham Has 6 Months to Renovate Ramsay McCormack Building or Face Fines, Attorney Says," AL.com, August 12, 2018, www.al.com/news/birmingham/2018/08/birmingham_has_6_months_to_ren.html.

70. Jon Paepcke, "REV Birmingham Receives Contract to Revive Ramsay McCormack Building," MSN, November 20, 2018, https://www.wvtm13.com/article/rev-birmingham-receives-contract-to-revive-ramsay-mccormack-building/25243994#.

71. Urban Impact Birmingham, www.urbanimpactbirmingham.org/.

72. REV Birmingham, http://revbirmingham.org/.

73. Andrew Manis, "Alabama Christian Movement for Human Rights," Encyclopedia of Alabama, October 9, 2017, www.encyclopediaofalabama.org/article/h-2594.

74. Melissa Albert, "Fred Shuttlesworth," Britannica.com, last updated October 1, 2019, www.britannica.com/biography/Fred-Shuttlesworth.

CHAPTER 4

1. The Official Website of Arthur Ashe, quotes by Arthur Ashe, https://www.cmgww.com/sports/ashe/quotes/.

2. William Bates, personal communication at Community Forge, formerly Johnston Elementary School, November 30, 2018.

3. Frederick Douglass, "Douglass' Narrative," chapter 6, http://utc.iath.virginia.edu/abolitn/abaufda8t.html.

4. Eric Klinenberg, *Palaces for the People* (New York: Crown, 2018).

5. Ibid., 5.

6. Susan Aud and others, *The Condition of Education 2013* (Washington, DC: National Center for Education Statistics), 241.

7. "Wilkinsburg to Lay Off 43 Workers, Close School," TribLIVE, https://triblive.com/home/2100748-74/budget-close-district-board-million-teachers-wilkinsburg-decided-elementary-employees.

8. Alex Zimmerman, "Wilkinsburg, Aliquippa School Districts Put on Watch List," *Pittsburgh Post-Gazette*, March 16, 2013, www.post-gazette.com/news/education/2013/03/16/Wilkinsburg-Aliquippa-school-districts-put-on-watch-list/stories/201303160131.

9. Ethan Lott, "Unionville-Chadds Ford School District Top School District in Pennsylvania," *Pittsburgh Business Times*, April 10, 2015, www.bizjournals.com/

pittsburgh/news/2015/04/10/chester-county-district-ranks-no-1-in-pennsylvania
.html.

10. "Communities Prepare for Wilkinsburg, Westinghouse School Merger,"
Wilkinsburg School District, August 26, 2016, www.wilkinsburgschools.org/
communities-prepare-for-wilkinsburg-westinghouse-school-merger/; Molly Born,
"Wilkinsburg-Westinghouse Merger Started with Frenetic Pace, but Has Come
Together with Time," *Pittsburgh Post-Gazette*, April 9, 2017, www.post-gazette.
com/news/education/2017/04/09/Wilkinsburg-Westinghouse-merger-started-
with-frenetic-pace-but-has-come-together-over-time/stories/201704070172.

11. Rebecca Nuttall, "Pittsburgh Westinghouse Will Welcome Wilkinsburg
Students in 2016, but Will the Benefits Outweigh the Drawbacks in the Long
Run?" *Pittsburgh City Paper*, November 4, 2015, www.pghcitypaper.com/pittsburgh/
pittsburgh-westinghouse-will-welcome-wilkinsburg-students-in-2016-but-will-
the-benefits-outweigh-the-drawbacks-in-the-long-run/Content?oid=1866129.

12. Emma Brown, "In a Disadvantaged District, a Parable of Contemporary
American Schooling," *Washington Post*, October 29, 2015, www.washingtonpost.
com/local/education/in-a-disadvantaged-district-a-parable-of-contemporary-
american-schooling/2015/10/29/9a7782c4-783d-11e5-b9c1-f03c48c96ac2_story.
html.

13. Center for Research and Education Outcomes, "Lights Off: Practice and
Impact of Closing Low-Performing Schools," Stanford University, https://aefpweb.
org/sites/default/files/webform/AEFP2018_school_closure_CREDO.pdf.

14. Elizabeth Behrman, "Community Space Planned for Former Johnston
Elementary School," *Pittsburgh Post-Gazette*, June 23, 2017, https://www.post-
gazette.com/local/east/2017/06/23/Wilkinsburg-Johnston-Elementary-building-
purchased/stories/201706230021.

15. William Zehner and others, "Business Incubation in the USA," in Dariusz
M. Trzmielak and David Gibson, eds, *International Cases on Innovation, Knowledge
and Technology Transfer, First Edition* (Lodz, Poland: University of Lodz, 2014), 17.

16. Ian Hathaway, "Accelerating Growth: Startup Accelerator Programs in
the United States," Brookings, February 17, 2016, www.brookings.edu/research/
accelerating-growth-startup-accelerator-programs-in-the-united-states/.

17. Ibid.

18. Ibid.

19. Pui-Wing Tam, "How Silicon Valley Came to Be a Land of 'Bros,'" *New
York Times*," February 5, 2018, www.nytimes.com/2018/02/05/technology/silicon-
valley-brotopia-emily-chang.html.

20. Andre Perry, "Opinion | Who Gets Left Out of the Urban Tech Boom?"
New York Times, July 21, 2018, sec. Opinion, www.nytimes.com/2018/07/19/
opinion/amazon-hq2-google-pittsburgh-jobs.html.

21. Fast Facts, Data Snapshot and Video Archive, National Center for Education Statistics, https://nces.ed.gov/fastfacts/dailyarchive.asp.

22. Henry M. Levin and others, "The Costs and Benefits of an Excellent Education for All of America's Children," 2007, https://doi.org/10.7916/D8CF9QG9.

23. "Statistic of the Month: How Much Time Do Students Spend in School?" NCEE, February 22, 2019, http://ncee.org/2018/02/statistic-of-the-month-how-much-time-do-students-spend-in-school/.

24. Quoctrung Bui and Conor Dougherty, "Good Schools, Affordable Homes: Finding Suburban Sweet Spots," *New York Times*, March 30, 2017, sec. The Upshot, www.nytimes.com/interactive/2017/03/30/upshot/good-schools-affordable-homes-suburban-sweet-spots.html.

25. David Kall and David Ebersole, "Illinois: Population Continues to Decline, Eroding the Tax Base," January 18, 2018, https://mcdonaldhopkins.com/Insights/Blog/Tax-and-Benefits-Challenges/2018/01/18/Illinois-Population-continues-to-decline-eroding-the-tax-base.

26. "Wilkinsburg: A Call for Sustainability," (Fall 2007) Systems Project, H. John Heinz School of Public Policy and Management Carnegie Mellon University, www.wilkinsburgpa.gov/wp-content/uploads/2017/01/WBG_Final_Compiled.pdf.

27. PEW Charitable Trusts, "Philadelphia and Other Big Cities Struggle to Find Uses for Closed Schools," February 11, 2013, https://www.pewtrusts.org/-/media/assets/2013/02/11/philadelphia_school_closings_report.pdf?la=en&hash=962B0A36AE84D210B253504AC53704C1591732A2.

28. Megan Guza, "In Mon Valley Steel Towns, Shrunken Communities and an Increase of Crime," Point Park News Service, July 8, 2014, www.wesa.fm/post/mon-valley-steel-towns-shrunken-communities-and-increase-crime.

29. Michael Skirpan, personal communication at Community Forge, formerly Johnston Elementary, in Wilkinsburg, Pennsylvania, November 30, 2018.

30. Gwen's Girls, website, www.gwensgirls.org/.

31. Kontara Morphis and Calina Womack, personal communication at Community Forge, formerly Johnston Elementary School, in Wilkinsburg, Pennsylvania, November 30, 2018.

32. Ibid.

33. Erin Perry, personal communication at Community Forge, formerly Johnston Elementary, in Wilkinsburg, Pennsylvania, November 30, 2018.

CHAPTER 5

1. Jane Arnold Lincove, Nathan Barrett, and Katharine O. Strunk, "Did the Teachers Dismissed after Hurricane Katrina Return to Public Education?" Education Research Alliance for New Orleans, May 31, 2017, https://education-researchalliancenola.org/publications/did-the-teachers-dismissed-after-hurricane-katrina-return-to-public-education.

2. Andre M. Perry and Michael Schwam-Baird, "School by School: The Transformation of New Orleans Public Education," in *Resilience and Opportunity*, edited by Amy Liu and others, Lessons from the U.S. Gulf Coast after Katrina and Rita (Brookings Institution Press, 2011), 31–44, www.jstor.org/stable/10.7864/j.ctt127x5f.6.

3. Jess Clark, "How New Orleans Schools Created a Segregated City," New Orleans Public Radio, May 17, 2018, www.wwno.org/post/qa-how-new-orleans-schools-created-segregated-city.

4. Ibid.

5. *The Daily Show* via Twitter: "Is there a tape of Trump saying the N-word? If it surfaces, will there even be consequences? @roywoodjr breaks it down, " August 15, 2018, https://twitter.com/TheDailyShow/status/1029900364030595072.

6. "Why Were All the Teachers Fired Post-Katrina?" MSNBC.com, August 31, 2015, www.msnbc.com/msnbc/watch/why-were-all-the-teachers-fired-post-katrina-516431427591.

7. Erik W. Robelen, "New Orleans Eyed as Clean Educational Slate," *Education Week*, September 21, 2005, www2.edweek.org/ew/articles/2005/09/21/04katreform.h25.html.

8. Christian Buerger and Douglas Harris, "How Can Decentralized Systems Solve System-Level Problems? An Analysis of Market-Driven New Orleans School Reforms," *American Behavioral Scientist* 59, no. 10 (September 1, 2015): 1246–62, https://doi.org/10.1177/0002764215591182.

9. Phoebe Ferguson, *Perfect Storm: The Takeover of New Orleans Public Schools*, June 22, 2016, www.youtube.com/watch?v=2RgSICjKe5k.

10. Daryl Purpera, "Recovery School District's Modular Campus Construction Program," Louisiana Legislative Auditor, April 3, 2013, A.2, https://app.lla.state.la.us/PublicReports.nsf/D37141BC3E866E5586257B42006D57FE/$FILE/00031562.pdf.

11. U.S. Department of Labor, "Union Members Summary," Bureau of Labor Statistics, January 18, 2019, www.bls.gov/news.release/union2.nr0.htm.

12. Sarah Reckhow and Megan Tompkins-Stange, "'Singing from the Same Hymnbook': Education Policy Advocacy at Gates and Broad," February 5, 2015, https://education.msu.edu/epc/library/papers/WP-50-The-Role-of-Foundations-in-school-reform-Reckhow-Stange.asp.

13. Corey Mitchell, "What Happened to New Orleans' Veteran Black Teachers?" Education Week, August 19, 2015, https://neworleans.edweek.org/veteran-Black-female-teachers-fired/.

14. Lincove, Barrett, and Strunk, "Did the Teachers Dismissed after Hurricane Katrina Return to Public Education?"

15. Jo-Ann Armao, "The Big Easy's School Revolution," *Washington Post*, April 27, 2012, sec. Opinions, www.washingtonpost.com/opinions/the-big-easys-school-revolution/2012/04/27/gIQAS4bDuiT_story.html.

16. Thomas S. Dee, "Teachers, Race, and Student Achievement in a Randomized Experiment," *Review of Economics and Statistics* 86, no. 1 (February 2004): 195–210, www.jstor.org/stable/3211667.

17. Seth Gershenson, and others, "The Long-Run Impacts of Same-Race Teachers," Bonn, Germany: Institute of Labor Economics, March 2017, http://ftp.iza.org/dp10630.pdf.

18. Adam C. Wright, "Teachers' Perceptions of Students' Disruptive Behavior:

The Effect of Racial Congruence and Consequences for School," 1–42, Paper presented at the 2015 Association of Education Finance and Policy Annual Conference, Washington, D.C., 2015, https://aefpweb.org/sites/default/files/webform/41/ Race%20Match,%20Disruptive%20Behavior,%20and%20School%20Suspension .pdf.

19. Adam C. Wright, Michael A. Gottfried, and Vi-Nhuan Le, "A Kindergarten Teacher Like Me: The Role of Student-Teacher Race in Social-Emotional Development," *American Educational Research Journal* 54, no. 1 (April 2017): 78–101, https://doi.org/10.3102/0002831216635733.

20. Sarah Carr, "How Strict Is Too Strict?" *The Atlantic*, November 17, 2014, www.theatlantic.com/magazine/archive/2014/12/how-strict-is-too-strict/3822 28/.

21. Ibid.

22. Mónica Hernández, "The Effects of the New Orleans School Reforms on Exlusionary Discipline Practices," Education Research Alliance for New Orleans, March 19, 2019, https://educationresearchalliancenola.org/files/ publications/03192019-Hernandez-Effects-of-the-New-Orleans-School-Reforms-on-Exclusionary-Discipline-Practices.pdf.

23. Seth Gershenson, Stephen B. Holt, and Nicholas W. Papageorge, "Who Believes in Me? The Effect of Student-Teacher Demographic Match on Teacher Expectations," *Economics of Education Review* 52 (June 2016): 209–24, www. sciencedirect.com/science/article/abs/pii/S0272775715300959.

24. Betty Achinstein, and others, "Retaining Teachers of Color: A Pressing Problem and a Potential Strategy for 'Hard-to-Staff' Schools," *Review of Educational Research* 80, no. 1 (March 2010): 71–107, https://doi.org/10.3102/0034654309355994.

25. Alice Quiocho and Francisco Rios, "The Power of Their Presence: Minority Group Teachers and Schooling," *Review of Educational Research* 70, no. 4 (485AD): 2000, www.jstor.org/stable/pdf/40658446.pdf?refreqid=excelsior%3Ab630475b0 e44d48c9886662a1d6e94f.

26. Jo-Ann Armao, "The Big Easy's School Revolution," *Washington Post*, April 27, 2012, www.washingtonpost.com/opinions/the-big-easys-school-revolu tion/2012/04/27/gIQAS4bDmT_story.html.

27. Patrick R. Gibbons, "Constitutional Change Made New Orleans Reform Possible," RedefinED, November 30, 2015, www.redefinedonline.org/2015/11/ constitutional-change-made-new-orleans-educational-transformation-possible/.

28. Armao, "The Big Easy's School Revolution."

29. "The Test Score Gap," FRONTLINE PBS, www.pbs.org/wgbh/pages/ frontline/shows/sats/etc/gap.html; "Stereotype Threat Widens Achievement Gap," American Psychological Association, July 15, 2006, www.apa.org/research/action/ stereotype.

30. William C. Hiss and Valerie W. Franks, "Defining Promise: Optional Standardized Testing Policies in American College and University Admissions" (Arlington, VA: National Association for College Admissions Counseling, February 5, 2014), www.luminafoundation.org/resources/defining-promise.

31. Andre M. Perry and others, "The Transformation of New Orleans Public Schools: Addressing System-Level Problems without a System," Data Center Research, August 2015, https://s3.amazonaws.com/gnocdc/reports/TheData-Center_PublicEducation.pdf.

32. Danielle Dreilinger, "New Orleans Special Education Settlement given Preliminary OK by Federal Judge," nola.com, January 9, 2015, www.nola.com/education/2015/01/new_orleans_special_education_1.html.

33. Nick Anderson, "Education Secretary Duncan Calls Hurricane Katrina Good for New Orleans Schools," *Washington Post*, January 30, 2010, www.washingtonpost.com/wp-dyn/content/article/2010/01/29/AR2010012903259.html.

34. "New Orleans Schools Before and After Katrina," PBS NewsHour, November 1, 2005, www.pbs.org/newshour/show/new-orleans-schools-before-and-after-katrina.

35. "After Katrina, Fundamental School Reform in New Orleans," *National Review*, August 11, 2015, www.nationalreview.com/2015/08/new-orleanss-education-revolution/; "New Orleans Education System Remade After Hurricane," NPR.org, August 24, 2010, www.npr.org/templates/story/story.php?storyId=129404355.

36. Thomas Toch, "The Big Easy's Grand Experiment," *US News & World Report*, August 18, 2015, www.usnews.com/opinion/knowledge-bank/2015/08/18/lessons-from-new-orleans-post-katrina-charter-school-experiment.

37. Kristen McQueary, "Chicago, New Orleans, and Rebirth," *Chicago Tribune*, August 13, 2015, www.chicagotribune.com/news/opinion/commentary/ct-chicago-katrina-financial-disaster-landrieu-new-orleans-mcqueary-emanuel-pers-20150813-column.html.

38. Neerav Kingsland, "The City Fund," Relinquishment, July 31, 2018, https://relinquishment.org/2018/07/31/the-city-fund/.

39. Matt Barnum, "With Big Names and $200 Million, the City Fund Will Push for 'Portfolio Model,'" Chalkbeat, July 31, 2018, https://chalkbeat.org/posts/us/2018/07/31/the-city-fund-portfolio-model-200-million/.

40. Jonathan Chait, "How New Orleans Proved Urban-Education Reform Can Work." Intelligencer, August 24, 2015, http://nymag.com/intelligencer/2015/08/how-new-orleans-proved-education-reform-can-work.html.

41. Douglas N. Harris and Matthew F. Larsen, "What Effect Did the New Orleans School Reforms Have on Student Achievement, High School Graduation, and College Outcomes?" Education Research Alliance for New Orleans, July 15, 2018, https://educationresearchalliancenola.org/publications/what-effect-did-the-new-orleans-school-reforms-have-on-student-achievement-high-school-graduation-and-college-outcomes.

42. Jessica Williams, "Former Employee Charged with Stealing $31,000 from Military Academy," The Lens, December 3, 2013, https://thelensnola.org/2013/12/03/former-employee-charged-with-stealing-31000-from-new-orleans-military-and-maritime-academy/.

43. Cindy Chang, "Ellenese Brooks-Simms Gets Sentence Reduced as

Reward for Helping Prosecutors," Nola.com, March 12, 2010, www.nola.com/crime/2010/03/ellenese_brooks-simms_got_sent.html.

44. "The State of Racial Diversity in the Educator Workforce," Policy and Program Studies Service, Office of Planning, Evaluation and Policy Development, U.S. Department of Education, July 2016, 42, https://www2.ed.gov/rschstat/eval/highered/racial-diversity/state-racial-diversity-workforce.pdf.

45. "A Rich Source for Teachers of Color and Learning: Minority Serving Institutions," Penn GSE CMSI, April 18, 2016, https://cmsi.gse.upenn.edu/content/rich-source-teachers-color-and-learning-minority-serving-institutions.

46. Brent Staples, "Opinion | Where Did All the Black Teachers Go?" *New York Times*, December 22, 2017, sec. Opinion, www.nytimes.com/2017/04/20/opinion/where-did-all-the-black-teachers-go.html.

47. Motoko Rich, "Where Are the Teachers of Color?," *New York Times*, December 21, 2017, sec. Sunday Review, www.nytimes.com/2015/04/12/sunday-review/where-are-the-teachers-of-color.html.

48. Autumn A. Arnett, "Funding at HBCUs Continues to Be Separate and Unequal," Diverse, May 31, 2015, https://diverseeducation.com/article/73463/.

49. Wilborn Nobles, "Educators Get $13 Million Grant to Recruit 900 Teachers by 2020," Nola.com, November 14, 2017, www.nola.com/education/2017/11/13_million_for_orleans_teacher.html.

50. Ashley Griffin and Hilary Tackie, "Through Our Eyes: Perspectives and Reflections from Black Teachers," The Education Trust, November 3, 2016, https://edtrust.org/resource/eyes-perspectives-reflections-black-teachers/.

51. Andre M. Perry, "The Education-Reform Movement Is Too White to Do Any Good," *Washington Post*, June 2, 2014, sec. PostEverything, www.washingtonpost.com/posteverything/wp/2014/06/02/the-education-reform-movement-is-too-white-to-do-any-good/.

CHAPTER 6

1. "Infant Mortality," CDC, www.cdc.gov/reproductivehealth/maternalinfanthealth/infantmortality.htm.

2. Rachel Jones, "Can the Lives of Mothers Giving Birth Be Saved?" Culture & History, December 13, 2018, www.nationalgeographic.com/culture/2018/12/maternal-mortality-usa-health-motherhood/.

3. "Reproductive Justice," SisterSong, www.sistersong.net/reproductive-justice.

4. Christopher Bergland, "More Proof that Skin-to-Skin Contact Benefits Babies' Brains," *Psychology Today*, March 16, 2017, www.psychologytoday.com/us/blog/the-athletes-way/201703/more-proof-skin-skin-contact-benefits-babies-brains.

5. "Pregnancy Mortality Surveillance System," CDC, January 16, 2019, www.cdc.gov/reproductivehealth/maternalinfanthealth/pregnancy-mortality-surveillance-system.htm; "Maternal Mortality," ACOG, www.acog.org/

About-ACOG/ACOG-Departments/Government-Relations-and-Outreach/
Federal-Legislative-Activities/Maternal-Mortality?IsMobileSet=false.

6. Matthew Clair and Jeffrey S. Denis, "Racism, Sociology Of," *International Encyclopedia of the Social & Behavioral Sciences* (Elscvier, 2015), 857–63, https://doi.org/10.1016/B978-0-08-097086-8.32122-5.

7. Gilbert C. Gee and Chandra L. Ford, "Structural Racism and Health Inequities," *Du Bois Review : Social Science Research on Race* 8, no. 1 (April 2011): 115–32, https://doi.org/10.1017/S1742058X11000130.

8. Kilolo Kijakazi, "50 Years after Martin Luther King's Death, Structural Racism Still Drives the Racial Wealth Gap," Urban Institute, April 6, 2018, www.urban.org/urban-wire/50-years-after-martin-luther kings-death-structural-racism-still-drives-racial-wealth-gap.

9. Sheri Fink, "Study Links Poorer Hospital Care to Racial Segregation," ProPublica, March 4, 2009, www.propublica.org/article/study-links-poorer-hospital-care-to-racial-segregation.

10. Fan Qu and others, "The Association between Psychological Stress and Miscarriage: A Systematic Review and Meta-Analysis," *Scientific Reports* 7 (May 11, 2017), https://doi.org/10.1038/s41598-017-01792-3.

11. Douglas Almond, Kenneth Y. Chay, and Michael Greenstone, "Civil Rights, the War on Poverty, and Black-White Convergence in Infant Mortality in the Rural South and Mississippi," SSRN Scholarly Paper (Rochester, NY: Social Science Research Network, December 31, 2006), https://papers.ssrn.com/abstract=961021.

12. Ibid.

13. Nancy Krieger, "Methods for the Scientific Study of Discrimination and Health: An Ecosocial Approach," *American Journal of Public Health* 102, no. 5 (March 15, 2012): 936–44, https://doi.org/10.2105/AJPH.2011.300544.

14. Maeve Wallace and others, "Separate and Unequal: Structural Racism and Infant Mortality in the US," *Health & Place* 45 (2017): 140–44, https://doi.org/10.1016/j.healthplace.2017.03.012.

15. Joint Center for Political and Economic Studies, *Place Matters for Health in Orleans Parish: Ensuring Opportunities for Good Health for All. A Report on Health Inequities in Orleans Parish, Louisiana,* June 2012, www.nationalcollaborative.org/wp-content/uploads/2016/02/PLACE-MATTERS-for-Health-in-Orleans-Parish.pdf.

16. Brian D Smedley and others, *Promoting Health: Intervention Strategies from Social and Behavioral Research* (Washington, D.C.: National Academy Press., 2000), http://public.eblib.com/choice/publicfullrecord.aspx?p=3377451; Brian D. Smedley, "Moving Beyond Access: Achieving Equity in State Health Care Reform," *Health Affairs* 27, no. 2 (March 1, 2008): 447–55, https://doi.org/10.1377/hlthaff.27.2.447.

17. Nancy Krieger and others, "Using the Index of Concentration at the Extremes at Multiple Geographical Levels to Monitor Health Inequities in an Era of Growing Spatial Social Polarization: Massachusetts, USA (2010–14)," *Interna-*

tional Journal of Epidemiology, March 7, 2018, https://doi.org/10.1093/ije/dyy004.

18. Brittany D. Chambers and others, "Using Index of Concentration at the Extremes as Indicators of Structural Racism to Evaluate the Association with Preterm Birth and Infant Mortality—California, 2011–2012," *Journal of Urban Health*, June 4, 2018, https://doi.org/10.1007/s11524-018-0272-4.

19. Alicia Lukachko, Mark L.Hatzenbuehler, and Katherine M.Keyes, "Structural Racism and Myocardial Infarction in the United States," *Social Science & Medicine*, 103 (February 2014), www.sciencedirect.com/science/article/abs/pii/S0277953613004206.

20. "Stigma—An Overview," ScienceDirect Topics, www.sciencedirect.com/topics/social-sciences/stigma.

21. Alison Young, John Kelly, and Christopher Schnaars, "Hospitals Blame Moms When Childbirth Goes Wrong. Secret Data Suggest It's Not That Simple," USATODAY, November 13, 2019, www.usatoday.com/in-depth/news/investigations/deadly-deliveries/2019/03/07/maternal-death-rates-secret-hospital-safety-records-childbirth-deaths/2953224002/.

22. "Deadly Deliveries Childbirth: Complication Rates at Maternity Hospitals," USAToday.com, www.usatoday.com/maternal-mortality-harm-hospital-database/.

23. Monique Tello, "Racism and Discrimination in Health Care: Providers and Patients," Harvard Health, January 16, 2017, www.health.harvard.edu/blog/racism-discrimination-health-care-providers-patients-2017011611015.

24. Kelly M. Hoffman and others, "Racial Bias in Pain Assessment and Treatment Recommendations, and False Beliefs about Biological Differences between Blacks and Whites," *Proceedings of the National Academy of Sciences of the United States of America* 113, no. 16 (April 19, 2016): 4296–4301, https://doi.org/10.1073/pnas.1516047113.

25. K. H. Todd and others, "Ethnicity and Analgesic Practice," *Annals of Emergency Medicine* 35, no. 1 (January 2000): 11–16; Karen O. Anderson, Carmen R. Green, and Richard Payne, "Racial and Ethnic Disparities in Pain: Causes and Consequences of Unequal Care," *Journal of Pain: Official Journal of the American Pain Society* 10, no. 12 (December 2009): 1187–1204, https://doi.org/10.1016/j.jpain.2009.10.002; Hoffman and others, "Racial Bias in Pain Assessment and Treatment Recommendations, and False Beliefs about Biological Differences between Blacks and Whites," *PNAS* 113 (16) 4296–4430, https://www.pnas.org/content/113/16/4296.

26. Monica R. McLemore, "To Prevent Women from Dying in Childbirth, First Stop Blaming Them," *Scientific American*, May 1, 2019, https://www.scientificamerican.com/article/to-prevent-women-from-dying-in-childbirth-first-stop-blaming-them/.

27. Matt Sledge, "New Orleans Jail Population Cut in Half: Here's How Trend Can Continue, Landrieu's Office Says," The Advocate, April 4, 2018, www.theadvocate.com/new_orleans/news/courts/article_0f3d3c3c-4755-11e8-b58d-5f5a2ece5825.html.

28. "Unified Housing Policy Update and Inclusionary Zoning Text Amendment," www.ci.minneapolis.mn.us/cped/WCMSP-214876.

29. Rebecca Bellan, "$23 Billion Education Funding Report Reveals Less Money for City Kids," CityLab, March 27, 2019, www.citylab.com/equity/2019/03/education-nonwhite-urban-school-districts-funding-tax/585691/.

30. Andrea S. Christopher, "Single Payer Healthcare: Pluses, Minuses, and What It Means for You," Harvard Health, June 27, 2016, www.health.harvard.edu/blog/single-payer-healthcare-pluses-minuses-means-201606279835.

31. J. Daar and others, "Disparities in Access to Effective Treatment for Infertility in the United States: An Ethics Committee Opinion," *Fertility and Sterility* 104, no. 5 (November 1, 2015): 1104–10, https://doi.org/10.1016/j.fertnstert.2015.07.1139.

32. Ibid.

33. Black Mamas Matter Alliance, "About," https://blackmamasmatter.org/about/.

34. Sunshine Muse, "Setting the Standard for Holistic Care of and for Black Women," Black Mamas Matter Alliance, April 2018, http://blackmamasmatter.org/wp-content/uploads/2018/04/BMMA_BlackPaper_April-2018.pdf.

CHAPTER 7

1. Jim Galloway, "Politics, Parents and Candidates with Sabotaged Childhoods," AJC, October 6, 2017, www.ajc.com/blog/politics/politics-parents-and-candidates-with-sabotaged-childhoods/wkgd7PjoLNOmhIqfaaXQ1N/.

2. Keisha Lance Bottoms for Mayor, *Keisha Lance Bottoms – Horse & Buggy*, September 26, 2017, www.youtube.com/watch?v=Jfvbh5JRH9w&amp=&t=63s.

3. Andre M. Perry, "Analysis of Black Women's Electoral Strength in an Era of Fractured Politics," Brookings, September 7, 2018, www.brookings.edu/research/analysis-of-black-womens-electoral-strength-in-an-era-of-fractured-politics/; Andre M. Perry, "Black Women Are Looking Forward to the 2020 Elections," Brookings, January 9, 2019, www.brookings.edu/research/black-women-are-looking-forward-to-the-2020-elections/.

4. Kelly Dittmar, *The Status of Black Women in American Politics*, The Higher Heights Leadership Fund and the Center for American Women and Politics, Rutgers University, 2014, http://d3n8a8pro7vhmx.cloudfront.net/themes/51c5f2728ed5f02d1e000002/attachments/original/1404487580/Status-of-Black-Women-Final-Report.pdf?1404487580.

5. Andre M. Perry, "Alabama Is a Precursor to the Black Vote's Value in 2018 and 2020," Brookings, December 13, 2017, www.brookings.edu/blog/the-avenue/2017/12/13/alabama-is-a-precursor-to-the-black-votes-value-in-2018-and-2020/.

6. Rebecca Jennings, "Two Newly Elected Congresswomen Have Talked about Their Lipstick. Here's Why That's Important," Vox, November 7, 2018, www.vox.

com/the-goods/2018/11/7/18071900/alexandria-ocasio-cortez-ayanna-pressley-red-lipstick-election.

7. Katharine Q. Seelye, "Ayanna Pressley Upsets Capuano in Massachusetts House Race," *New York Times*, November 1, 2018, sec. U.S., www.nytimes.com/2018/09/04/us/politics/ayanna-pressley-massachusetts.html.

8. Darren Sands, "One of the Democratic Stars of 2018 Sharply Rebuked Her Party in A Private Meeting," BuzzFeed News, December 11, 2018, www.buzzfeednews.com/article/darrensands/one-of-the-democratic-stars-of-2018-sharply-rebuked-her.

9. Shane Croucher, "This Woman Just Dumped a 10-Term House Incumbent in a Democratic Primary," *Newsweek*, September 5, 2018, www.newsweek.com/ayanna-pressley-massachusetts-congress-capuano-democratic-1105277.

10. Kate Knibbs, "Stacey Abrams Is Still Fighting for Fair Elections," *The Ringer*, December 14, 2018, www.theringer.com/2018/12/14/18139572/stacey-abrams-voter-suppression-2018.

11. John P. Sarbanes, "Text – H.R.1 – 116th Congress (2019–2020): For the People Act of 2019," webpage, March 14, 2019, www.congress.gov/bill/116th-congress/house-bill/1/text.

12. Amanda Michelle Gomez, "House Forms First Black Maternal Health Caucus," ThinkProgress, April 9, 2019, https://thinkprogress.org/house-forms-first-ever-black-maternal-health-caucus-alma-adams-lauren-underwood-32791417ffd7/.

13. Lisa Mascaro, "Roy Moore: America Was Great 'When Families Were United—Even Though We Had Slavery,'" LAtimes.com, December 8, 2017, www.latimes.com/politics/washington/la-na-pol-essential-washington-updates-roy-moore-america-was-great-when-1512758057-htmlstory.html.

14. Stephanie McCrummen, Beth Reinhard, and Alice Crites, "Woman Says Roy Moore Initiated Sexual Encounter When She Was 14, He Was 32," *Washington Post*, November 9, 2017, www.washingtonpost.com/investigations/woman-says-roy-moore-initiated-sexual-encounter-when-she-was-14-he-was-32/2017/11/09/1f495878-c293-11e7-afe9-4f60b5a6c4a0_story.html; "Opinion | Roy Moore Is Not a Pedophile," *Washington Post*, November 19, 2017, www.washingtonpost.com/opinions/roy-moore-is-not-a-pedophile/2017/11/19/1a9ae238-cb21-11e7-aa96-54417592cf72_story.html.

15. Terence Burlij, "The 7 Most Revealing Findings in the Alabama Exit Polls," CNNPolitics, December 13, 2017, www.cnn.com/2017/12/13/politics/revealing-alabama-exit-polls/index.html.

16. Richard Fausset, "Black Voters Could Sway an Alabama Senate Race Rocked by Scandal," *New York Times*, January 20, 2018, sec. U.S., www.nytimes.com/2017/11/29/us/doug-jones-roy-moore-black-voters.html.

17. Terry M. Neal and Thomas B. Edsall, "Democrats Fear Loss of Black Loyalty," washingtonpost.com, August 3, 1998, www.washingtonpost.com/wp-srv/politics/campaigns/keyraces98/stories/keydem080398.htm.

18. Fast Facts, Data Snapshot and Video Archive, National Center for Education Statistics, https://nces.ed.gov/fastfacts/dailyarchive.asp.

19. Sonja C. Tonnesen, "Hit It and Quit It": Responses to Black Girls' Victimization in School," Race, Racism and the Law, racism.org/index.php/articles/intersectionality/gender/1664-blackgirlsvictimization?showall=&start=1.

20. Kimberlé Williams Crenshaw, *Black Girls Matter: Pushed Out, Overpoliced and Underprotected*, African American Policy Forum, Center for Intersectionality and Social Policy Studies, 2015, https://www.law.columbia.edu/sites/default/files/legacy/files/public_affairs/2015/february_2015/black_girls_matter_report_2.4.15.pdf.

21. Edward J. Smith and Shaun R. Harper, "Disproportionate Impact Of K-12 School Suspension and Expulsion on Black Students in Southern States," August 25, 2015, 92, https://www.issuelab.org/resource/disproportionate-impact-of-k-12-school-suspension-and-expulsion-on-black-students-in-southern-states.html.

22. ACLU via Twitter: "Today Is #BlackWomensEqualPay Day, when Black women's pay finally catches up to what white men made in 2016, July 31, 2017, https://twitter.com/ACLU/status/892022285028270080.

23. Nina Martin, "U.S. Has The Worst Rate of Maternal Deaths in The Developed World," NPR, May 12, 2017, www.npr.org/2017/05/12/528098789/us-has-the-worst-rate-of-maternal-deaths-in-the-developed-world.

24. Black Girls Rock, website, https://blackgirlsrock.com/.

25. Black Girls Run!, website, https://blackgirlsrun.com/.

26. Malcolm X, "Who Taught You to Hate Yourself?" Genius, https://genius.com/Malcolm-x-who-taught-you-to-hate-yourself-annotated.

CHAPTER 8

1. The Love Chopperetta via Twitter: "I'm not a fan of gogo but the dudes down at Metro PCS on Georgia have stopped playing their music. Apparently, the new yt neighbors were complaining about the "noise". Simply saying gentrification is sickening is an understatement," April 7, 2019, https://twitter.com/heroinej__/status/1114780952771874816.

2. John Legere via Twitter: "I've looked into this issue myself and the music should NOT stop in D.C.! @TMobile and @MetroByTMobile are proud to be part of the Shaw community—the music will go on and our dealer will work with the neighbors to compromise volume," April 10, 2019, https://twitter.com/JohnLegere/status/1116008146902736897.

3. Tisha Lewis, "Howard University Students Say New Neighbors Have Been Using the Campus like It's a Dog Park," WTTG, April 18, 2019, www.fox5dc.com/news/local-news/howard-university-students-say-new-neighbors-have-been-using-the-campus-like-it-s-a-dog-park.

4. *Times Picayune* staff, "Plan Shrinks City Footprint," nola.com, December 15, 2005, www.nola.com/politics/2005/12/plan_shrinks_city_footprint.html.

5. Michelle Krupa, "Many Areas Marked for Green Space after Hurricane Katrina Have Rebounded," nola.com, August 24, 2010, www.nola.com/katrina

/2010/08/many_areas_marked_for_green_space_after_hurricane_katrina_have_re
bounded.html.

6. Devon McCurdy, "Forty Acres and a Mule," Black Past, December 15, 2007, https://blackpast.org/aah/forty-acres-and-mule.

7. "Nagin Apologizes for 'Chocolate' City Comments," CNN.com, January 17, 2006, www.cnn.com/2006/US/01/17/nagin.city/.

8. William H. Frey, "The New Great Migration: Black Americans' Return to the South, 1965–2000," Brookings, November 30, 2001, www.brookings.edu/research/the-new-great-migration-black-americans-return-to-the-south-1965-2000/.

9. Donald J. Trump via Twitter: "….and viciously telling the people of the United States, the greatest and most powerful Nation on earth, how our government is to be run. Why don't they go back and help fix the totally broken and crime infested places from which they came. Then come back and show us how….," July 14, 2019, https://twitter.com/realdonaldtrump/status/1150381395078000643.

10. Kathleen Parker, "Trump's Tweets Are a Distraction for Something Else He Doesn't Want Us to See," *Washington Post*, July 16, 2019, www.washingtonpost.com/opinions/trumps-tweets-are-a-distraction-for-something-else-he-doesnt-want-us-to-see/2019/07/16/4274a34c-a811-11e9-9214-246e594de5d5_story.html.

Index